M A L L

C I T Y

M A L L

C I T Y

HONG KONG'S DREAMWORLDS OF CONSUMPTION

Edited By Stefan Al

 University of Hawai'i Press
Honolulu

Published for distribution in Asia by:
Hong Kong University Press
The University of Hong Kong
Pokfulam Road
Hong Kong
www.hkupress.org
ISBN: 978-988-8208-96-8

Published for distribution outside Asia by:
University of Hawai'i Press
2840 Kolowalu Street
Honolulu, HI 96822-1888
http://www.uhpress.hawaii.edu/
ISBN: 978-0-8248-5541-3

Library of Congress Cataloging-in-Publication Data

Names: Al, Stefan, editor.
Title: Mall city: Hong Kong's dreamworlds of consumption / edited by
    Stefan Al; contributing editors: Carolyn Cartier, Cecilia Chu, Stan Lai,
    Gordon Matthews, Adam Nowek, David Grahame Shane, Barrie Shelton,
    and Jonathan Solomon.
Description: Honolulu: University of Hawai'i Press, [2016] | Includes
    bibliographical references.
Identifiers: LCCN 2015046965 | ISBN 9780824855413 (pbk. : alk. paper)
Subjects: LCSH: Shopping malls—China—Hong Kong. | Consumption
    (Economics)—China—Hong Kong.
Classification: LCC HF5430.6.C6 M35 2016 | DDC 381/.11095125—dc23 LC
    record available at http://lccn.loc.gov/2015046965

21 20 19 18 17 16   6 5 4 3 2 1

Designed by Anthony Lam

Printed and bound by Paramount Printing Co., Ltd. in Hong Kong, China

CONTENTS

ACKNOWLEDGMENTS

Publishing an academic book rich in visual content is challenging. I am deeply appreciative of Michael Duckworth, publisher of the University of Hawai'i Press, for his continuing support. I also thank Hong Kong University Press's publisher Malcolm Litchfield for arranging co-publication, and acquisitions editor Eric Mok and copy editor Jessica Wang for managing the production. Nathan Tseng helped choose case studies and the graduate students in urban design of the University of Hong Kong rigorously documented them. Finally, I am very grateful to Anthony Lam for lending the design of this book with his graphic expertise.

CONTRIBUTORS

Stefan Al is an associate professor of urban design at the University of Pennsylvania. He is the author of *The Strip: Las Vegas Architecture and America* (2017), and edited a number of books including *Factory Towns of South China: An Illustrated Guidebook* (2012) and *Villages in the City: A Guide to South China's Informal Settlements* (2014). Besides his academic career, Al worked as a practicing architect on projects including the 600-meter-tall Canton Tower in Guangzhou, and served as an advisor to Hong Kong government's Harbourfront Commission and Environment Bureau.

Carolyn Cartier is a professor of Human Geography and China Studies at the University of Technology, Sydney. She is the author of *Globalizing South China* (2001) and the co-editor of *The Chinese Diaspora: Space, Place, Mobility and Identity* (2003) and *Seductions of Place: Geographical Perspectives on Globalization and Touristed Landscapes* (2005). Her article in *Urban Geography*, "Production/Consumption and the Chinese City/Region: Cultural Political Economy and the Feminist Diamond Ring" (2009) develops a gendered perspective on urban restructuring and luxury consumerism in Hong Kong and China. She is working on a book on consumerism, urban change, and the Hong Kong–China relationship.

Cecilia L. Chu is an assistant professor in the Department of Urban Planning and Design at the University of Hong Kong (HKU). Her research interests include history and theory of architecture and urbanism, cultural landscape studies, heritage conservation, and interdisciplinary approaches to the study of the built environment. Before joining HKU, Chu taught at the Department of Architecture at the University of California in Berkeley, the School of Design at the Hong Kong Polytechnic University, and the Architectural Conservation Programme at the University of Hong Kong. She has also been involved with several NGOs on policy research relating to urban design and urban conservation. Her writings have been published in several academic journals, including *Urban Studies, Habitat International, Design Issues, Journal of Historical Geography, Traditional Dwellings and Settlements Review*, and *Geoforum*.

Tung-Yiu Stan Lai is an associate professor in the Department of Architecture, Chu Hai College of Higher Education (CHARCH). Lai completed his PhD at the University of Hong Kong. He is a specialist in urban morphology of historic market towns and buildings. His teaching focuses on sustainable design in urban environments, modern architectural theories, and the history of Chinese and Hong Kong architecture. His research interests cover various architectural types ranging from walled villages, *cha chaan teng* (Hong Kong–style cafés), shopping malls, and cinemas to multilevel transportation systems. Lai has frequently been invited by universities, NGOs, museums, and various high-profile institutions around the world to present his research. He has authored a broad range of academic papers on topics such as "From Resistance to Participation: Clanship and Urban Modernization in the Wuyi Rural Market Towns during the Republican Era," "The Architectural and Urban Transformation of Yau Ma Tei Wholesale Fruit Market," "Eisenstein and Moving Street: From Filmic Montage to Architectural Space," "Mapping the Geographical Distribution of Duanfen Markets," and "Social and Religious Space: The Central Axis of Nga Tsin Wai Village."

Gordon Mathews is a professor and chair of the Anthropology Department at the Chinese University of Hong Kong. He is the author of *What Makes Life Worth Living: How Japanese and Americans Make Sense of Their Worlds* (1996), *Global Culture/Individual Identity: Searching for Home in the Cultural Supermarket* (2001), *Hong Kong, China: Learning to Belong to a Nation* (with Eric Ma and Tai-lok Lui, 2008), and *Ghetto at the Center of the World: Chungking Mansions, Hong Kong* (2011). He has also edited a number of books, including *Japan's Changing Generations: Are Young People Creating a New Society?* (with Bruce White, 2004), *Pursuits of Happiness: Well-Being in Anthropological Perspective* (with Carolina Izquierdo, 2009), and *Globalization from Below: The World's Other Economy* (with Gustavo Lins Ribeiro and Carlos Alba Vega, 2012). He has been teaching a class of asylum seekers every week in Chungking Mansions.

Adam Nowek is an urban researcher and architectural photographer. His primary areas of research are Vancouverism, pop-up city-making, and high-rise residential architecture. In 2014, Adam edited *Pop-Up City: City-Making in a Fluid World* by BIS Publishers. His photography focuses on comparative studies of architectural typologies and documenting urban spaces in transition.

David Grahame Shane studied architecture at the Architectural Association, London, and graduated in 1969. He continued to study for MArch in Urban Design (1971) and then PhD in Architectural and Urban History (1978) with Colin Rowe at Cornell University. He taught Graduate Urban Design at Columbia University and Town Planning at Cooper Union from 1992 to 2012. He is a visiting professor at the Polytechnic in Milan, and has participated in the Urban Design PhD program at the University of Venice since 2000. This fall he taught the Landscape Urbanism PhD program at Copenhagen University in Aarhus, Denmark. He has lectured widely and published in architectural journals in Europe, the United States, and Asia. He co-edited with Brian McGrath *Sensing the 21st Century City: Close-Up and Remote* (November 2005). He is the author of *Recombinant Urbanism: Conceptual Modeling in Architecture, Urban Design and City Theory* (2005) and *Urban Design Since 1945: A Global Perspective* (2011). His most recent publication is *Block, Superblock and Megablock: A Short History* (2014).

Barrie Shelton is an honorary associate professor at the Faculty of Architecture, Design and Planning, the University of Sydney, where he earlier directed urban design programs. His expertise is in urban morphology, history, theory, and design, following an education that spanned from planning, geography to architecture. He has a special interest in East Asian culture and built form, which is reflected in his recent books: *Learning from the Japanese City: Looking East in Urban Design* (2012), the expanded Japanese version, *Nihon no toshi kara manabu koto* (2014), and the co-authored *The Making of Hong Kong: From Vertical to Volumetric* (2011). Shelton has been a Japan Foundation Fellow, a visiting professor at English and Japanese universities, and an associate professor specializing in urban design at the Universities of Melbourne and Tasmania. For more information, see http://urbantransmedia.blogspot.com.au/.

Jonathan D. Solomon is director of the Department of Architecture, Interior Architecture and Designed Objects at the School of the Art Institute of Chicago, and editor of the art and design journal *Forty-Five*. His recent book, *Cities without Ground*, was reviewed by publications including *The Wall Street Journal, The Guardian*, and *Der Spiegel*. Solomon had edited the influential series *306090 Books* for over a decade and served as curator of the US Pavilion at the 2010 Venice Architecture Biennale. Solomon holds a BA from Columbia University and a MArch from Princeton University, and is a licensed architect in the State of Illinois.

HONG KONG / 5,606

SINGAPORE / 4,023

NETHERLANDS / 253

MALTA / 231

JAPAN / 125

UNITED KINGDOM / 120

UNITED STATES / 76

LUXEMBOURG / 75

SLOVENIA / 69

SWITZERLAND / 69

Top 10 mall-densest countries
(in m² gross leasable mall area per km² land area)

INTRODUCTION

MALL CITY: HONG KONG'S DREAMWORLDS OF CONSUMPTION

Stefan Al

Hong Kong is a city of malls. With about one mall per square mile it is the world's mall–densest place,[1] only trailed by Singapore, the other consumer–oriented city–state.[2] This immense mall concentration is proof that retail lies at the core of Hong Kong's urban economy, with most people employed in the retail and wholesale sector—about one in four people, compared to New York where the sector employs one in nine.[3] Shopping alone is seen as a valid reason for a visit to the city that for decades has enjoyed the reputation as "Asia's Shopping Paradise." A place where all brands can be found and fakes can be avoided, Hong Kong has become *the* retail destination for China, the fastest growing consumer market on earth. Global brands now see Hong Kong worthy of a flagship, where they are free of sales and import taxes, but have to cough up the world's highest–priced retail space: in 2013, its high-end shopping malls rented for an average yearly $4,328 per square foot, twice as high as New York's Fifth Avenue, four times more than Paris's or London's upscale retail districts.[4]

Hong Kong is also a city of skyscrapers. The city ranks the world's number one with 1,309 skyscrapers, almost twice as many as New York City, its closest competitor.[5] Hong Kong's skyscrapers are a representation of the world's highest real estate prices, artificially kept up by the government's monopoly on land from which it derives a large portion of its revenue, and pumped up by foreign real estate investors: take a short stroll in central Hong Kong and touts will flog you with flyers featuring for-sale apartments. Skyscrapers are the *raison d'être* behind the city's top two ranking tourist attractions: the Peak, a mountain on Hong Kong Island that gives a panorama view over hundreds of concrete high-rise towers, and the Symphony of Lights, the world's largest permanent lightshow that so deliriously animates the city's most iconic skyscrapers with pulsating lasers, under a soundtrack.

This concrete jungle of malls and skyscrapers has become the breeding ground of a lucrative cross-fertilization. Malls are rarely found in isolation. In the residential areas of the New Territories, they tend to attach to residential towers and transit hubs; in Hong Kong Island and Kowloon, they are known to reside under office and hotel towers.

It is a fruitful symbiosis. The broad mall, designed to seduce and bring people in, prefers to sit on the ground where it maximizes its shop-window façade like a Venus flytrap. Its tentacles reach deep into the ground to attach to subway systems, or bind to other malls with an ivy-like mesh of sky-bridges. The tall skyscraper, designed to move people up, accommodates thousands efficiently but requires some distance: set backs between other skyscrapers to allow for air and light. Together, the mall provides the skyscrapers with extended entry points, an elevated base, and a private roof deck, while the skyscrapers offer the mall an icon visible from far away and a large economy of residents to feed the mall, and establish a self-sufficient ecosystem. For these and other reasons, the Big Box and the High Rise tend to mate.

The government has named the more recent permutations with a vague and deceiving term: a "Comprehensive Development Area" (CDA). It stands for a planning control mechanism that streamlined large mixed-use Transit Oriented Developments (TOD), and helped the mall become more dominant. But this book coins this urban typology—defined by a cluster of residential or office towers standing on a podium shopping mall, often integrated with railway infrastructure—with a more honest designator: a Mall-Oriented Complex (MOC), or "mall city."

This new term recognizes the centrality of the mall and the vastness of the complex. These mall-oriented developments are cities in and of themselves; they accommodate captive audiences of up to tens of thousands of people who live, work, and play within a single structure, without ever having to leave. The mall is deliberately placed on the intersection of all pedestrian flows, between all entry points into the structure and the residential, office, and transit functions—impossible to miss.

The mall city has become one of the basic units of urban development in Hong Kong, like what the skyscraper has become of New York City. As these insular developments multiplied, they connected to one another and formed clusters, turning Hong Kong into an archipelago of mall cities—with important implications for people's lives.

The consequence of this urban form is that, for millions of people, entering a mall has become an inevitability, not a choice. It has set in stone a culture of consumerism in which everyday life is increasingly played out on the terrain of the mall, and the private shopping atrium takes on the role of the public square. And besides, Hong Kong's apartments are small, its summer climate hot and humid, so why not meet at the mall where space is plenty and air-conditioning is free? And while being there, although one might not need to shop for anything specific, one might as well have a look around, and spend some money.[6]

In this respect, Hong Kong's mall cities achieve the maximum potential of the "Gruen Transfer." This term refers to the moment when the mall's undulating corridors deviate consumers from their original intentions, leading them to shop for shopping's sake, rather than looking for a product specifically. It was named in "honor" of architect Victor Gruen, who designed the first mall, the 1956 Southdale Center in Minnesota—fully enclosed and climate controlled, complete with anchor stores, escalators, and interior atrium. Ironically, the Austrian immigrant, who had changed his name from Grünbaum to Gruen (German for "green"), had more idealistic purposes. He envisioned the mall as a new town center—supplemented with apartments, offices, a park, and schools—as a dense antidote to the rather solitary American suburbs. His invention backfired when malls in America remained insular, and nourished the frantic consumerism he was trying to reduce, like a Frankenstein's monster.

"Those bastard developments,"[7] Gruen exclaimed as he revisited his American creations. They had ditched community functions and surrounded themselves not with other buildings, but with "the ugliness and discomfort of the land-wasting seas of parking."

But unlike their American counterparts, Hong Kong's malls lie closer to Gruen's original intentions. They are part of a high-density, mixed-use community. Even better than Gruen's imagination, they are integrated in mass transit and have stunning tall vertical atria—all the while being highly profitable.

Moreover, in Hong Kong Gruen's creation would reach an entirely new order of magnitude. The 1966 Ocean Terminal, the first in what was called the "malling" of Hong Kong, planted the seed.[8] Preceding mass consumerism, it was built for tourists. Even if the locals did not shop at Ocean Terminal, it acculturated them in window-shopping and brand value. After China's Open Door Policy in 1978 Hongkongers quickly became consumers, their economy upgraded from manufacturing to providing commercial and financial services to Mainland China.

Malls now catered to the growing middle class and were integrated into new town developments, transit stations, and office complexes. They quickly became the most visited malls in the world.

By the twenty-first century, with wealth skewing to a narrower segment of the population, new malls abandoned the masses for luxury markets. They grew from a couple of floors to 26-story structures, their height an indicator of escalating retail rents. Moreover, mainland shoppers now flood the city, many of them with same-day return tickets and empty suitcases—in 2012, 35 million Chinese nationals visited Hong Kong, 20 million of which returned the same day. With China expected to overtake the United States as the world's largest consumer economy in 2016, the fate of Gruen's invention will take another turn. Developers in the Mainland and other places now closely copy Hong Kong's mall cities, aiming to achieve compact, transit-oriented, and lucrative developments.

Mall City is an investigation of this interesting and influential urban typology. The third in a book series about contemporary urban forms in China, including Factory Towns of South China and Villages in the City, it explores the city from a multidisciplinary and visual angle. Essays from experts provide insight from different disciplines, including architecture, urban planning, geography, cultural studies, and anthropology. They offer explanations of how the mall city came into being, what it means for Hong Kong communities, and what we can learn from this development.

This book is also a catalog of Hong Kong's mall cities, including a structured list of key developments. In contrast to the other two books, in which the case studies were sampled to explore the various forms across different regions—laid out as guidebooks—the cases here are sampled in such a way as to show how the type has evolved over time. This historical typological classification of mall development in Hong Kong not only provides structure for the book, it also shows how shopping has become imbricated into the city's politics and people's everyday lives.

The catalog begins with an early version: a single large residential block, Chungking Mansions, which was converted into a mixed-use shopping center with guesthouses and offices. The second category is the residential estate with a podium, which revamped Corbusier's "towers in the park" into "towers on the mall." The third includes office towers on a podium mall, whereas type four, "T4," is the most potent of them all: it includes residential, hotels, and office towers into an ever more encompassing complex, all the while the mall continues to be at the nexus of the development. The evolution of this type shows a clear logic: the mall city quickly grew in size and complexity, with an ever clearer laser-sharp focus: getting people to shop.

The layout of the book attempts to simulate the very urban experience of this high-density and interconnected city it describes. Drawings, pictures, and portraits help readers experience the bewildering, intertwining, and congested city. Readers will encounter various shoppers and shop-owners, like mainland Chinese close to the border, wheeling home suitcases filled with toiletries and diapers. Or South Asian and African traders at Chungking Mansions, buying cheap cellphones and exchanging money. Or Filipino domestic workers at World Wide House, remitting currency. These encounters reveal that mall cities are not just homogenous. Within the microcosm of each mall city appear different socio-economic groups, and products that remind people of Hong Kong's past reputation of good value, beyond its current status as an Elysium of luxury handbags.

To help evaluate each mall city variation, urban design graduate students from the University of Hong Kong made a series of drawings. The exploded view is key. It shows the dynamic interrelations between floors and circulation systems. To facilitate easy reading, different uses are marked with different colors: blue stands for office, yellow for residential, but you will find that red is the dominant color—the code for shopping—always at the intersection of functions, impossible to avoid in the maze of mall cities.

Shopping is seamless in Hong Kong. Metro exits lead directly into malls and footbridges connect different malls so that pedestrians remain in a shopping continuum, not contaminated by the public realm. The drawings also visualize the interior mechanism of the complex, and the important decisions developers need to make about program composition, distribution, and circulation. How much retail makes a development successful, and what should be the programmatic mix? How should the program be distributed through the complex, and where is the best location to place the "anchor" tenants? And most importantly: how can circulation systems be placed in such a way as to "irrigate" the mall with a solid stream of shoppers, nourishing retail rents from top to

In this logistical equation, exterior architecture is a mere after-effect. Overall architectural form is chiefly a result of maximizing Gross Floor Area (GFA), at times simply by the literal extrusion of a plot. Ground-level façade design is often an exercise of fortification, the deliberate dismissal of urban context to introvert the mall, by maximizing the "blank wall ratio": the percentage of bare, windowless walls decorating the ground floors. Residential towers typically have floorplans the shape of a diamond or crucifix to cram in as many apartments as possible. To further increase square footage developers squeeze bay windows (excluded from the maximum gross area set by the government) onto the buildings' outer face, like putting pimples on a tower.

In opposition to the plain exterior and the small apartments stand spacious and beautiful atria, the site of activities, special exhibitions, and community gatherings, where many feel at "home." These interior spaces, as the cutaway drawings reveal, generate a unique type of urbanisms, where shopping is juxtaposed with ice rinks, and corridors and escalators transport people into a three dimensional spatial universe. These lavish spaces stand in sharp contrast to, and are at times at odds with, the sidewalks of the public realm.

The drawings also reveal the location of the Privately Owned Public space (POPs), the few open spaces within the complex that are a consequence of the government allowing developers to build more floor space, if they provide open space to the public. In this ambiguity between private management and public interests the POPs can be found on places including rooftops, so that they are only accessible through the maze of the mall. Meanwhile, at the POPs in front of the mall, the extensive use by the public is discouraged. For instance, Hong Kong's Times Square has deliberately provided uncomfortable chairs for sitting, along with "over-zealous" guards preventing people from lingering too long.[9] Times Square is "open to use by public" but "subject to rules on display," including the outlawing of demonstrations, dogs, birds, and musical instruments. In short, the trick is to place the POP to get people to shop.

The essays in the book provide a deeper analysis of the mall city. For instance, why did the mall city emerge in Hong Kong? In the first essay, Barrie Shelton explains how Hong Kong is "predisposed towards mall cities," thanks to regional historic building typologies such as the Hakka Village and the Guangdong shophouse, as well as local patterns of living, including the custom of occupying roofs and the habit of multilevel complexity stemming from contorting buildings to Hong Kong's hillsides.

In the second essay, David Grahame Shane provides an international background to Hong Kong's mall complex. He traces the evolution of Hong Kong's retail malls from nineteenth-century European department stores to 1970s Tokyo malls situated above railway junctions. In Hong Kong, retail manifested itself in isolated towers and department stores first, then as malls within new towns, and finally to central Hong Kong's three-dimensional meshwork of shopping corridors, footway bridges, and subway connections. These recent developments are true megastructures, cities in and of themselves, realizations of what 1960s avant-garde architecture groups could only dream of, and a high-density and transit-oriented urban form that is perhaps a model for future cities.

Zooming into Hong Kong's vertical malls, Tung-Yiu Stan Lai shows in the third essay how they are increasingly rising upward, stacking up floors of shopping as high as the Big Ben. But how do architects deal with the challenge to bring shoppers to upper floors? Lai shows how particularly designer Jon Jerde has succeeded in ensuring high retail rent values throughout, thanks to a variety of innovations including very large glass atria, a "spiral," and "expresscalators."

Nevertheless, as exciting as these developments may be architecturally, they radically restructure the existing physical and social fabric of the city. In the fourth essay, Carolyn Cartier shows how they become part of a process of gentrification that drives up rents and introduces high-end brands in industrial or working-class areas, while destroying historical landscapes. Developers and government have converted waterfronts, industrial areas, heritage areas, and working-class neighborhoods into retail space. And as Hong Kong developers export their models to other places including Shanghai and Beijing, mall city–style consumerism quickly spreads.

Chungking Mansions is an odd exception to this gentrification. In the fifth essay, Gordon Mathews writes about how this development became a low-cost heaven of cheap guestrooms, meals, phones, and computers. At the same time, with its unique South Asian and sub-Saharan African clientele, he argues it is "probably the most globalized building in the world." Mathews finds clues to the building's peculiarity in its unique history, including its large South Asian population and lack of a unified ownership structure.

In the sixth essay, Cecilia L. Chu challenges the conceptualization of malls as solely a commercialized space eroding the traditional spheres of community. Focusing on New Town Plaza, Chu shows how community development is key to the mega malls of the early 1980s, as developers provided locals with billiards, bowling arenas, ice skating rinks, and fountains. To many residents of new towns, the mall became more than just a capitalist space for making profits, but a place they attached sentiment and meaning to, on their own terms. Ironically, as the mega malls that used to be places of mass consumption strive to be more exclusive today, they formed the basis for resistance to development, since local community groups protest against further changes.

Jonathan D. Solomon, in the seventh essay, questions the notion that Hong Kong's malls are anti-urban by default, like many Western examples. Not all developments fulfill the stereotype of the "glo-cal bypass," like Union Square, which links directly to the airport but has little local connections. The International Finance Centre (IFC), on the other hand, is an example of a "global village," more integrated globally and locally, the crossroads between the airport, railway, ferry, and local neighborhood—partly because of a unique set of footbridges. In his intricate drawings of the networks, IFC stands at the intersection of a new type of public urban space network of shopping centers and footbridges that have the potential to create new class encounters, like Baudelaire once observed on Parisian boulevards.

In short, the mall has the dual potential to either erode urban public life or to contribute to it. At times it fragments the city with monotonous development, at other times it hyper-connects the urban fabric and enthralls it with diversity.

At worst, Hong Kong's mall cities represent a dystopian future of a city after the "Shopapocalypse."[10] They are the built structures of a state-of-the-art post-Fordist society in which people prefer to be in the mall as often as possible, not only to quench their shopping thirst but also to breathe in fresh air. According to a research conducted by the Environmental Protection Agency in 2010, the indoor levels of particulate matters of Hong Kong's malls were 70 percent lower than outdoor, thanks to their large ventilation systems. Malls offer consumers an oasis away from the smog, a place where they are not confronted with the undesired side effects of their consumerism: the nitrate-saturated air from neighboring South China factories.

The fundamental structure of a hypermodern society appears to be a medieval form of urbanism in which private enclaves stand as fortresses in the landscape, fragmenting the city in a series of high-rise gated communities, only accessible from shop-flanked gateways. Streets outside the enclave suffer, faced by the blank walls of introverted buildings, at best masked by architectural make-up. Devoid of life, streets are demoted to a place where people come to stand in line to get into the luxury shops—Canton Road has permanent queues into Louis Vuitton—as an affirmation of true brand veneration.[11]

At best, Hong Kong's mall cities are vibrant, diverse, and interconnected developments contributing to the public realm. Solid podium malls are broken into pieces that integrate with the city fabric, intersected by open streets and courtyards that increase and improve public open space in the city. They enable natural air ventilation, let in landscape and vegetation to naturally cool down the buildings and lessen heat island effects. The podium roofs are interconnected with footbridges so that residents enjoy the elevated level continuously. Podium edges are not blank walls but shop fronts that activate the street, or the podium lies underground as a base for open space. Finally, breaking the mall can occur on the level of a shop, by providing opportunities not just for formulaic flagships of global retailers, but for everyday shop owners that add to a diversity of products, for instance, in Argyle Centre's small stores, or in the tiny "cube boxes" in Sino Centre that anyone can rent for a little over a hundred dollars a month, with "no commission."

The time is right for Hong Kong's mall cities to reinvent themselves. Mainland shoppers might lose their appetite for Hong Kong's malls soon since they can find similar products and experiences at home: in 2012, three Chinese cities constructed the largest amount of new retail space in the world, and the city of Tianjin had more retail space under construction than the existing shopping space of any European city (except for Paris and Moscow).[12] Macao, by 2018, will have shopping space more than 15 times compared to a decade ago.[13] Will this fast-developing retail sector in Mainland China and in Macao's casinos make Hong Kong's shopping malls unnecessary?

Meanwhile, in the United States, the birthplace of the mall, there are many sightings of "dead malls." There, observers herald the end of the mall,[14] victims of high vacancy rates, "ghostboxes" (empty anchor stores), and "label scars" (still existing signage of a previous tenant). Retail increasingly leaves the mall to return to cities, streets, and markets. Yet, Hong Kong still builds more malls, while it eliminates its markets and streets.

During the Umbrella Movement, Hong Kong's 2014 protest for universal suffrage, students occupied neither the quasi-public spaces on top of malls, nor the interior atriums, but the little of what is left of Hong Kong's public space on the ground. They placed their tents smack in front of the malls, on top of highways. Their recuperation of public urban space expressed the street's democratic importance. Good urban space, and its capacity for inclusiveness, difference, spontaneity, as well as for contestation, is vital to any city—like the Ancient Greek "agoras" were places to buy goods *and* discuss politics, and became the birthplace of democracy.

In addition, public space appears attractive to retail as well, as shown by the shopping trends that offer alternatives to enclosed malls. Beijing's new Taikoo Li Sanlitun is a thriving retail district with shop-lined streets. Hong Kong's popular Star Street features local artisan shops mixed with restaurants. While these streetscape environments are arguably equally retail-centric as malls, they nevertheless benefit from the identity, diversity, and spontaneity of the streets.

Since the Hong Kong government owns most of the land, in contrast to most other places, it can actually exert its influence and break up the mall with the possibility of creating new exciting types of urbanism. This does not mean it needs to abandon the mall city altogether, but to swing the balance more in favor of the public realm. It needs to supplement the mall with a dose of public open space, just like it has used escalators, an export from the mall, to inject flavor into the city—for instance, the Central-Mid-Levels escalator, the world's largest outdoor covered escalator, which led to the vibrant "Soho" district, and now plays a major role in Hong Kong's cultural identity.

Whatever the future holds, this book features contemporary Hong Kong as a unique rendering of an advanced consumer society. Retail space has come a long way since the nineteenth-century Parisian arcades—according to Walter Benjamin, the birthplace of capitalist spectacle, where for the first time luxury goods had been put on secular display. It has morphed from the Ur-form of the arcades to the department stores,[15] and from the mall into the mall city: fully intertwined into people's everyday lives. Hong Kong's mall cities represent a new moment in the phantasmagoria of commodities, in which shopping is ubiquitous and mall atria are ever more mesmerizing, aiming to perpetuate a constant consciousness of shopping. If Paris was the paradigmatic consumer city of the nineteenth century, then Hong Kong is the consumer capital of the twenty-first century: a high-density "dreamworld" of mall cities.

NOTES

1 Data of leasable retail area per country taken from the International Council of Shopping Centers.

2 "City-state" is a politically contentious term in Hong Kong, which has become a Special Administrative Region within the People's Republic of China since 1997.

3 PwC, *PwC's Cities of Opportunity: Through a Retail and Consumer Lens* (December 2012), 13.

4 CBRE Research, *Hong Kong Prime Retail: Marketview*, Q1, 2013.

5 Emporis, "Most Skyscrapers," at http://www.emporis.com/statistics/most-kyscrapers (accessed June 14, 2013). Emporis defines a skyscraper as a multistory building at least 100 meters tall.

6 Researchers found that spending is directly related to the amount of time people spend at shopping centers. See Jon Goss, "The 'Magic of the Mall': An Analysis of Form, Function, and Meaning in the Contemporary Retail Built Environment," *Annals of the Association of American Geographers* 83.1 (1993), 18–47.

7 Jeffrey Hardwick, *Mall Maker: Victor Gruen, Architect of an American Dream* (Philadelphia: University of Pennsylvania Press, 2010), 216.

8 Tai-lok Lui, "The malling of Hong Kong," in Gordon Mathews and Tai-lok Lui (eds.), *Consuming Hong Kong* (Hong Kong: Hong Kong University Press, 2001), 25.

9 Diana Lee, "Pushy Times Square Guards Raise Hackles," *The Standard*, March 5, 2008.

10 The term "Shopapocalypse" was coined by Reverend Billy and the Church of Stop Shopping, a secular anti-consumerist performance group.

11 Katie Hunt, "Chinese Luxury Labels to Challenge Western Counterparts," *BBC News*, December 14, 2011.

12 CBRE Global Viewpoint, "Shopping Centre Development: The Most Active Global Cities," June 2012.

13 Muhammad Cohen, "Amid Casino Woes, Macau Retail Shines, At Least For Las Vegas Sands," *Forbes*, August 12, 2014.

14 For instance, Tony Dokoupil, "Is the Mall Dead?" *Newsweek*, November 11, 2008; Ellen Dunham-Jones and June Williamson, *Retrofitting Suburbia: Urban Design Solutions for Redesigning Suburbs* (New York: Wiley, 2008).

15 The development of retail in Hong Kong and other Asian cities has also been influenced by the advent of the department store in the early twentieth century. See Kerrie MacPherson (ed.), *Asian Department Stores* (Honolulu: University of Hawai'i Press, 1998).

Protesters recuperate public space in front of the malls in central
Hong Kong during the Umbrella Movement, 2014
Photo by Jimmy Ho

NEW TOWN PLAZA

MEGABOX

MEGABOX

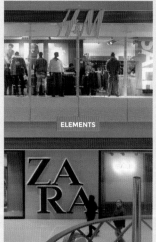

ELEMENTS

HOMOGENEITY

H&M
in Hong Kong

CITYPLAZA

LANGHAM PLACE

ELEMENTS

CITYWALK

CITYPLAZA

LANGHAM PLACE

CITYPLAZA Café

PARK CENTRAL

HOMOGENEITY

McDonald's
in Hong Kong

GRAND CENTURY PLACE

SHUN TAK CENTRE

ELEMENTS

MEI FOO SUN CHUEN

Part 1

ESSAYS

Figure 1.5 Roof as ground
Here, the roof of a nine-floor walk-up building is "ground"
for further building.

1. PREDISPOSED TOWARDS MALL CITIES

Barrie Shelton*

The typical mall city has two primary components: malls and towers, looking respectively big and boxy, and tall and slender. The former refers to the large volume of commerce and multidirectional connections (vertical, horizontal, and diagonal), and the latter to the upright residential tree structures of lifts and landings that link the floors within each tower. Together, side-by-side or towers over mass, they accommodate very high densities of both activity and residents, and their juxtaposition is now *the* ubiquitous sight in the city. These mall-city forms contribute to Hong Kong's standing as one of world's densest and tallest cities. It is the world's third densest. While it is unable to lay claim on the world's tallest tower, it surpassed New York for tallness long ago in that it has many more towers of 122 meters or higher than the "big apple"—558 to New York's 360.[1] In a similar vein, although it does not have the biggest malls (they are to be found elsewhere in Asia), I would be surprised if it did not have the most malls per unit area of urban land. Density works in Hong Kong because of a public transport system that is a wonder of today's urban world. Public transport accounts for nine out of ten Hong Kong vehicular journeys and the Mass Transit Railway (MTR) system accounts for a staggering 43 percent of those.[2] Public transport interchanges are close-by, if not incorporated in most malls, and MTR stations are sufficiently common to be considered the third component of major mall-city complexes. Further, these tripartite assemblages are powerful examples of compact urbanism. (Figure 1.1)

Over the five decades of mall cities in Hong Kong, the tower component has extruded skywards: in the 1960s the number of floors was typically less than 20 while today 50 or more is not uncommon. At the same time, the mass of the mall has expanded to envelop more levels and voids—15 levels in one instance. It is with some irony that these main components can be related to ideas that grew out of or were intended for very different settings. The mall links to a concept formalized by an Austrian émigré to the United States of America in the context of America's low-density suburban flatlands: Victor Gruen's "shopping town."[3] This was married to the Corbusian tower, with a cross- or Y-shaped plan (to minimize circulation space) and serrated edges (to maximize floor area and windows for adequate light), and advocated to stand tall and straight in the purity of plentiful parkland.[4] Hilberseimer's

Figure 1.1 Common podium-and-tower relationships
Towers rise above or beside the podium

* Thanks to Dr. Dan Li whose discussions of volumetric urbanism and graphic assistance were much appreciated during my preparation of this essay.

idea of the city as a series of bridge-connected podia, each covering a street-block and topped by high-rise residential slabs,[5] is another related model. "Streets in the air" concepts of various members of Team 10 may be seen as elements that link many malls to each other and their surrounds;[6] likewise Metabolist-like multilevel infrastructure, as introduced in the work of Kawazoe et al.,[7] can be seen to play similar roles. (Figure 1.2)

These are some of the more obvious international ideas that lurk, consciously or otherwise, behind Hong Kong's mall cities and their ancillary forms. However, there are other sources, in part more general but also more immediate, including local patterns of living, precedent local and regional forms, local topographic conditions, prevailing climate, and the nature of the city's policies that have embraced an odd mix of capitalism and control; some predate British colonization. This essay identifies this *background*: there follows a short overview of salient *changes in form* and a discussion that links the two together.

Background

Circa 1840, when the British sought to establish a trading post on the edge of China, they needed sheltered waters for their ships, mercantile and naval, and a site for an adjacent settlement, with merchant *go-downs* and a military garrison. That order of priorities is evident in their choice, which was a 2-kilometer-wide channel of water backed by a small but rugged island of just 80 km² but rising to over 500 meters—a safe and spacious harbor for vessels and a squeezed and steeply sloping "barren rock" (in the words of the British foreign secretary of the time) from which to defend them and on which to build a town. This was the original colony of Hong Kong; and it was on the island's north side that Victoria Harbour *and* the City of Victoria (which includes today's Wan Chai, Causeway Bay, Admiralty, Central, and Sheung Wan) were *together* shaped following possession in 1841. Just two decades later, concerns for defense of the harbor triggered further acquisition, this time a miniscule piece of the Chinese mainland. It was 9 km² of the peninsula that faced the island settlement across the water, resulting in the "twin cities" of island Victoria and peninsular Kowloon with control of the channel in between.

After another four decades, the territory extended again, this time not by one-tenth but tenfold: more "mainland" was leased from China beyond the peninsula plus some nearby islands. In 1898, Hong Kong's land area jumped from slightly under 100 km² to a little over 1,000 km², the new nine-tenths gaining the perfunctory title of "New Territories"—"new" to the colonialists though not to a scatter of village and clan communities. This time, there was no sudden extension. Blocking the head of Kowloon Peninsula runs a ridge of rugged hills that remained outlaw and big cat country until after World War II. Urbanism did not suddenly jump over the hills: instead, Kowloon and Victoria intensified between the ridge backing the peninsula and that stretching the length of Hong Kong Island. Peaks rise on both sides to over 500 meters while the channel in between sinks to more than 40 meters below the waterline. Even after World War II, Hong Kong intensified between these ridges for well over two decades, until the first road tunnels were run through Lion Rock ridge (1965 and 1978) to fuel the development of Sha Tin new town, which was a sign of things to come. Today, high-density high-rise Sha Tin (population 630,000) is a conglomerate of mall cities—TODs (Transit-Oriented Developments) in the parlance of New Urbanism.

From early British settlement, Europeans were greatly outnumbered by Chinese, whose culture dominated the region and Hong Kong. A relatively short journey upstream of about 150 kilometers via channels of the Pearl River delta was Canton (today's Guangzhou), which was already home to over three quarters of a million people and one of the world's three largest cities in 1800, together with Beijing and London.[8] A common sight in Canton was shophouses, of two or three generous levels in row formations, with narrow frontages and deep plans, and sometimes back-to-back. As the name implies, they mixed commercial *and* residential uses, and were often multi-tenanted. As a general type the form is said to have migrated to Southeast Asia, most famously to Singapore and Penang, where it was regularized in the 1820s by Sir Stamford Raffles to include a "five-foot way" across the front of each building. Thus a continuous covered "way" occurred for shopping along the street to provide shelter from the sun and showers in a hot wet climate.

Initially Hong Kong adopted the shophouse form, known locally as *tong lau* or *kee lau* from the Guangdong region. Early forms were generally without colonnades. These were around 4 meters wide, a dimension determined by the spanning capacity of local timbers, but three or four times as deep. Later came influence of the colonnaded form[9] and from the 1880s, colonnaded *tong lau* had a long life in Hong Kong, remaining the common building type until well after World War II.[10] Southeast Asian shophouses tended to be family occupied and divided into rooms. Guangzhou's buildings appear to have been mixed with many containing whole floors of free space[11] for subdivision and subtenants. Likewise in Hong Kong shophouse floors generally had no discrete rooms, each level being completed as uninterrupted space, except for a utilities strip at the back. In Hong Kong, each floor would then be occupied by a master tenant who would sublet in the form of "cabins," cocklofts or even bunk levels to individuals, groups, and families—an extremely dense division. Except during World War II, a continuously expanding population forced the building of taller shophouses and by the mid-twentieth century, the norm was four or five stories, with commerce, small industrial practices, and domestic living all mixed within but with predominately shops in high-ceilinged ground levels, often incorporating mezzanines. Hence covered shopping (colonnade *plus* open-fronted shop *and* mezzanine) was a standard Hong Kong experience. (Figures 1.3a and 1.3b)

Meantime, timber floors and tiled roofs gave way to concrete, bringing flat and usable roofs, which were inviting as *surrogate ground* in a squeezed city: few roofs escaped buildings. Statistician Robert Schmidt[12] drew attention to the number of very high-density districts in 1961: he observed 11 census districts with densities of 5,000 people or more per hectare. Here were thousands of

Figure 1.2 Hilberseimer's early modern precedent, 1924
Residential slab blocks rise above connected podia accomodating commercial and other uses.

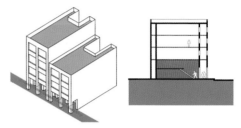

Figures 1.3a and 1.3b Shophouses
Common features of the shophouse were the covered way (colonnade), open front, ground space mezzanine, and commercial ground level with residential above.

Figure 1.4a Crossing contours: an early building (above)
This drawing from a late nineteenth-century government report shows the relationship between a building and a "stepped street," a section through the same building on an excavated hillside, and the "cockloft" division of space within floors (source: Colonial Office, "Mr Chadwick's Report on the Sanitary Conditions of Hong Kong," London, 1882).

Figure 1.4b Crossing contours: a modern building (left)
Modern Sai Ying Pun Market shows a complex "circulation facade," which is a response to the steep site.

Figure 1.4c Crossing contours: podium and tower (right)
This diagram of the Hopewell Centre shows entrances from the ground at both podium and tower levels—some 16 floors apart.

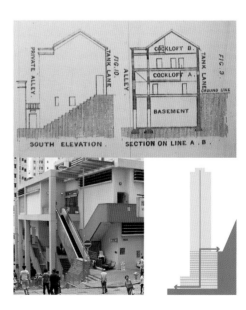

residents per hectare in mixed-use buildings above covered shopping. (Note also that 1961 saw the completion of the earliest of the later case studies, Chungking Mansions.)

While high densities were quick to take root, so were aspects of Victoria's morphology, which displayed a very distinctive structure. The city was long and thin following the first important "global" road, Queen's Road, which curved with the contour close to the water. Above, narrow streets climbed the hills more or less at right angles, and with such steepness that steps commonly substituted for pavements and even for whole streets. In this setting, the buildings in between would also step and contort according to landform to bring multilevel assemblages and complex links—a phenomenon of which the 1980 Hopewell Centre may be considered an exaggerated simplification: it is possible to enter the building at podium level on natural ground and exit above from the cylindrical tower also on natural ground, a full 16 levels above. (Figures 1.4a, 1.4b and 1.4c)

Hong Kong met its greatest city-building challenge after World War II when China was in revolutionary mode and the territory suffered huge influxes of refugees (more than 100,000 per year), with accommodation in perpetual crisis. For more than two decades, flows were unstoppable and squatter huts, fragile and fire-prone, blanketed hillsides. This prompted new sets of building regulations allowing higher buildings, and the colonial government's debut into mass public housing with some fascinating results. The legislation in 1956 allowed an extruded variation of the shophouse to "climb" to nine levels. The roofs of these buildings would also act as building lots with squatter dwellings mushrooming there too, to add to the height. Nine plus two squatter levels on two amalgamated shophouse lots would give a width to height ratio of around 1:5: this was an extreme in vertically extruded lift-less living. I am also aware of "holes" having been cut into walls between adjacent houses to give "neighborly" shared access and so free up stairwells as useful space. Lateral circulation between buildings would occur within and over them to become a multidirectional network— rather than a line of staircase culs-de-sac. The notorious example of this kind of set-up and density was the self-built mixed-use labyrinth of Kowloon Walled City: on a site area of 2.63 hectare, and supporting over 10,000 people in 1971 (census), over 14,500 (census) a decade later,

and approximately 33,000 (government survey) in 1987,[13] it had respective densities of 3,800, 5,560, and 12,550 people per hectare. It was a mass that rose to 14 levels, which was conspicuous in the landscape and prominent in the colony's consciousness. Roof areas certainly served as important gathering, recreational, and movement places.[14] Yet it should not be so singled out as the difference between some street blocks and the self-built walled city was of degree rather than kind. The point is that massive buildings, high-density population, mixed uses, and multidirectional movement were engrained early in Hong Kong urban life. (Figure 1.5)

Following devastating fires in squatter settlements in the early 1950s, the government initiated a building type of striking but basic form and built them in staggering quantities: the famous H-block. Each consisted of a pair of six- or seven-level slab blocks of tiny serviceless back-to-back flats of approximately 11 m^2: these were accessed along 1.2-meter-wide perimeter decks and linked at their middle by a stack of connecting decks and communal latrines and wash places—giving the overall H-plan. Though intended only as dwellings, the flats *and* balconies quickly became both homes *and* hotbeds of cottage commerce and industry. When the latter became excessive or too noxious, the government built an almost replica building type in larger format for factory purposes and with ramp access to all floors. In the residential blocks, a pertinent development was the placement of school buildings on their roofs, used also for other community purposes. Thus the H-block was effectively transformed into a massive mixed-use "podium" for school-cum-community buildings. Altogether the blocks had balcony decks around their perimeters, roofs as building sites, and stairwells connecting all. These were powerful and memorable no-nonsense multilevel forms that everywhere buzzed with activity. After these, with few exceptions, Hong Kong public housing settled for the familiar forms of slabs and towers, with access via lifts and lobbies or corridors. (Figure 1.6)

Meantime, new legislation in the early 1960s spawned another building type that vastly outsized the extruded shophouse: it ranged typically in height between 12 and 20 floors and its breadth might cross a whole street block. Light wells and indentations excepted, these appropriately named "massive blocks" were built to the boundaries of amalgamated lots, while inside were complex configurations of corridors connecting numerous tiny apartments, which might also be sublet above ground levels of commerce. These structures pushed the limits of cavernous living and contorted corridors, and over-burdened city infrastructure. Of themselves, they are here of little interest, but the forms, following from the legislation that was a reaction to the massive blocks' deficiencies, are important to the emergence of mall cities. New regulations of 1966 permitted building to the boundaries at lower levels (where the concern was for maximum volume and street front commerce), *and* set-back towers above (where the aim was for light and air to residential apartments). In other words, they framed a podium-and-tower form. At its most basic, the podium could occupy just two shophouse plots with a setback tower above—hardly a mall city but perhaps a miniature prototype.

Another building type that cannot be ignored is the square or circular "stacked settlement" of the Hakka people, of which examples still stand in Guangdong and Fujian Provinces. This form was a three or four floors building around a court or atrium and a conspicuous feature in the region's rural landscape well before British settlement. Outer walls were solid with peephole openings but the inside supported balcony decks allowing for upper level circulation around the court. Ground level was for work and ceremony. Some settlements consist of clusters of such structures; and it is occasionally possible to move between two or more of these at upper levels. These are truly volumetric with movement occurring around courts on and between balcony decks, and even between blocks. Many mall atria work in much the same way while the earlier mentioned H-block is a kind of inversion of the form. Slightly more tangential is a form that has been part of Chinese culture for millennia: it is the building of massive plinths that are effectively "podia" for further building. For instance, the rectilinear mass of the expanded section of a city wall to make a gatehouse plinth: such constructions, and many variations on the theme, have commonly provided elevated sites for buildings. (Figure 1.7)

To these formal phenomena we should add at least two other contextual circumstances as influential. First is the simple climatic factor. And second is the extraordinarily strong power of control over land development held by both British and Chinese administrations (which may seem inconsistent given Hong Kong's image

Figure 1.5
Here, the roof of a nine-floor walk-up building is "ground" for further building.

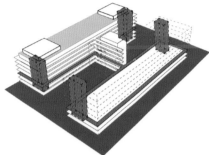

Figure 1.6 The H-block
The H-block consists of two slab blocks, rising through six or seven floors, of one-room back-to-back units, and a stack of communal washing facilities in between. Perimeter decks and four stairways link all units and floors. The roof is "ground" for school buildings.

Figure 1.7 Hakka village
This is a three-level round version of a building type that can be round or rectilinear. Circulation occurs on decks around the court at all levels. The house units occur "like segments of an orange"* with each rising to three or four levels; stairs connect decks at three or four points with stairs also within each dwelling. It is an unusual example of communal *and* private multilevel permeability.
* Kazutoshi Katayama, "Spatial Order and Typology of Hakka Dwellings," International Symposium on Innovation and Sustainability of Structures in Civil Engineering, Xiamen University, China, 2011, available at http://www2.cemr.wvu.edu/~rliang/ihta/papers/12%20FINAL%20katayama_paper_workshop.pdf (accessed March 19, 2013).

Figure 1.8 Expanding malls, extruding towers
There has always been considerable variation in the size of developments at any particular time, depending on situation. Nevertheless, the diagram is indicative of relative tower heights and podium volumes from the 1970s to 2000s: towers in mall-city complexes rose from 20 to 50 or more levels over a 30-year period. (Commercial towers and occasional residential towers could be considerably more.) The street block (of approx. 105 m x 35 m) is a pre-World War II Yau Ma Tei street block.

0   50m   100m

as a capital of capitalism). Hong Kong has a subtropical climate with prolonged heat and humidity for more than half the year, and an unstable mix of storm and sunshine. An early response was to build a city with a network of streets flanked by colonnades and covered shopping. The metropolis of malls extends this "sheltered street" tradition. The colonnade as a condition of development was easy to orchestrate in a place where floor space is at a premium: extending upper floors above the colonnade was an attractive model for all concerned. Second, with one church site excepted, all of Hong Kong is owned by the state (now the People's Republic of China) and leased for development by the Chief Executive (of the Special Administrative Region). Further, much of the urban land is actually "made by the government" through extensive coastal reclamation. The state has used its hold on this most basic resource to shape the city through land creation and sale of development rights (with conditions attached) but *not* sale of the land itself: that is leased, with the proceeds being a vital and permanent source of revenue. In recent decades, the state has also been the planner and major shareholder in mass transit and associated land development, which extends further its control. Thus in Hong Kong, the intensive development of land *and* movement by mass transit are *together* central parts of government policy *and* of the economic system: large-scale centers, incorporating shopping and other functions such as medical, commercial, and transport services, *and* associated residential and commercial towers are the essential components—as malls/podia and towers. Hong Kong is a territory of little more than 1,000 km² and a population of more than seven million yet

has retained 40 percent as country parks: this is indicative of strong control. In short, it is a *highly planned* territory, with the *mall city* as a model typology and major arm of urban strategy.

Changes in Form

The above offers a summary of experience, conditions, and tangible forms that have predisposed Hong Kong towards volumetric and vertical living. Mall cities are the product of overseas models, regional practice, and local circumstance. Since their 1960s appearance, their forms have evolved within a certain trajectory. Early commercial podia and residential towers appeared on older street block sites ranging in size from those occupying a few shophouse sites to larger amalgamations over the greater part of a street block. Early and well known as a podium *and* towers development, and of a size to perhaps warrant the term "mall city," is Chungking Mansions (see case study, p. 144). Completed in 1961, it is indicative of the form at its most basic with three 16-level towers over a podium that occupies the whole of a broad L-shaped site—or five towers if you regard two pairs of them as conjoined, which they are. The podium has a street facade and entrance leading to a grid of aisles-and-booths over three commercial levels and is embedded into the street block structure. On top of the podium, but clearly delineated from it while occupying most of its surface, are the towers. In fact, these bulky objects are more like bunched-up "massive blocks." As each of the five towers has its separate circulation, these are tree structures. The podium roof (what little remains around the towers) is left-over space.

Figure 1.9 A "through" position
At Tsing Yi, two lines penetrate the podium beneath residential towers at 2nd and 4th floor levels within a 7-level podium, including "ground." Maritime Square mall is integrated with and an extension of the station volume.

Since those early days, there have been changes to mall-city form: some are more matters of scale, others of evolution of the concept. Today's malls can encompass many more levels than two or three: the 1980s saw the mall component rise to eight (nine with roof garden) in New Town Plaza, Sha Tin, while in the last decade that of Langham Place, Mong Kok, climbed to fifteen. Similarly, tower heights pushed steadily upwards: while permitted height is determined by the dimensions and position of the particular site, heights of residential towers on less constrained sites were commonly 20 floors in the 1970s, 30 plus by the mid-1980s, and 50 or more in the early years of this century. Between tower and podium is the latter's roof, which has been used increasingly as surrogate ground. In early mall-city buildings, roof areas were not extensive and often unused, in effect "lost space": roofs not only became ground but also progressed from relatively passive and flat (some greenery, children's play area, place for tai chi, and perhaps a view to "borrowed scenery" as at Tai Koo Shing) to more active and even "contoured" (with pools and other extensive recreational opportunities) though this is often only for residents. Sometimes towers would hover Corbusian-style over the podium level on piloti. (Figure 1.8)

Since the opening of the first MTR subway line in 1979, stations have featured increasingly as

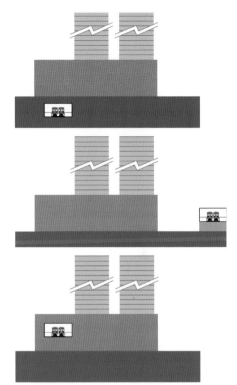

Figure 1.10 Podia/malls and stations
A station may run under, beside or through a podium/mall building.

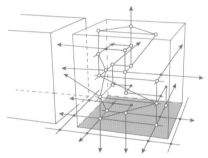

Figure 1.11 Volumetric networks
Connection is increasingly multidirectional within large mall/podia volumes: sometimes these multilevel connections extend to neighboring developments. Occasionally links also occur between towers. These developments highlight the potential for truly multidirectional (or volumetric) networks of links and nodes across cities. (Already three substantial networks of upper-level walkways line up almost end-to-end across the Central, Admiralty, and Wan Chai districts of the old City of Victoria—a straight line distance of some three kilometers.)

Figure 1.12 External links
Typical features of early podium and towers developments may be seen here in Tsuen Wan: residential towers, a landscaped roof, a multilevel commercial podium, and at least two levels of commercial premises opening to both street and deck: ramps, stairs, and bridges link levels and buildings.

Figure 1.13 "Breaking down the scale"
As malls became larger and more internalized, facades became potentially more forbidding: attempts were made to "break down the scale" of the building mass by expressing parts or simply diversifying facade elements (Festival Walk, Kowloon Tong).

Figure 1.14 Visual connection
This podium (Langham Place, Mong Kok) has a 15-level ascent/descent within: while much of the perimeter is blank and impermeable, the atrium itself offers broad view out to the surrounding streets and buildings.

an element of mall cities though their place and relationships to malls and towers may vary considerably. The common position is alongside or beneath. Extremes may be seen in Olympian City, which stands as a lonely island station in an archipelago of mall cities that are held together by thin strands of bridge (up to 150 meters long) in a landscape of transport infrastructure. On the other hand, the two-level interchange station of the fast Airport Express and standard Tung Chung lines at Tsing Yi penetrates the podium (with towers above) as a railway might penetrate a hill town from a viaduct. (Figures 1.9 and 1.10)

Such description raises the crucial matter of urban connection. It is a subject highlighted by Jacobs[15] and Alexander[16] in the 1960s and one we have come to know better in recent years from the work of Hillier,[17] Marshall,[18] and Salingaros,[19] although all seem reluctant to extend their concepts to embrace multiple levels, which are a defining quality of both mall cities and Hong Kong. The nub of their ideas is that urban vitality depends on the number and quality of connections within and across scales (much like creativity depends on the network of links and nodes in the brain). With Hong Kong's mall cities this translates into links between all main components: stations, malls/podia, towers, levels including podia roofs, and surrounding streets and parks. With mall cities, spaces and uses were initially layered rigidly with few physical and limited visual connections both within and between towers. Mall levels became more punctured by spacious courts and atria or took more arcade-like forms: at first these tended to be rectilinear but later often more curvaceous. Levels became more visible to each other. Stairs and escalators were given more exposure and even feature status to emphasize movement: in turn, escalators became differentiated between "standard" and "expresscalators" for short and long ascents. (At the same time, old city districts "borrowed" from mall cities with the escalator street joining the stairway street as components of the urban network.) (Figure 1.11)

Bigness can exaggerate both positive and negative characteristics of form. With malls, size can bring insularity: more connection within is often accompanied by less external connection: that is, with much blank wall to the outside and few and controlled entrances. In many early podia, the edges to streets were strings of shops, each with their own door, often at more than one level and with outside deck-access at upper levels (similar to the H-block but with wider decks). Further, decks extended into bridges to join with other structures across the streets. These arrangements are to be seen at Tseun Wan, Sha Tin, and parts of Mei Foo. But malls became more internalized and more fortress-like outside: to compensate, attempts were made to mask external blankness by fragmenting the facade ("breaking down the scale") as at Festival Walk, Kowloon Tong though this can be largely cosmetic. Even in the heart of busy Mong Kok, where Langham Place has a super-tall atrium and major entrances that are visible from the street, it also has long stretches of blank edge at street level where pedestrian activity is patchy when compared with the milling that occurs along the pavements around nearby shop-fronted street blocks. Langham Place is also interesting because the shopping "walk" passes through 15 levels within a very constrained space, as elaborated by Stan Lai in the essay "The Rise of Tall Podia and Vertical Malls": although this condition is perhaps attractive only in a city where hillside shopping has long been a fact.[20] (Figures 1.12, 1.13 and 1.14)

As malls expanded, towers nosed skywards gaining floors and height in what are effectively extended culs-de-sac: apartments became more isolated—from each other, the podium, neighboring towers, and from the wider city—by virtue of their location in slender single-use stacks. Ken Yeang,[21] in his discussion of vertical urban design, brought our attention to the limitations of uninterrupted repetitive stacking of identical floor plates and the need for "centers" and sky gardens within towers (to which we may add bridges) to form networks. While sky gardens have started to appear in some Hong Kong towers, bridges barely feature.

Recently, space has started to become organized more as a pile of intersecting volumes than a layering of single-use floors. If Chungking Mansions represents early layering, then its near neighbor, iSQUARE, is indicative of a more volumetric spatial organization—a step towards dissolution of boundaries between podium and tower. While iSQUARE does not include an office, hotel or apartment tower (and is therefore not a mall city as described here), it is indicative of a different set of spatial relationships. It is a collection of volumes and has multiple entrances, atria, and passages (not just at ground level) that connect two MTR stations (at the most central point in Hong Kong), Nathan Road (the spine of the peninsula network), and its own retail,

cinema, and restaurant volumes. Further, most parts are highly visible to each other, with views extending to the interior from city streets and vice versa. Perhaps "iCube" would be a more appropriate name, with lessons for mall cities?

Conclusions

Commercial podia and residential towers emerged in Hong Kong within an unusual topographical, cultural, and political-economic context. The territory was small, mostly steep, and squeezed for building space. In the post–World War II decades, refugees poured into that difficult space at a frantic pace. The pressure for living accommodation, shopping and other services, and the challenge of building were enormous. There were government responses, but the results were not always as intended. A combination of legislation and unofficial improvisation brought shophouses of nine plus two informal levels. Direct government intervention produced H-blocks of mixed rather than the intended residential use. Both were super dense hives of activity. They were also basic, unique, and "made in Hong Kong." Mall cities, together with associated multilevel infrastructure, emerged in the wake of this local experience. They also followed from knowledge of overseas urban precedents and models (from Europe, America, and Japan), whose arrival was assisted by a new department of architecture at the University of Hong Kong and an associated international architectural culture.[22] It was during the 1960s and 1970s that typological futures for urban structure and built form, especially mall cities and new towns, were cast.

Mall-city forms were consistent with local experience of spatial form and organization in several important ways. High densities and convenient services were hallmarks of Hong Kong. Covered shopping, incorporating open-front shops and mezzanine interiors, was common practice. Residential and other uses above retail were the norm and the ratio of ground floor shops to dwelling floors in a slender 9-11 level variation of the shophouse is similar to that of a 4-level retail and service podium and a 40-floor residential tower, about 1:10. The extensive use of roofs as ground and ambiguity of real and surrogate grounds was familiar. Constant changes of level in moving about the city were the Hong Kong way-of-life. Experience of the vertical and multilevel conditions embodied in twentieth-century overseas urban design ideas and models were probably greater in Hong Kong than in the places from which these were sourced. Development pressures were more acute, resistances fewer, and the hand of government in development stronger. The city's propensity for the vertical and volumetric, and mall city should not surprise.

Finally, mall cities are discussed here mostly in their physical dimensions. There is little mention of associated issues such as public accessibility. In their various forms, mall cities remain quasi-public rather than real public spaces where access and behavior can be restricted by corporate management. While authorities have always accepted density in Hong Kong, they have also favored simplicity and orderliness, including separated and stratified uses, which

mall cities reflect. However, the people of Hong Kong have acted otherwise: for instance, the presence of mixed uses and location of schools on roofs in H-blocks were sources of tension between residents (who wanted them) and government/management (which did not). The emphasis here on a certain kind of form and propensities for that form is neither to ignore nor to excuse its limitations. The combination of stratified mall and cul-de-sac towers is, by various criteria, a fragmented form of urbanism. There are, however, no perfect forms and a better integrated, more publicly accessible, and multifunctional mall city (including connected towers) with greater scope for public improvisation remains a worthy urban design goal and model—with Hong Kong predisposed to the challenge. (Figure 1.15)

Figure 1.15 Glimpsing the future? This proposal (for Melbourne Australia) includes a variform podium of parts with connected towers. The whole has a structure that is related to the broader city structure and a vast variety of uses: here are replaceable buildings *within* towers *within* a mega-structure *within* the city (source: Lok Ho Tin, "Megastructure: Metabolising over 'Lost Space,'" Independent Design Thesis, Master of Architecture program, University of Melbourne, 2012. Significantly, the author is from Hong Kong and his work is, by implication, a critique of conventional podium and tower forms.)

NOTES

1 Skyscraper Museum Exhibition 2008, available at: http://wwww.skyscraper.org/EXHIBITIONS/VERTICAL_CITIES/vc-pr.pdf (accessed February 24, 2013).

2 Land Transport Authority, Singapore, "Passenger Transport Mode Shares in World Cities," *Journeys*, Issue 7 (2011): 60–70, available at: http://ltaacademy.gov.sg/doc/JOURNEYS_Nov2011%20Revised.pdf (accessed November 25, 2013); and Global Mass Transit Report (2013), available at: www.globalmasstransit.net/archive.php?id=11965 (accessed February 24, 2013).

3 Victor Gruen and Larry Smith, *Shopping Towns USA* (NY: Reinhold, 1960).

4 Le Corbusier, *The City of Tomorrow and Its Planning* (originally published as *Urbanism* in 1929, translated by Frederick Etchells; London: Architectural Press, 1947).

5 Ludwig Hilberseimer's High-Rise City Project was made in 1924 and published in his book, *Großstadt Architektur*, in 1927. This is reported in Marisol Rivas Velazquez and Diego Barajas, *Ludwig Hilberseimer: Radical Urbanism*, available at http://138.232.99.40/atvo06s_bl_pdfs/hilberseimer%20research%20 072dpi.pdf (accessed February 26, 2013).

6 Alison Smithson (ed.), *Team 10 Primer* (London: Studio Vista, 1968).

7 Noboru Kawazoe et al., *The Proposals for a New Urbanism* (Tokyo: Bitjsutu Shuppansha, 1960).

8 Matt T. Rosenberg, sourced from Tertius Chandler, *Four Thousand Years of Urban Growth: An Historical Census* (Lewiston, NY: Edwin Mellen Press, 1987), available at http://geography.about.com/library/weekly/aa011201a.htm (accessed February 24, 2013).

9 It should be remembered that, in addition to the Rafflesian "five-foot way" in Southeast Asia, the colonnade was also a fashionable element in urban design in England through the Regency period.

10 A range of *tong lau*, including the colonnaded type, are to be found in Lee Ho Yin, "Pre-War *Tong Lau*: A Hong Kong Shop-House Typology," available at http://www.heritageworldmedia.com/downloads/pdfs/Hoyin%20Tong%20Lau.pdf (accessed February 24, 2013).

11 A variety of Guangzhou houses/shophouses are shown in Lu Yuandin and Wei Yanjun, *Guangzhou Minju* (Beijing: Zhongguo jianzhu gongye chubanshe, 1990).

12 Robert Schmidt, "Implications of Density in Hong Kong," *Journal of American Planners* 29 (3) (1963): 210–16.

13 Density Atlas (2011), available at http://densityatlas.org/casestudies/profile.php?id=110 (accessed February 24, 2013).

14 Makoto Kikuchi et al. show the process of Kowloon Walled City buildings "growing vertically and extending sideways to make lateral connections" in their "Case Study Gunkanjima and Kowloon City," in Hajime Yatsuka, *Hyper den-City* (Tokyo: INAX Publishing, 2011), 86.

15 Jane Jacobs, *The Death and Life of Great American Cities* (New York: Random House, 1961).

16 Christopher Alexander, "The City Is Not a Tree," *Design*, No. 206 (1966): 46–55.

17 Bill Hillier, *Space Is the Machine: A Configurational Theory of Architecture* (Cambridge: Cambridge University Press, 1999).

18 Stephen Marshall, *Streets and Patterns* (London: Spon, 2005)

19 Nikos Salingaros, *Principles of Urban Structure* (Amsterdam: Techne Press, 2005).

20 Barrie Shelton, Justyna Karakiewicz, and Tom Kvan, *The Making of Hong Kong: From Vertical to Volumetric* (London/New York: Routledge, 2011), 129.

21 Ken Yeang, *Reinventing the Skyscraper: A Vertical Theory of Urban Design* (London: Wiley Academy, 2002).

22 The Department of Architecture commenced at the University of Hong Kong in 1950, and graduation of its first student intake occurred five years later. The formation of the Hong Kong Society of Architects (forerunner to the Hong Kong Institute of Architects) followed in 1956. Further, for the first quarter century of architecture department at the university, chair professors (R. Gordon Brown, 1950-1957; and W. G. Gregory, 1958-1976) and some other staff came from England, where post-war education was promulgating a spectrum of Modernist ideas. Also, international figures visited Hong Kong and some practitioners had been trained overseas. The department and the library would have been an invaluable source of ideas.

Figure 2.2
Norman Foster, HSBC and Statue Square, 1986.
Courtesy of Norman Foster

2. A SHORT HISTORY OF HONG KONG MALLS AND TOWERS

David Grahame Shane

As more and more of the world population moves to cities, Hong Kong stands out as an important ecological model because of its emphasis on public transportation linked to high-rise residential and commercial developments, both in the center and in a network of new towns. As a result Hong Kong's per capita energy consumption is among the lowest for any city in the world, providing an important global model.[1] (Figure 2.1)

Throughout its modern history designers of Hong Kong drew elements of the unique high-density solution from around the world. Local designers began in a colonial fashion replicating metropolitan models from Europe, but quickly had to develop novel solutions under pressure in the new towns to house hundreds of thousands of immigrants who lived on boats in Tsuen Wan Bay and in self-built shacks around the village. MTR designers, Hong Kong Housing Authority designers, and New Territory planners all adapted American suburban malls to new purposes largely reliant on public transportation and a web of skybridges like Minneapolis. Designers then ported the new hybrid mall, podium, bridges, and housing towers that emerged to central downtown. Here Hongkong Land (HK Land) first layered skybridges between their office blocks, later working with the city to connect to super tall office towers above megamalls in Central and Kowloon (displacing typical American megamall theme park anchors to new towns near the new airport).[2]

This short history will trace the recombination of department stores, malls, skybridges, super blocks, megablocks, and towers in Asia, Europe, and America, with an especial focus on developments in Central and Tsuen Wan, the first new town in Hong Kong. The port and naval functions long dominated Hong Kong life, each with its own morphology, large enclaves for dockyards and barracks for the military, and fine-grained market streets and shophouses for the merchants. Larger offices and warehouses along the quayside served the big trading companies. By constant infilling along the waterfront Hong Kong succeeded in mutating from a colonial base into an imperial manufacturing powerhouse and then global financial hub in 50 years. This remarkable, accelerated transformation through recombination and reinvention is an important global model as many other Asian and African cities attempt to follow the same transformative path.

The Metropolitan Model in the CBD and New Towns: Street, Podium, and Square (1945–1980)

Hong Kong's impressive ecological transport footprint is the accidental by-product of an enormous planning effort, a great shortage of land, intense land speculation, and a massive immigrant influx after 1949 from Mainland China. Hong Kong's Central District in 1949 could not compare to Shanghai's Bund, with its many Art Deco Towers and eight department stores along Nanjing Road shopping street. Sir Patrick Abercrombie, author of the County of London Plan with Forshaw (1944) and Greater London Plan (1945), visited the colony in 1947, issuing a report in 1948. This report, though widely ignored in its details, framed the goals of the Hong Kong colonial administration until the 1990s. Abercrombie proposed that the large military installations in the city center at Central and Admiralty be moved elsewhere, allowing for the proper development of a modern central business district (CBD). He proposed that a road tunnel be built under the harbor between Central and Kowloon, and that the airport be removed from neighboring Kai Tak to allow for new development. In addition, Abercrombie proposed the development of two new towns to house new immigrants, one at Tsuen Wan behind Kowloon, associated with new factory

district and a proposed commercial port facility that would grow into one of the largest container ports in the world. Abercrombie recognized the special land holding structure of Hong Kong Crown Leases from the colonial period, giving long ground leases to large landholders, as in London, and creating a powerful group of land-owning companies, like HK Land, that would play a leading role in any transformation, as well as the municipality, port authorities, and the military.[3]

Abercrombie's metropolitan sketch provided the framework for the transformation of Hong Kong into a modern metropolitan center with a new CBD and industrial base. Hong Kong began its CBD modernization importing both Art-Deco architects and tower styles from Shanghai in the 1940s. Hong Kong long retained its Venetian, palatial waterfront with naval and military installations, while Shanghai's Bund erupted in Art-Deco skyscrapers during the 1920s and 1930s. In the center of colonial Hong Kong the big banks occupied the north of the Statue Square, the civic hub, while colonial administrators filled the western edge with courts and legislative chambers, as well as the Hong Kong Club (1897). This exclusive private cultural organization overlooked Cenotaph Square and the British war memorial (1922). The Shanghai firm Palmer and Turner designed the first fully air-conditioned, 14-story skyscraper for the Hongkong and Shanghai Bank in 1935 dominating the Statue Square. Moving from Shanghai after 1949, the same firm designed the subsequent two bank towers around the square in the same Art-Deco style, the 17-story Bank of China tower to the east in 1950 and the 20-story Standard and Chartered Bank to the west in 1957. In 1986 Foster's hyper-modern, free-standing, 47-floor Hongkong and Shanghai Banking Corporation (HSBC) building, with its rooftop helipad, replaced the earlier Art-Deco tower.[4]

Three enormous Victorian office buildings containing the big British trading companies like Jardine, Matheson, and Swire occupied the eastern edge of the honorific colonial center. Here the Queen's Building (1899), Prince's Building (1904), and King's Building (1905) shared a common cornice height, facing the domed, civic Legislative Building (formerly Supreme Court, Webb and Bell, 1912). The 1960s landfill provided the opportunity to redevelop the eastern commercial edge of the square at the same time as the new City Hall in the east. First Jardine's HK Land replaced the Victorian Prince's Building with a new 29-story block, then the neighboring Queen's Building became the site of HK Land's 26-story luxurious Mandarin Oriental Hotel (1963). In 1967 HK Land built the first pedestrian bridge connecting these two new buildings. Both office and hotel buildings completely filled their small blocks as their Victorian predecessors had done. But the introduction of the pedestrian bridge began to hint at the formation of a new CBD cluster with an upper deck of private circulation, a miniature equivalent of London examples of upper decks begun in the 1956 London Wall proposal and Chamberlin Powell and Bon's Barbican Scheme (1965–1976).

London was clearly a metropolitan model, with its ring and radial roads and infrastructure adapted by colonial planners to the archipelago of Hong Kong's islands and ferries. In the City of London Plan (1947 with William Holden), Holford, Abercrombie's colleague from Liverpool University, imagined 12-story modernist towers in the new CBD around St Paul's Cathedral's dome as in his Paternoster Square (1961–1999). The new 12-story City Hall in Hong Kong was the first modernist downtown skyscraper (Phillips and Fitch, 1956–1962) designed in a clean, Scandinavian, rectilinear style, following the SOM Lever House tower and podium model from New York.[5] Quickly dwarfed by the opposite Jardine Tower (see below), this heterotopic civic tower contained a disparate collection of public cultural facilities, a public library, and marriage bureau. Covered arcades around a memorial garden for Chinese civilians killed in the Second World War linked the tower base to a lower block in the west containing an exhibition hall, concert hall, and art gallery. A new army headquarter and barracks (28 floors, 1979) terminated the vista to Admiralty in the west beyond the public Chater

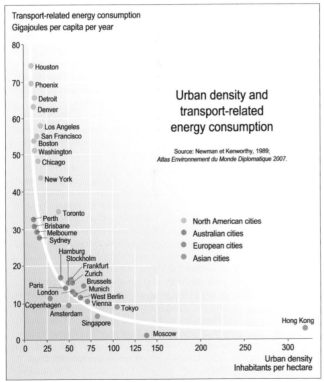

Figure 2.1
Urban density and transport-related energy consumption. Newman et Kenworthy, 1989; *Atlas Environnement du Monde Diplomatique*, 2007.

Garden park created on the old private Hong Kong Cricket Club grounds. In 1982 the Hong Kong Club employed the Australian architect Harry Seidler to design an isolated, new hybrid office tower and club house, with dining club rooms, exhibition halls, and an auditorium under a 28-story tower, financed by HK Land next door to the colonial City Hall[6] (Figure 2.2).

Many contemporary, post-war designers looked to Scandinavia for models of high-quality, modern public space and design, visiting Stockholm's open-air Hotorget downtown development (1952–1956) and Vallingby new town shopping center (1952). Sven Markelius, the Swedish planner responsible with others for both Stockholm designs, developed the section of SOM's New York Lever House (1951), where a low podium base shielded a courtyard garden at street level. Markelius combined the skyscraper tower base plinth into a low layered podium of shopping creating a new city section (Figure 2.3). Markelius's 1952 downtown Stockholm podium embedded a 200-meter (600 feet) pedestrianized, open-air armature in multiple layers of shopping, with bridge skywalks and roof gardens above connecting to the five office skyscrapers marking the city skyline. The pedestrian street led from the old Haymarket open-air square and theater to the new subway stop and traffic roundabout, in front of the new municipal building containing a library, theater and coffee house, arts complex, with a small, multilevel public pedestrian plaza in front for democratic meetings. Beneath a new subway connected to the new towns beyond the green belt a buried highway gave access to underground parking.[7]

As the Hong Kong civic and commercial center transformed into a modern CBD, so did the surroundings. Here the housing that once served the Chinese workers in the military barracks, docks, and company warehouses stretched up towards the Peak, an area reserved exclusively for wealthy European villas. In the Mid-Levels the small-scale shop-front merchant houses and stepped street markets absorbed many immigrants, creating an intense, crowded commercial hub that began to sprout small residential, finger towers on tiny shophouse lots. Later further uphill developers would build larger 40-story towers for the emerging middle

class along Robinson Road at very high densities. This Hong Kong hybrid model of high-density small lots and high-rise, high-density middle-class towers transformed Abercrombie's Garden Suburb model in Tsuen Wan, the first new town. Following the example of Central, the project radically altered the landscape, capping mountains to make landfill in shallow bays for new construction. Begun in 1963 the former fishing village grew to accommodate half a million inhabitants by 1975, beside one of the world's largest Kwai Tsing Container Terminal (1969). The first phase of the new town looked to Scandinavian models with small apartment buildings along open air streets and a covered communal market forming a small grid nested between the two industrial estates, with attached schools, a hospital, and public park.[8] The huge public Fuk Loi Estate (1967) provided modernist slab block mass housing, schools, and athletic fields. In the second phase the big private landholding companies of Hong Kong, Jardine, Henderson, Swire, HK Land, Sun Hung Kai, and Cheung Kong Holdings all built housing complexes around the new MTR station (1981). The original Sam Tung Uk walled village was moved out of the way and turned into a museum (opened 1990).

The Megalopolis in CBD and New Town: Department Stores, Bridges, and Towers (1960–1990)

The designers of the second phase of new towns, following on Tsuen Wan, not only accommodated the subway leading to Central, but also incorporated highways and shopping malls as around the Tsuen Wan subway terminal. Instead of following the ring radial web of highways and green belts imagined by Abercrombie, Hong Kong planners in the 1960s shifted to accommodate the car on a network of wide, American-style thruways with enormous clover leaf intersections and by passes as in the second development stage of Tsuen Wan (1981). Public transportation to Central still played a major role, but in a second-generation new town like Sha Tin, shopping malls, offices, and cultural centers linked by raised walkways became a standard administrative solution, following the megalopolis model advocated by Colin Buchanon in the London-based report *Traffic in Towns* (1963).

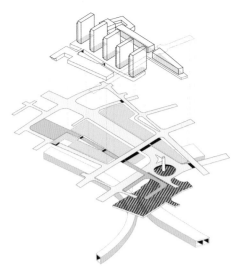

Figure 2.3
Axonometric diagram of Sven Markelius et al., Hotorget development, Stockholm, 1952. D. G. Shane and Uri Wegman

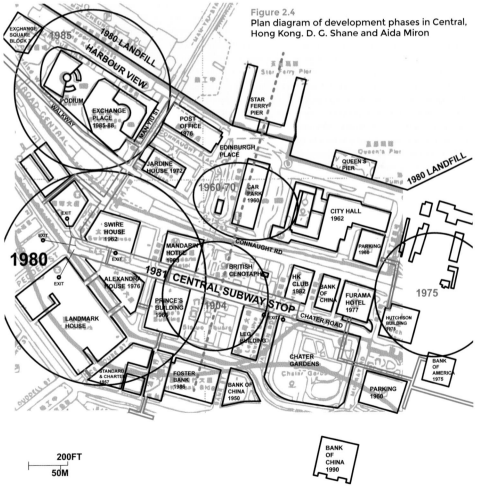

Figure 2.4
Plan diagram of development phases in Central, Hong Kong. D. G. Shane and Aida Miron

Jean Gottmann in *Megalopolis* (1961) had described the East Coast corridor of America as a single city stretching 400 miles and containing 32 million people, based on the old metropolitan railway system and the new highway-based suburban expansions. Within this vast city-territory Gottmann highlighted agricultural areas and watersheds that were protected to provide essential food supplies and ecological supports. He also highlighted the new single-family home with detached suburban life style that was obviously impossible in the new territories.

Planners and designers struggled to accommodate the automobile in rebuilding the central CBD. HK Land, for instance, continued to demolish the neighboring King's Building and York House beside the new Prince's Building to make way for the 52-story Jardine House (1972) on the new landfill.[9] This gigantic, modern, free-standing American-style skyscraper on the plaza designed by Palmer and Turner towered above the recently built new City Hall (1962) opposite. An enormous at-grade car park originally surrounded its base. The municipality built a new two-story public car park in Edinburgh Place between the Jardine and City Hall towers, blocking the historic view from Statue Square. Beyond this car park, built on new landfill, the new Star Ferry piers stood on axis with the HSBC tower (Figure 2.4).

Influenced by Colin Buchanon in the 1960s and 1970s HK Land extended their small skybridge system between Mandarin Oriental Hotel (1963) and Swire House (1962, redeveloped as Chater House KPF in 2003) to the triangular 36-story Alexandra House (1976) and Landmark Building (1970).[10] This connective network was self-enclosed and separate from the city, like the skybridges and mall at the base of the IDS Center, Minneapolis, USA (1968–1972). Later HK Land's network extended to the Stock Exchange in the base of their twin-tower Exchange Square development (1986–1988) built over a new bus station. Further to the west of Statue Square along Chater Road towards Admiralty a similar system of skywalks beyond the Hong Kong Club tower linked a public car park to a contemporary cluster of isolated towers: the 24-story Hutchison House (1975), the 38-story Bank of America Tower (1975), and the 33-story Furama Kempinski Hotel with its rotating skyline restaurant (1977, demolished in 2001 for the KPF AIG (AIA) Tower).

Figure 2.5
Tsuen Wan MTR station, mall with housing above, 1981–1982. Atwanist, Wikipedia Commons

In Hong Kong planners sought to construct an Asian megalopolis model by connecting the harbor tunnel from Central to a network of highways in the New Territories serving the new towns, while also providing provision for future subways. As in Central, a similar cluster of developments accommodating basement car parks connected the first phase of the new town uphill to the second phase site of the MTR subway in Tsuen Wan. Unlike Central, the big land companies built here a series of interior shopping malls leading from the main shopping street, Sha Tsui Road, towards the new station. The same big land companies filled out the second phase of the new town plan with huge private housing estates on the flattened mountain tops. The new MTR railway station, for instance, linked directly to HK Land and Jardine's Luk Yeung

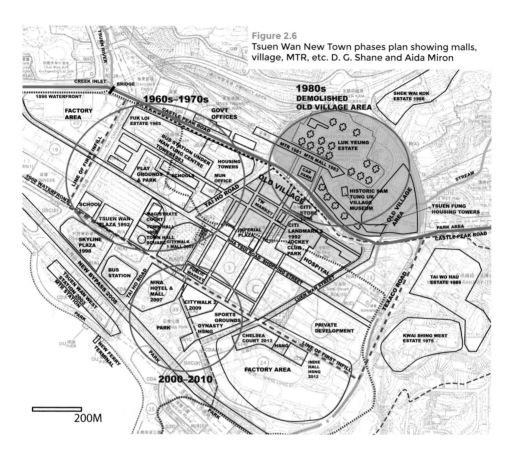

Figure 2.6
Tsuen Wan New Town phases plan showing malls, village, MTR, etc. D. G. Shane and Aida Miron

Galleria (1983), attached to the huge 17-tower high-rise Luk Yeung estate (1983-1984).[11] A system of second-level, air-conditioned bridges linked southwards to the older new town center along Sha Tsui Road via Henderson's Citi Landmark malls 1+2 and hybrid Citistore (1986 with a housing tower above). (Figures 2.5 and 2.6)

The Fragmented Metropolis in CBD and New Town: The Hybridization of the Mall, Tower, Podium, and Street (1980–2015)

It is easy to overlook the radical nature of the recombinant hybridization of European, Japanese, and American models in the small, fragmentary malls of early Tsuen Wan, linked to public transportation. In the European metropolitan tradition both Sigfried Giedion

and Walter Benjamin wrote about the modern department store as a temple of bourgeois, industrial consumption, following the glass and steel, transparent structure of Paxton's Crystal Palace in the 1851 Great Exhibition held in London, the first World's Fair. Benjamin and Gideon both highlighted French department stores for their innovations in the 1860s, where the staff of sales girls often lived in company accommodation under the roof, creating a heterotopic miniature city in the city. Benjamin linked the origins of the department store to the earlier Passages, covered interior pedestrian streets of Paris, cited by J. F. Geist (1983) as the origin of the modern, linear shopping mall.[12]

Japan was the first Asian nation state to industrialize and import such beacons of modern consumption as prominent markers on the wide boulevards cut across older, wooden cities, in imitation of Paris and American temples of consumption (Jinnai, 1995). European colonial outposts, such as Melbourne or Sidney in Australia, or Shanghai in China, incorporated branch stores of prominent European department stores prompting local copies. The British David Jones branch in Sidney, for instance, inspired Ma Ying Piu, the founder of the Shanghai Sincere department store chain, as his model in 1900.[13] By 1900 eight department stores lined the main commercial street Nanjing Road. The multistory, glass-covered atriums of these emporiums sealed the link between shopping, transparency, glass, light, and modernity. Sincere still operates department stores in Hong Kong, recently opening a store in the Citywalk 2 Mall in the Tsuen Wan new town.

Gottmann in his later research collected in *Since Megalopolis* (1990) described an Asian variant of the megalopolis giving the Tokyo to Osaka corridor with its 32 million inhabitants as the classic example of a global city based on high-speed railways, sponsored by the national government planning. Here the megalopolis morphed into a fragmented system of sub-centers spread across a network. The Japanese National Railway Company, for instance, developed the railway hub and high-rise shopping center district at Shinjuku. After the Second World War Japanese industrial conglomerates like Mitsubishi diversified into construction and commercial development, along with the national railway system. The result was the multiple department stores and later malls perched above the new planned, commercial sub-centers as at the Shinjuku railway junction in the 1970s. Each store contained its own restaurants and services, including exhibition halls, auditoria, and art galleries as cultural attractions. Bridges over the tracks connected the department store complexes.[14]

When American suburbia expanded into the car-based megalopolis, American department store companies like Allied and Hudson's played a significant role in the mutant development of the shopping mall between two rival, suburban, "magnet" department stores. In 1950 Graham & Company's design of the open-air Northgate Shopping Center in Seattle provided the

first hyper-successful demonstration of the effectiveness of the regional mall formula.[15] In *The Heart of Our Cities* (1964) the early mall architect Victor Gruen described the regional mall formula precisely: half a million people in 20 minutes' driving distance, 40 acres for parking, two department stores 600 feet (200 meters) apart along a pedestrianized armature. The intention of this open-air dumbbell layout was to force people out of their cars so they would spend more than 20 minutes at the mall when the so-called "Gruen effect" would induce shoppers to forget their intended purchases and buy impromptu, irrational items influenced by advertising. Gruen went on to outline the evolution of the regional shopping mall design from the open-air prototypes like Northgate, Seattle, to his indoor armature at Southdale, Medina, Minneapolis (1954-1956).

Gruen in *The Heart of Our Cities* took pride in how he improved on Seattle's Northgate by enclosing the 600-foot mall armature under a glass roof at Southdale, creating the world's first interior mall. In addition, Gruen emphasized how he doubled the size of the mall, while keeping it compact and 600 feet (200 meters) in length by creating split-level parking on one side to access a second story. The mall was also climate-controlled (engineers heated the enclosed two-story pedestrian armature in winter and cooled it in summer). Fifty years later this American mall archetype, reminiscent of Benjamin's Parisian Passage and glass-enclosed arcades like the Milan Galleria (1860s), still continued to draw customers.[16] Gruen attempted to implant his enclosed, two-story, suburban, dumbbell model in an old downtown in his first mall and mixed-use tower development at the Rochester Midtown Center (1956-1962).[17] It was the transformation of the interior of this mall model that provided the two-story, air-conditioned, linear, armature between Phase 1 and Phase 2 of Tsuen Wan new town in Hong Kong in the early 1980s, leading to the MTR station.

In Central, Hong Kong, the 1981 arrival of the underground subway system (MTR) at downtown Central Station on Statue Square, the terminus of the line linking to Tsuen Wan new town, also prompted HK Land in 1983 to rebuild Landmark House as a twin-tower office complex above a new podium mall so that all their downtown

Figure 2.7
Kohn Pedersen Fox, Landmark shopping mall, Central, Hong Kong, 2002 (original structure 1983).
Photo by D. G. Shane, 2009

landholdings connected directly to the new station, as well as two other subway lines, following the Japanese model.[18] I. M. Pei's nearby 1000-foot isolated megatower Bank of China (1990) soon overshadowed HSBC on the city skyline symbolizing Hong Kong's arrival as a global financial center. Later KPF redesigned the Landmark complex again (2002–2005) as a 4–5-story podium atrium with a Mandarin Oriental hotel tower and office tower above, still linking the network to the subway and the Hong Kong Station (1998) linked to the new airport designed by Foster.[19] The central, sky lit atrium served as the forecourt to a high-end Harvey Nichols department store, as well as housing a terrace for a restaurant, marking the transformation of the banking and government enclave into a mixed-use, modern, luxurious, global CBD as in Shinjuku (Figure 2.7).

The Megacity/Metacity in CBD and New Town: The Hybrid Mall, Hybrid Tower, Podium, and Street Architecture (1990–2015)

Before the handover of Hong Kong to China in the 1990s the British colonial administration

pushed to complete many of the proposals outlined by Abercrombie 50 years earlier. These planners realized that Hong Kong would no longer be isolated in the Pearl River Delta (PRD) and that Abercrombie's plans for a new airport and station would have to be at a new, global, mega scale, especially at the planned new railway station at Kowloon Central. This big new transportation hub would mirror and rival Hong Kong Central, connecting like Central to the new airport directly by rail and housing the terminus of the high-speed rail lines connecting through Shenzhen and Guangzhou to Beijing. Macao, the ex-Portuguese colony, on the other bank of the city territory estuary, to be linked by a new bridge, also emerged as a mega-scale entertainment and gambling hub overtaking Las Vegas in the size of its fantasy architecture and revenues.

British town planning operated at a European city-region scale, very different from the megalopolis infrastructure planning of the American highway system and different again from the mega-scale planning of the Chinese Mainland. The United Nations recognized Hong Kong and the PRD as one of the emerging "megacities" of the world, based on an urban concept first outlined in 1976 by Janice Perlman to describe unmapped, informal development in Rio.[20] The UN definition of what was a city then shifted from the metropolis to include informal settlements and also peripheral rur-urban areas known as "desakotas" or "village-cities" in Asia, first identified by the Canadian geographer Terry McGee in Jakarta in the late 1960s. The UN definition of the city shifted again later to include the vast scale of the new Chinese planned megacities, cities that included enormous agricultural preserves and green belts. McGee created a simple diagram to represent this situation, linking its hybrid small-scale mixtures both to ancient Asian rice farming traditions in deltas and to the enormous new scale of megastructures (factories, megamalls, gated communities) needed in the new megacities.[21] Rem Koolhaas and his Harvard students also documented the hybrid small-scale rural and urban mega-scale of the PRD city territory.[22] At the boundary with China the stark contrast of the productive rice paddies, saved by Hong Kong as a military and agricultural buffer, confronted the fast expanding towers of the new Chinese industrial and commercial center of Shenzhen new town.

Joining the small-scale, village-like structures together with megastructural three-dimensional transport hubs formed one of the strange juxtapositions of the Asian development model, as shown early at Tokyo's Shinjuku hub, abutting the Golden Gai village-like redlight district. In Tsuen Wan the innovation consisted of aligning several mall complexes in a long linear sequence to connect the main shopping street of the early, small-scale grid of the Phase 1 new town to the mega-scale of the new MTR station and its mall above the tracks. In Central during the same period the municipality also sought to connect the older, shophouse fabric to the new towers and new ferry piers. As at Tsuen Wan, a long linear finger connected from the Mid-Levels to the HK Land cluster of towers past the plaza of the Jardine Tower, the new Post Office (1976) to the new ferry terminal. Another long elevated passage along Connaught Road connected the new Exchange Square bus station to the base of the Mid-Levels escalator system (1993) at Hang Seng House. These escalators provided a long linear connection, as in Tsuen Wan, between

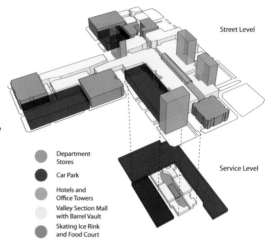

Street Level

Service Level

- Department Stores
- Car Park
- Hotels and Office Towers
- Valley Section Mall with Barrel Vault
- Skating Ice Rink and Food Court

Figure 2.8
HOK, Houston Galleria axonametric diagram, first megamall, 1967. Photo by D. G. Shane and Uri Wegman

the small-scale fabric of the older small towers and shophouses of the 1960s and the emerging mega-scale of the global system on the new waterfront infill.

Reyner Banham in his *Megastructures: Urban Futures of the Recent Past* (1976) noted the Asian origin of the term "megastructure" as a structure that contains a city within. Banham attributed the new term to Fumihiko Maki at the 1960 World Design Conference in Tokyo, attended by the Smithson's and Louis Kahn (both members of Team 10 who had designed large urban systems with complex, three-dimensional nodes and bridges).[23] Maki contrasted the megastructure, such as those designed by his Metabolist colleagues from Kenzo Tange's workshop, with both Modern and Beaux-Arts formal layouts, and with informal, small-scale, repetitive fractal patterns he called "group forms," creating urban villages as described by Jane Jacobs (1961).[24] Maki himself designed small-scale shopping villages, as at the Hillside Terrace, Shibuya, Tokyo (1967–1979). The Smithson's had incorporated small office towers in the 1958 Berlin Hauptstadt competition entry, attached to a network of raised, mall-like "Finger Buildings" with walkways on their roofs, a source of inspiration for Buchanon and Hong Kong.[25] In the same period the American landscape architect Lawrence Halprin also admired small-scale, detailed design, having traveled to Vallingby in Stockholm, filling his 1950s notebooks with sketches (published in 1969). In this spirit Halprin created the first downtown, multistory, open-air Festival Mall in Ghirardelli Square at Fisherman's Wharf, San Francisco (1964) around a cascading, landscaped staircase.

Banham, despite his Los Angeles chapters on highways, malls, and the "Art of the enclave," did not include either festival-or mega-malls in his *Megastructures* of 1976.[26] He did highlight Geoffrey Caldicott's design for Cumbernauld New Town Centre in Scotland (Phase 1 completed in 1967) as an early megastructure. This project followed up on the ideas of the unbuilt Hook New Town Plan (1961), forming a new commercial megamall center contemporary with the early 1960s Japanese Metabolist megastructural designs. Cumbernauld's vast interior shopping mall pioneered multilevel, mixed-use housing and office development above a highway and bus

station. The Singapore-based Design Partnership designed another sophisticated, air-conditioned version in their mixed-use megastructural mall, office, and housing complex Woh Hup (Golden Mile) at Kallang, Singapore (completed in 1973).[27] Cumbernauld did not incorporate an office or residential tower above the shopping armature, like Hotorget in Stockholm (1952) or Rochester Plaza (1956). In the 1960s American regional mall developers, like Gerald Hines in oil rich Houston, began to describe their projects as "New Downtowns" that would replace the old CBDs in 15 years including towers.

In Texas, Hines built the first American megamall in installments. His Houston Galleria Mall (HOK 1967–1970) started around an open-ended dumbbell scheme with an Olympic size skating ring below a glass barrel vault, with office and hotel towers attached. At one end the high-end Neiman Marcus store with its valet parking included an atrium capable of showing small aircraft and luxury yachts, as well as Ferraris. The second phase of Houston Galleria (1976) incorporated an atrium reaching up into the financial center offices above, as in John Portman's contemporary Peach Tree Center, Atlanta. Hines added the Transco (now Williams) tower, the size and height of the Empire State Building in New York, beside Neiman Marcus in 1983. The third phase Galleria (1986) incorporated a more arcade-like armature with indoor gardens, bringing the total square footage up to 1 million square feet, forming the first super regional megamall, attracting customers from all over Latin America.[28] In 2003 Hines added Galleria IV, bringing the total area up to 2.4 million square feet of retail shopping visited by 35 million people in 2011 (Figure 2.8). Megamalls of over 1 million square feet acted like Disneyland, advertised in the media, attracting shoppers from around the world. Jon Jerde perfected this formula in his 2.5-million-square-foot Mall of America (1992) outside Minneapolis. This megamall combined four department stores and four themed, multilevel mall armatures around an enormous, indoor, central theme park, within a single, large multistory megablock complex.

Jerde ushered in a themed, immersive, scenographic revolution in American malls, starting with the colorful, open-air Horton Place in San Diego (1985). The Jerde Partnership

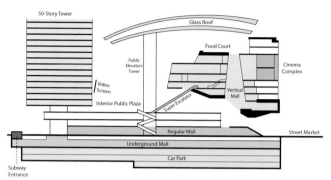

established a global brand for high-end mall design, after their spectacular successes in Las Vegas at the Treasure Island Casino (1993), The Fremont Street Experience (1995), and Bellagio casino (1998). Malls became places of spectacle and entertainment beyond shopping, including cinemas and even dinner theaters, bars, and more restaurants (Crawford, 1999). Jerde designed many dynamic, three-dimensional mall complexes in Asia, including Canal City Hakata, Fukuoka (1996), and the giant Rippongi Hills development in Tokyo (2003), as well as Langham Place in Mong Kok, Kowloon, Hong Kong (2004). Here a 59-story office tower and 42-story hotel tower hover above a 15-story mall (600,000 sq ft). The mall opens into a basement mall connected to the MTR subway, to an open-air street market and has a public plaza at the fourth level, above which a spiral of boutiques forms another mall connected to a multiplex cinema and top-level food court[29] (Figure 2.9).

In Central, Hong Kong, the International Finance Center (IFC) mall design represented a new hybrid development at a mega-scale, incorporating a mega-node connecting to earlier developments, a megamall and a supertall tower. In the 1990s Sun Hung Kai and Henderson Land, which controlled the rights to the landfill to the west of Statue Square, employed Rocco Yim, Arups, Pelli, and others to develop their huge IFC development, beside the new MTR Hong Kong station (1998). Together the megamall and supertall tower formed a massive megablock. The IFC

Figure 2.9
John Jerde, section diagram of Langham Place, Mong Kok, Hong Kong, 2009. D. G. Shane and Uri Wegman; Photo collage, D. G. Shane

designers, in typical Hong Kong fashion, quickly adapted the American suburban megamall with its four armatures layout, replacing the four department stores usually placed in the corners with three towers and an entry to the subway and skywalk system further west. Instead of the theme park that Jerde might have placed at the center of an American megamall, the MTR placed its new Hong Kong station at the center. Here a high-speed rail connection took 25 minutes to get to the new airport, as well as the neighboring Disneyland theme park. The 39-story IFC 1 tower opened in 1999 above the first phase of the mall while Pelli's over 1000 feet high IFC-2 opened in 2003 above the second phase, followed by an associated 60-story Four Seasons Hotel tower (2005) to the east.[30] (Figure 2.10)

The long curve of the IFC Mall between tower bases opened to a spectacular roof-top view out over the harbor at its midpoint, echoing Pelli's success at the World Financial Center (WFC) Palm Court, New York (1986). The landward side of the IFC Mall wrapped the back of the new MTR Hong Kong airport express station connecting via four bridges into the open-air, raised plaza at the base of HK Land's earlier Exchange Square 1, 2, and 3 developments (1986–1988). From there skybridges of the old HK Land system lead back to their Landmark mall (1983, remodeled in 2003–2005) and the connection to the MTR Central station (1981). The MTR built an underground tunnel connecting between the Hong Kong and Central stations (1998) while HK Land was slow to add a new connective mall (2011) beneath the Exchange Square towers.[31] Across the harbor a similar mega-scale development by the MTR and same mega-developer partnership at West Kowloon placed the 500,000 square feet Elements mall (2007) above another high-speed airport railway stop. Above the Union Square megablock scheme circled the mall's rooftop garden with a ring of 46+-story office, residential, and hotel towers. KPF's International Commerce Center tower (2010) capped the Pelli's IFC 2 (2003) tower across the harbor by 180 feet at 1,588 feet. At the same time in connection with IFC 2 and thanks to further landfill for a new waterfront park at Admiralty, the center of Hong Kong's government has shifted to a new symbolic core located at the Tamar Government Centre, the scene of many recent protests.[32]

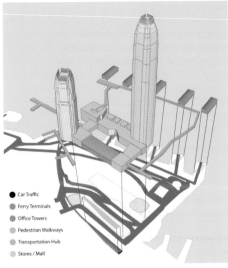

● Car Traffic
● Ferry Terminals
● Office Towers
● Pedestrian Walkways
● Transportation Hub
● Stores / Mall

Figure 2.10
Pelli et al., axonametric diagram of IFC 2 mall, podium, and tower, 2009. D. G. Shane and Uri Wegman

In Tsuen Wan, the 1998 construction of the MTR from Hong Kong to the new airport at Lantau Island with a new station on Tsing Yi Island prompted the new development. Above the MTR station the four-story Maritime Square mall supported the 3,500-unit Tierra Verde housing tower development on its roof (2003). New tower developments on the surrounding hills helped fill in the bay, where parks and sports facilities lead to the waterfront as a result of the 1980s citizen resistance to polluting uses earlier located there like the Esso oil terminal and early power station. New bridges connected to the Tsuen Wan new town waterfront across Rambler Channel. Here a second MTR station Tsuen Wan West (2003) sparked the fourth phase of development. In a massive jump in scale, Sino Land's 80-story Nina Tower and L'Hotel above a shopping mall base (2007) connected by air-conditioned, second-level walkways to their Citywalk 1 (2007) and Citywalk 2 (2009). Both of these multistory malls had huge, high-rise housing developments on their roofs, like the five 50-story towers of Vision City 1 (2007) above Citywalk 1 containing 1,500 condo units.[33]

Conclusion

Hong Kong's remarkable ecological profile for transportation concentration and efficiency is the product of an extraordinary set of circumstances. Such calculations never take into account the massive amount of energy embodied in the multi-year construction of the landfill so necessary to Hong Kong's success, capping mountains and filling bays in Tsuen Wan and Central. In the case of Central, Kowloon, Tsuen Wan, and Tsing Yi designers exploited the infrastructural advantages of the public transportations system, landfill concentrations, high-density living style, and low-cost housing finances to create a unique solution of global significance.

In each phase of the city's development designers recombined and scaled up or down a set of urban elements drawn from around the world, as well as from local sources like shophouses and stepped village streets. Military and colonial installations provided large scale land holding structures where urban designers could assemble department stores, office blocks and towers on plazas as symbols of modernity. Later department stores sponsored podium mall developments centered on subways, reworking the Japanese model, while also looking back to Scandinavian innovations at Hotorget and Vallingby. MTR designers, Hong Kong Housing Authority designers, and New Territory planners all adapted American suburban malls to new purposes largely reliant on public transportation and a web of skybridges like in Minneapolis. Later developers and the MTR supersized these urban elements, following the success of Jerde's scenographic mall innovations, creating megablock developments above huge regional transportation interchanges connected to a global airport hub.

Part of the fascination of the Hong Kong mall and tower story is how the skywalk system provided connections to a very different, small scale and heterogeneous, older urban fabric in neighboring sites like the Mid-Levels in Central, or the street market beside Citywalk 1 in Tsuen Wan. This variety of scale gave Hong Kong a degree of flexibility in the global market, so the city could accommodate many facets of the global market, including large agricultural and parkland reservations in the New Territories, preserved thanks to the concentration of population in new towns.

It remains a question whether the Hong Kong model of compact, high-rise development, new towns, and green agricultural belts can be exported to other cities, in China or around the world. Hong Kong undoubtedly has great lessons to teach to the developing cities of the world, but few have been able to replicate the disciplined administration, rapid industrialization, and concentrated economic power that provided mass-produced, industrialized housing to millions through various financial housing schemes. Informal self-built housing is the post-colonial norm in many cities of the global south, without any hope that an industrialized system could ever catch up with global needs. It is impossible to see the future, but the creative recombination of tower, mall, and walkway in Hong Kong inspires hope that creative designers in the city may yet provide a solution to the climate changes of the new Anthropogenic age.

NOTES

1 P. W. G. Newman and J. R. Kentworthy, "Gasoline Consumption in Cities: A Comparison of US Cities with a Global Survey," *Journal of American Planning*, Vol. 55, no. 1 (1989), available at http://www.des. ucdavis.edu/faculty/handy/LUT_seminar/Readings/Newman_and_Kenworth_1989.pdf (accessed June 15, 2013). See also E. G. Pryor and S. H. Pau, "The Growth of the City-A Historical Review" and "A New City Emerges," in V. L. Lampugnani (ed.), *Hong Kong Architecture: The Aesthetics of Density* (Munich and New York: Prestel, 1993), 97-140.

2 For key developments the many Wikipedia entries on Hong Kong and malls worldwide provide much useful information about date of development, land ownership, designers, and finance. Almost every project included in this essay has a Wikipedia entry. For metropolis, megalopolis, and megacity/metacity, see D. G. Shane, *Urban Design since 1945: A Global Perspective* (London: Wiley, 2011).

3 L. Wai-Chung, "Reflections on the Abercrombie Report 1948: A Strategic Plan for Colonial Hong Kong," *Town Planning Review*, Vol. 70, no. 1 (1999): 61-87. Stable URL: http://www.jstor.org/stable/40113529 (accessed January 22, 2015).

4 See http://www.p-t-group.com (accessed June 15, 2013) and for Foster http://www.fosterandpartners. com/projects/hongkong-and-shanghai-bank-headquarters/ (accessed June 15, 2013).

5 For Lever house, see https://www.som.com/project/lever-house; for Hong Kong City Hall, see http://www.epd.gov.hk/eia/register/report/eiareport/eia_0552001/report/vol2/eia_0552001appendix_w. pdf (accessed June 15, 2013).

6 H. Seidler, *Seidler: Selected and Current Works* (Mulgrave, Australia: The Images Publishing Group, 1997) and http://seidler.net.au/?id=24 (accessed June 15, 2013).

7 D. G. Shane, *Urban Design Since 1945: A Global Perspective* (Chichester: Wiley Academy, 2011), 116-19; O. Hultin, B. O. Johansson, J. Martelius, and R. Waern, *The Complete Guide to Architecture in Stockholm* (Stockholm: Arketektur Forlag, 2004).

8 New Territories Development Department, Public Works Department Hong Kong, *Hong Kong's New Towns: Tsuen Wan* (Hong Kong: Government Printer, 1972) and http://ebook.lib.hku.hk/HKG/B35835898.pdf. See also housing in HA, *Public Housing in Hong Kong* (Hong Kong: Hong Kong Housing Authority, 1996); for historic village, see http://www.amo.gov.hk/en/monuments_10.php (accessed January 22, 2015).

9 J. Gottmann, *Megalopolis: The Urbanized North Eastern Seaboard of the United States* (New York: Twentieth Century Fund, 1961). For Jardine House, see http://www.p-t-group.com.

10 J. Rotmeyer, 2010, "Publicness of Elevated Public Space in Central, Hong Kong: An Inquiry into the Publicness of Elevated Pedestrian Walkway Systems as Places and Non-places" (PhD dissertation, http://hub.hku.hk/handle/10722/174362, accessed February 26, 2016).

11 X. Yuan, "Hong Kong a Linked City: A Holistic Approach to Footbridge Design," master's thesis, Urban Design Department, the University of Hong Kong, 2012; see also MTR Tsuen Wan station mall at https://www.mtr.com.hk/en/corporate/properties/twl_tsuenwan.html (accessed January 22, 2015).

12 J. F. Geist, *Arcades: The History of a Building Type* (Cambridge, MA: MIT Press, 1983).

13 H. Jinnai, *Tokyo: A Spatial Anthropology* (Berkeley: University of California Press, 1995); and Shanghai Municipal Archives, *Forerunners of Modern Chinese Department Stores—Collected Archival Materials of the Four Great Department Stores of Shanghai* (Shanghai: Shanghai Bookstore Press, 2010).

14 J. Gottmann and R. Harper (eds.), *Since Megalopolis: The Urban Writings of Jean Gottmann* (Baltimore: John Hopkins University Press, 1990). See also R. Cybriwsky, *Tokyo* (New York: Wiley, 1998) and D. G. Shane, *Urban Design Since 1945* (Chichester: Wiley Academy, 2011), 178-85. Also see S. Sassen, *Global Cities: New York, London, Tokyo* (Princeton: Princeton University Press, 1991).

15 M. L. Clausen, "Northgate Regional Shopping Center—Paradigm from the Provinces," *Journal of American Society of Architectural Historians* (*JASAH*), Vol. XLIII (May 1984): 144-61.

16 V. Gruen, *The Heart of Our Cities: The Urban Crisis—Diagnosis and Cure* (New York: Simon and Schuster, 1964), and M. Gladwell, "The Terrazzo Jungle: 50 Years Ago the Mall Was Born, America Would Never Be the Same," *The New Yorker*, March 15, 2004, available at http://www.newyorker.com/archive/2004/03/15/040315fa_fact1 (accessed June 15, 2013).

17 J. Hardwick, *Mall Maker: Victor Gruen, Architect of an American Dream* (Philadelphia: University of Pennsylvania Press, 2004).

18 Rotmeyer (2010), 37–47.

19 For Landmark, see http://casestudiesarchive.uli.org/EZPrint.aspx?j=8107&p=5 and http://www.hkland.com/en/properties/china/hong-kong/landmark-atrium.html (accessed January 22, 2015).

20 J. Perlman, *The Myth of Marginality: Urban Politics and Poverty in Rio de Janeiro* (Berkeley: University of California Press, 1976) and http://www.megacitiesproject.org. For UN shifts, see Shane (2011), 29–32.

21 T. McGee, *The Urbanization Process in the Third World* (London: Bell and Sons, 1971) and "The Spatiality of Urbanization: The Policy Challenges of Mega-Urban and Desakota Regions of South East Asia" (Tokyo: UNU–IAS, 2009), Working Paper No. 161.

22 C. J. Chung, J. Inaba, S. T. Leong, and R. Koolhaas, *The Great Leap Forward / Harvard Design Project on the City* (Cologne, Germany: Taschen, 2002).

23 R. Banham, *Megastructures: Urban Futures of the Recent Past* (New York: Harper and Row, 1976) and F. Maki, "Some Thoughts on Collective Form," in G. Kepes (ed.), *Structure in Art and Science* (New York: Braziller, 1966).

24 J. Jacobs, *Death and Life of Great American Cities* (New York: Modern Library, 1961).

25 Shane (2011), 154–55.

26 Ibid., 102 and 328. Also see L. Liauw (ed.), *World Architecture*, Vol. 208 (October 2007): 90–91.

27 R. Banham, *Los Angeles: The Architecture of 4 Ecologies* (New York: Harper and Row, 1971), 119–20.

28 S. Fox, *The A.I.A. Houston Architectural Guide* (Austin TX: Herring Press, 1990), 233ff; D. G. Shane, *Recombinant Urbanism: Conceptual Modeling in Architecture, Urban Design and City Design* (Chichester: Wiley Academy, 2005) and Shane (2011), 166.

29 M. Crawford, "The World in a Shopping Mall," in M. Sorkin (ed.), *Variations on a Theme Park: The New American City and the End of Public Space* (New York: Hill and Wang, 1992) and "The Architect and the Mall," in F. Anderson (ed.), *You Are Here: The Jerde Partnership International* (London: Phaidon, 1999), 44–54. See also Li Lin, "Indoor City and Quasi-Public Space: A Study of the Shopping Mall System in Hong Kong," *China Perspectives*, No. 39 (January–February 2002), French Center for Research on Contemporary China, available at http://www.ln.edu.hk/cultural/programmes/MCS/Symp%2013/S1P2.pdf (accessed June 15, 2013). For MTR Langham Place, see www.jerde.com/projects/projectphp?id=31 (accessed June 15, 2013), L. Liauw, "The Good, the Bad and the Ugly," in L. Liauw (ed.), *World Architecture*, Vol. 208 (October 2007): 90–91; and Shane (2011), 329–30.

30 IFC layout references history; see L. Liauw (2007), 89–90; Li Lin (2002), op. cit., and Shane (2011), 295–96.

31 J. Solomon, J. Wong, and A. Frampton, *Cities Without Ground: A Hong Kong Guidebook* (Barcelona: Oro Editions, 2012).

32 See Kowloon Central at http://www.terryfarrellco.uk/#/project/0097/ (accessed June 15, 2013); see also Shane (2011), 331. For Tamar Government Centre and new park, see L. Liauw (2009), 102–3.

33 See New Territories Development Department, Public Works Department Hong Kong (1972), op. cit. and http://ebook.lib.hku.hk/HKG/B35835898.pdf; for Tsuen Wan West Station, see https://www.mtr.com.hk/en/corporate/properties/wrl_tsuenwanwest.html; for Nina Towers see http://skyscraperpage.com/cities/?buildingID=1319 (accessed January 22, 2015) and http://www.ninatower.com.hk/eng/mall/floorplan.php (accessed January 22, 2015).

Figure 3.1
Advertisement of Langham Place on construction site fencing

3. THE RISE OF TALL PODIA AND VERTICAL MALLS

Tung-Yiu Stan Lai

The Megapodium and Tall Podium

This essay focuses on the extremely tall podium shopping malls, a unique typology of Hong Kong's vertical urbanism. The 1990s witnessed the rise of new "megapodia" below the towers. These huge podia, usually accommodating shopping malls and transport facilities, can be classified into two types in general: One is the broad podium developed above new railway stations, such as IFC and Union Square; another is the tall podium, smaller in scale but piled up with plenty of stories, usually at urban renewal sites like the Langham Place project.

A "podium" in the Hong Kong context means the broader bottom part of building under the slimmer tower(s). The standard podium height of 15 meters is derived from reg. 20(3) of the Building (Planning) Regulations. This regulation stipulates 100 percent site coverage for the lower part under 15 meters (podium) of a building,[1] but maximum 65 percent coverage for its upper part (tower) above its podium.[2] This standard has formed the general streetscape of buildings constructed after the 1970s in Hong Kong.

However, since the late 1990s the 15-meter podium-height restriction has been put aside in many large-scale developments for covered bus termini, railway stations, and other public transport facilities. In particular, new railway stations have formed broad megapodia. For instance, the podium of Union Square (1998) covers over 47,000 m² but measured only 20 meters tall, which is slightly higher than the standard 15 meters. On the other hand, with more gigantic urban renewals amalgamating several street blocks in recent years, the government has relaxed the podium-height restriction, which is often justified by other forms of concession like street-level open spaces. These have resulted in many extremely tall podia, such as Langham Place's 90-meter high podium.

From the 2000s onwards, almost all large-scale developments in Hong Kong's urban area were related to either the Mass Transit Railway Corporation (MTRC) or the Urban Renewal Authority (URA): IFC (Hong Kong Station) and Union Square (Kowloon Station) under MTRC; and Langham Place together with the ongoing Wan Chai, Kwun Tong, and Mong Kok projects under URA. These are well-known examples that are substantially changing the cityscape of Hong Kong. This trend will persist since public interests such as public transportation and the improvement of old districts are increasingly used as justifications for government-initiated property developments.

The underlying ideology of these developments becomes apparent in their marketing and public images. The Chinese language denominations of three residential estates in Union Square, i.e., "Arrival of the Emperor" (君臨天下 The Harbourside), "Royal Seal from Heaven" (天璽 The Cullinan), and "Peninsular Propping up the Sky" (擎天半島 Sorrento), all express the same desire for superior domination. An advertisement on the construction site fencing of Langham Place conveys a similar message. It shows a huge red high heel trampling over the fine grained urban fabric of Mong Kok, like Godzilla crushing Tokyo.

MEGAMALL TYPOLOGY

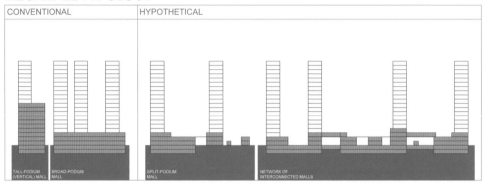

Figure 3.2
Megamall typology

The Twentieth-Century Hong Kong Vertical Malls

Compared to residential and office uses, shopping malls are constrained by their height. Except for restaurant customers, shoppers normally do not need an exterior view from the upper level. Moreover, they are usually reluctant to travel high, and prefer shopping closer to the ground. Therefore, the rent on the upper floors, unless for restaurants with nice views, is usually lower than the bottom floors. However, under conditions of high density, small sites, and high retail revenues, vertical mall design is a solution. This is why vertical malls are so rare in any places other than Hong Kong.

These abnormal conditions in Hong Kong led to decades-long experimentation with vertical malls (see Tables 3.1 and 3.2). In 1965, the five-story podium shopping mall of Prince's Building in Central District was the tallest. The regulations controlling site coverage and the 15-meter podium-height restriction did not apply here because they had not yet been enacted until the 1970s. Until the 1980s, all shopping malls generally complied with the podium-height restriction. However, New Town Plaza (1984) beside Sha Tin Railway Station, one of the largest malls in Hong Kong at that time, jumped to a total of ten mall stories including a G/F bus terminus and two underground cinema floors. Different from other smaller-block sites with podium height restricted to 15 meters, the super-

large site of this mall allowed it to be exempted from that standard restriction.

In the mid-1990s, the tallest mall in Hong Kong was the 1995-redevelopment of Lee Theatre in Causeway Bay with a total of 23 mall stories including 2 basement floors. However, its mall levels occupy part of the tower with less than 65 percent site coverage on top of the podium under 15 meters high. Hence, it is a case of a vertical mall complying with the standard podium-height restriction.[3] The second tallest mall was Times Square, which was redeveloped on the site of the original Causeway Bay Tram Depot in 1994, with a total of 15 mall stories including 3 underground floors. Its podium is about 70 meters high with almost 80 percent site coverage, so it is obviously not restricted by the standard 15-meter podium height. Over 20 percent of the site is covered by a street-level plaza, which might be the reason for the Buildings Department's relaxation of that restriction.

There are two contrasting mall ideologies developed by two important mall designers: Victor Gruen's (1903–1980) orderly, predictable, focused, and rational mall planning *versus* Jon Jerde's (the co-designer of Langham Place) shopping/entertainment hybrid, celebration of the chaos of the city, operation of the fun house with uncertain scale, orientation, and overall organization.[4] Times Square, designed by Wong & Ouyang (another co-designer of Langham Place),

Table 3.1 The tallest vertical malls in Hong Kong built in different decades

Decade of construction	Year of operation	Mall	No. of mall stories above ground	No. of mall stories underground	Total no. of mall stories
1960s	1965–present	Prince's Building	5	0	5
	1965–1987	Entertainment Building	3	2	5
1970s	1975–present	Hang Lung Centre	4	1	5
	1976–present	Alexandra House	3	1	4
1980s	1984–present	New Town Plaza	8	2	10
	1982–2010	New World Centre	4	2	6
1990s	1995–present	Lee Theatre	21	2	23
	1994–present	Times Square	12	3	15
2000s	2009–present	iSQUARE	24	2	26
	2007–present	MegaBox	19	0	19
	2006–present	Windsor House	17	1	18
	2006–present	wtc more	15	0	15
	2004–present	Langham Place	13	2	15
	2005–present	apm	10	1	11
2010s (until 2015)	2010–present	The ONE	22	2	24
	2012–present	Hysan Place	15	2	17
	2012–present	Domain	8	0	8

Table 3.2 Current tallest vertical malls in Hong Kong

Rank	Year of completion	Mall	No. of mall stories above ground	No. of mall stories underground	Total no. of mall stories	Exterior	Interior
1	2009	iSQAURE	24	2	26		
2	2010	The ONE	22	2	24		
3	1995	Lee Theatre	21	2	23		
4	2007	MegaBox	19	0	19		
5	2006	Windsor House	17	1	18		
6	2012	Hysan Place	15	2	17		
7	2006	wtc more	15	0	15		
8	2004	Langham Place	13	2	15		
9	1994	Times Square	12	3	15		
10	2005	apm	10	1	11		

demonstrates Gruen's style in comparison to Langham in Jerde's style (developed ten years later). In Times Square, an atrium on Level 3 spans over seven stories tall. Apart from the transparent bullet elevators overlooking the atrium, the vertical circulation mainly relies on single-story escalators.[5] Such ordered arrangement is suitable for rational shoppers, especially those having very clear targets of what they are shopping for.

Langham Place: Microcosmos of the Mong Kok Vertical Urbanism

In 2004, the 15-story Langham Place (13 aboveground stories plus 2 underground stories) became the second tallest mall in terms of aboveground stories. The project has become a model for the design of vertical shopping malls in Hong Kong. Its design not only represents a new order of magnitude in Hong Kong's vertical urbanism, but also particularly reproduces Mong Kok's dynamic streetscape into the mall.

As mentioned above, local architect Wong & Ouyang (HK) Ltd. and America-based The Jerde Partnership co-designed Langham Place. It was developed by the Land Development Corporation, which was later restructured as URA. This semi-governmental organization acquired the site after amalgamating the separated lots of old buildings on the original four street blocks into two. It closed off two original street segments and submerged them under two newly combined blocks. The western block accommodates a hotel and other communal facilities, while the eastern block is a shopping mall under an office tower.

Like most other URA projects, the result is a giant landmark that dwarfs surrounding buildings. From a distance, the 255-meter-tall office tower impresses with 59 stories. However, from up close, especially if you are accustomed to the standard 15-meter high podia in Hong Kong, the most striking part is its abnormally tall 90-meter high podium. The Buildings Department approved this unusual height since it considered the actual podium height only 17 meters tall, with its roof on Level 4 (the base floor of the Grand Atrium), rather than the existing vault-form roof above Level 13 of the mall. In other words, by deducting the transparent volume of the elevated Grand Atrium in the middle of the

shopping mall, the site coverage of the east block is under 50 percent, lower than the standard 65 percent.[6] This cunning justification realized Langham Place's two noteworthy architectural characteristics: An atrium that enhances the mall's verticality, and an "indoor" space that appears as "outdoor" urban space.

The Grand Atrium is placed on Level 4, instead of street level or underground station level, as a crucial node to draw customers to the upper floors all the way up to Level 13. First, it splits the long boring journey to the upper floors into two segments by providing a mental "restart" from the atrium. Second, its generous volume provides the space for a set of lower "Xpresscalators"—escalators spanning over four stories with direct connection between Levels 4 and 8. Third, this atrium provides every upper floor of the shopping mall, the so-called "Rock Pile," with an open view rather than an enclosed environment.

The uppermost Levels 12 and 13, named Ozone, house high-end restaurants and bars which benefit from the external views of higher levels. To draw the people to these two floors, another set of upper Xpresscalators, in addition to the lower one, is inserted. It continues the customer flow on Level 8 brought by the lower Xpresscalators from Level 4, and provides direct access to Level 12 through a smaller atrium known as the Spiral.

The biggest challenge is accessibility to Levels 9 to 11, which are bypassed by the upper Xpresscalators. The solution is to link up these three levels with the two ends of the upper Xpresscalators forming the Spiral—an atrium surrounded by five continuous spiral levels. The intention is to draw people up to Level 12, and then to pull them down via short stairs, ramps, and escalators back to Level 8. This reverse flow is revolutionary in vertical mall design. However, in contrast to its Xpresscalators that were widely used in later vertical malls, the complicated reverse circulation system has not been copied by others.

Apart from the more complicated vertical circulation system, Langham Place gives customers a different sensational experience that contrasts with the more rational Times Square. Langham Place reproduces Hong Kong's vertical

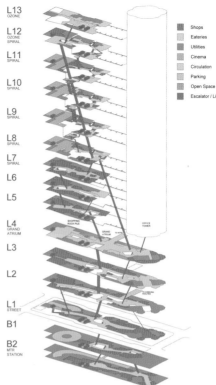

Figure 3.3
The large office tower and abnormally tall podium mall of Langham Place.

Figure 3.4
Isometric floor plans of Langham Place.

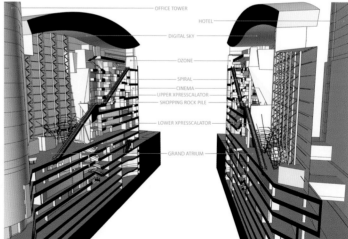

Figure 3.5
The plazalike Level-4 Grand Atrium of Langham Place with the "exterior" wall of the office tower as the background.

Figure 3.6
Sectional perspective of Langham Place.

Figure 3.7
The lower Xpresscalators in the Grand Atrium on Level 4 lead to the shopping Rock Pile of Langham Place.

Figure 3.8
Overlooking the shopping Rock Pile at the Grand Atrium of Langham Place.

Figure 3.9
The upper Xpresscalators through the Spiral of Langham Place.

Figure 3.10
The Spiral of Langham Place.

Figure 3.11
The Ozone of Langham Place.

urban space in an internalized and vertical mall setting. The mall spaces are piled up rather than stretched out, giving a tall atrium volume (Levels 4 to 13). This void space is surrounded by two glazed walls opening to the streetscape outside on two opposite sides, and by the shopping Rock Pile and the office tower on the other two opposite sides. Dark-blue reflective glass wraps the round office tower so that the boundary between the inside and outside of the atrium is almost invisible. The opposite shopping Rock Pile has similar detailing, but it is modified by irregular faceted faces of stone cladding. (Figure 3.12)

The ceiling of the atrium, the "Digital Sky," has video projections of a sky with floating clouds. The bottom of the atrium (Level 4) is a plazalike space with irregular kiosks of cafés and food stalls, the "Metal Trees" (treelike sculptures), lighting signposts, and temporary installations for promotional or seasonal occasions. Standing in the atrium, it feels like being in an outdoor plaza space that is raised above the street level of Mong Kok. If you raise your head to look at the

Figure 3.12
Expressions of invisibility of the atrium's external walls. *Left,* the joint between the glazed wall and the dark-blue reflective glass of office tower; *Right,* the joint between the glazed wall and the irregular stone cladding wrapping the shopping Rock Pile.

floating clouds in the blue sky, you may obtain an even stronger illusion of being outside. Under the same Digital Sky, a smaller plaza configuration exists on the top restaurant Levels 12 and 13.

The atrium of Langham Place offers a sanitized version of the real urban scenes of high-density Mong Kok. The district, especially the area surrounding Langham Place, was once famous for its nightclubs, massage parlours, mahjong parlours, brothels, and many criminal activities over the decades. Therefore, the developer and the designers of Langham Place had to face a serious problem of practically uncontrollable street activities surrounding the new development. Although an outdoor plaza like that of Times Square for commercial events can certainly draw pedestrian flows into the highly congested Mong Kok, it would also burden the management of Langham. Therefore, the Level-4 plaza has been internalized.

Although not publicly announced as a measure requested by Langham Place, the police conducted persistent operations against brothels, their signboards, and street prostitutes in the area surrounding the new mall, before its opening in 2003. Since then, brothels have been expelled from Langham's surrounding streets.[7] Instead, new businesses popped up including pubs, cafés, restaurants, beauty shops, and boutiques. These street shops or upper-floor shops are in similar business sectors to Langham but are generally of lower end. Today, more gigantic podia and towers are being redeveloped from amalgamated small lots and rising up like Langham within Mong Kok, radically altering the fine grain of the urban fabric.

The two opposite atrium glazed walls express the ambiguous attitude of the mall to the surrounding streetscape. On the one hand, from the major access to the mall—the congested junction of Nelson Street and Portland Street—you can see the restless flow of shoppers and the ever-changing clouds in the Digital Sky in the atrium through the first layer of the glazed wall, and then further see Langham Hotel behind through the second layer. On the other hand, inside the atrium, you can experience an illusion of trampling the energetic Mong Kok streets; when you are raised by the Xpresscalator, you can even see the close-up of the surrounding

buildings' windows and additional roof structures. Under your own "sky," in an air-conditioned urban space, on your "seat" moving along the escalators, you become an audience of the Mong Kok streetscape; but the heat or chill, the noise of vehicles, and the smell of cigarettes outside are all screened off by the glass. You are in Mong Kok, but not a part of Mong Kok; you become a visual consumer of the streetscape only.

The Post-Langham Malls in Hong Kong

Shopping malls built after Langham Place (2004) follow the irreversible trend of verticality. By the end of 2012, there are ten malls with over ten stories and three malls with over twenty stories. The fundamental reason is not architectural but economic. The influx of mainland Chinese tourists and the persisting depreciation of Hong Kong dollar have created the high demand for retail spaces over residential and office spaces in the property market these years.

In 2007, Jerde designed another vertical mall, MegaBox in Kowloon Bay in collaboration with Wong Tung & Partners. Its podium height is similar to Langham, which is about 90 meters. However, with totally 19 stories, its car parking spaces are spread to the peripheries of most of the shopping floors, and in fact Levels 16 and 17 are wholly used as carpark. This is another revolutionary circulation system in vertical mall design, which can reduce the driving shoppers' mental distance and height of access to the shops on the upper floors. Apart from this innovation, most of the design formulae of Langham were reused here, such as visual extension of external cityscape into the mall, express escalators spanning over several stories, and an optional (no longer compulsory as in Langham) reverse customer flow in downward direction. Nevertheless, the spatial continuity as in Langham is not as smooth in MegaBox due to the split of mall by the mid-level carparking floors and the lack of inter-floor visual connection via any atrium on the upper levels. In other words, the mall atmosphere can hardly extend further upward from the lower 14 levels.

Some of Jerde's formulae in Langham and MegaBox have also been adopted later in other vertical malls like iSQUARE, The One, Hysan

Figure 3.13
Nightclub signs in the red-light district of Mong Kok.

Figure 3.14
Portland Street. *Above*, businesses such as pubs, nighclubs, and bathhouses have been expelled from the area adjacent to the new Langham Place mall; *Below*, further from the mall neon signs still exist.

Figure 3.15
From the outside, through the first layer of the glazed wall, the restless flow of shoppers in Langham Place's atrium can be seen simultaneously with the buildings behind the second glass skin.

Figure 3.16
Inside the atrium of Langham Place shoppers get a panoramic view of Mong Kok.

Place, etc. Currently the tallest mall in Hong Kong is the 2009-built iSQUARE in Tsim Sha Tsui with a total of 26 mall stories including 2 underground floors. However, it is split into three quite independent portions with an exclusive cinema block on Level 11 (the 13th mall level from basement) bisecting the lower mall and the upper tower above the podium. Since this tower portion accomodates only restaurants, health care centers, and customer service offices that are solely elevator-accessed, it cannot really be regarded as part of the shopping mall. In fact, the number of shoppers substantially drops on the levels above the Level-6 atrium.

These recent vertical malls may have exhausted the feasible height limit of a shopping mall in Hong Kong. The 15-story Langham Place seems close to the limit. The difficulties in maintaining the continuous inter-floor visual connection and customer flow, which are crucial for successful vertical malls, are in direct proportion to height. As mentioned above, this vertical trend violates the typical customer's preference to shopping closer to the ground. If one day the demand for retail spaces in Hong Kong would decrease, megapodia in Hong Kong would deflate from tall to broad massing. In fact, there has been a trend of decreasing height of malls in Hong Kong since iSQUARE (2010) (see Table 3.1).

It may be that the site of a new bigger broad-podium mall will ultimately split into smaller blocks with reproduced street or plaza spaces in between (see hypothetical megamall types in Figure 3.2). This would possibly become a network of smaller malls with elevated, street-level, and underground interconnections. Indeed, at least three groups of proximate malls in Hong Kong have been renovated or repackaged as shopping networks under the same developers since 2012.[8] These malls in a network are interconnected by footbridges and/or underground tunnels. Despite being new in Hong Kong, this type of mall networks has already ocurred for years in Japanese cities with similar well-developed railway networks. Nevertheless, instead of only verticalizing or internalizing the shopping paths, Japanese also fuse railway lines, buildings, urban space, and landscape into the smooth pedestrian paths. For example, around Kyoto Station is an extensive underground mall network that connects railway

Figure 3.17
"Porta," the underground mall-network around Kyoto Station.

Figure 3.18
The Shinsaibashi covered arcade network, Osaka.

Figure 3.19
Jerde's "Namba Parks" mall, Osaka.

lines to surrounding commercial buildings, combining a transport terminus and shops into a plaza.

Sometimes, these networks are so extensive that they span over several railway stations within an entire district. The shopping network along the Shinsaibashi and Namba districts of Osaka, for instance, connects several malls, department stores, and stations of railway lines run by different companies. This gradually built-up vertical as well as lateral network is composed of underground and aboveground malls, covered arcades, open streets, plazas, canal promenades, elevated walkways, platforms, sky gardens, and other forms of urban spaces. Podia and towers are only one type of components in the whole system. Jerde's other project, Namba Parks (2003), is a landmark mall in this network. Placed under an office tower, a curvilinear open walkway splits the podium mall into two, while terraces carve out eight levels of cascading roof gardens all the way down to the street level.

The new trend in Hong Kong and progressive examples from Japan show that shopping malls do not have to be violently imposed to, they can also be seamlessly blended into the fabric of the city. In the old streets of Mong Kok, such an urban renewal approach could lead to a more sensitive transformation of the district: one that does not trample like a "high heel"—or rather big foot— onto the fine-grained urban fabric.

NOTES

1 The original regulation is: "Subject to the provisions of paragraph (4), the site coverage for a non-domestic building, or for the non-domestic part of a composite building, on a class A, B or C site may, whatever the height of the building, exceed the permitted percentage site coverage to a height not exceeding 15 m above ground level."

2 There are two conditions for the 65% site coverage: 1) building height over 61 meters; 2) class C site abutting on at least three streets.

3 The definition of Lee Theatre as shopping mall is arguable since almost all the floors above its four podium stories are single-tenant restaurants or beauty centers only accessed by elevators. This particular type of commercial buildings has also been popular since the 1990s, such as One Peking Road and Causeway Bay Plaza 1, which can be separately categorized.

4 Daniel Herman, "Jerde Transfer," in Chuihua Judy Chung et al. (eds.), *Harvard Design School Guide to Shopping* (Köln: Taschen; Cambridge, MA: Harvard Design School, 2001), 402–7.

5 There are three "express escalators" spanning more than one story added in the atrium of Times Square in recent years.

6 "Langham Place: Urban Oasis," Division of Building Science and Technology, City University of Hong Kong, p. 6, at http://bst1.cityu.edu.hk/e%2Dlearning/building%5Finfo%5Fpack/tall_building/langham.pdf (accessed October 21, 2015).

7 "朗豪坊效應打散紅燈區 旺角淫業3招應變求存" [Langham Place effect breaks up the red-light district; 3 strokes from the Mong Kok prostitution respond for survival], *Apple Daily*, May 5, 2006, at http://hk.apple.nextmedia.com/news/art/20060505/5893741 (accessed October 21, 2015).

8 The new shopping networks include (1) Landmark in Central district (composed of Landmark Atrium, Landmark Prince's, Landmark Alexandra, Landmark Chater, Jardine House, One, Two, and Three Exchange Square, and The Forum); (2) Lee Gardens in Causeway Bay district (composed of Hysan Place, Lee Theatre, 111 Leighton Road, 18 Hysan Avenue, One Hysan Avenue, Lee Gardens One, and Lee Gardens Two); and (3) Tai Po Mega Mall in Tai Po district (composed of Zones A to E).

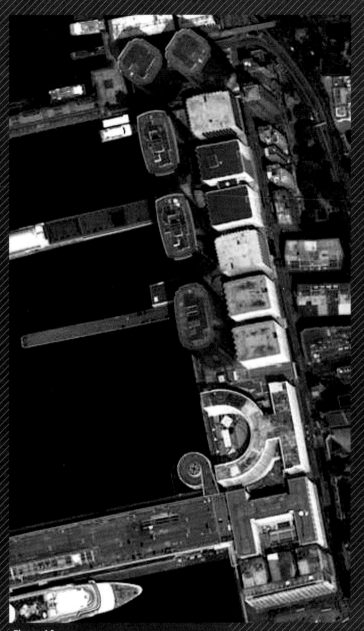

Figure 4.1
Harbour City, Tsim Sha Tsui. Google Earth, 2013

4. Restructuring Urban Space

THE MALL IN MIXED-USE DEVELOPMENTS

Carolyn Cartier

Urban redevelopment in Hong Kong seems like a process in perpetual motion. New building and construction projects periodically emerge in almost every district, whether in the planned new towns and industrial areas of the Kowloon Peninsula, or in the commercial centers of Hong Kong Island. The ongoing process of redevelopment drives the property industry and restructures urban space by transforming industrial areas into new residential and retail hubs. Ordinary places in out-of-the-way districts become new consumer destinations. On reclaimed land, property developers erect entirely new mixed-use built environments, virtual citadels on the shore. Predictably, every new mixed-use property development in Hong Kong contains a mall.

This essay focuses on malls in mixed-use developments to assess their contexts in the urban environment and impacts on urban restructuring. Mixed-use developments in Hong Kong provide residential, retail, and office space and often also contain a hotel or serviced apartments. Urban restructuring typically refers to how places change as a consequence of the declining of manufacturing and the rising of service industries, including retail.[1] Restructuring in a global city like Hong Kong makes consumerism a way of life. New malls in mixed-used developments often feature spectacular designs and symbolize urban modernity. But the global city is also characterized by social inequality. New property developments also represent the loss of everyday landscapes in historic neighborhoods, with impacts on local residents. This perspective of relational restructuring, or how change in one place and time is related to change in other places and times, also invokes spatial relations between development sites, the city, the nation, and the world.

Hong Kong is a global city of the world—Asia's world city. It is also the primary shopping destination for China at large. Since 2003, when the Hong Kong and mainland governments established the Closer Economic Partnership Arrangement and the Individual Visit Scheme, malls in Hong Kong have become the leading sites of consumer experience for visitors from Mainland China.[2] As showcases for urban design and new consumer culture, many Hong Kong malls have become well-known landmarks for new Chinese consumers. Property developers have capitalized on these relational expectations by building virtual models of Hong Kong's famous malls in Beijing and Shanghai. This essay develops a historical perspective on the mall in Hong Kong, and ultimately follows the Hong Kong mall to mainland cities.

Mixed-Use Redevelopment and Spatial Restructuring

Most of the largest mixed-use properties in Hong Kong co-locate with transit hubs. Development of mixed-used properties in Hong Kong rearranges the space of the city by co-locating residential, business, retail, leisure, and transport spaces. Placed purposefully at the crossroads of these multiple functions, malls in mixed-use developments become transition zones and spaces of daily life. The path to and from the high-rise home or flat to the MTR station segues through the mall, turning the mall's constituent spaces and establishments into regular zones of passing by, daily necessities, and social contact.

Extreme urban density in Hong Kong would appear to compel high-rise mixed-used property development, yet spatial determinism cannot explain the realities of urban restructuring. Investment in new mixed-use redevelopment sets in motion the process of spatial restructuring that drives economic growth through the construction industry, real estate development, and higher rents.[3] Large-scale mixed-use development restructures the city by increasing density and total rents, eliminating historical landscapes, and building "pre-demand" infrastructure by exceeding existing demand through sheer scale of capacity. For example, the outsize Kowloon Station, on the Tung Chung MTR and Airport Express lines under the massive Union Square development that contains the Elements mall, demonstrates such characteristics.

Iconic Malls of the 1980s and 1990s

Hong Kong's early malls were anchors of evolving mixed-use developments. Ocean Terminal was the largest mall in Hong Kong when it opened in 1966 to serve cruise ship passenger trade. It was a precursor to the worldwide strategy of waterfront redevelopment, converting dockside space into new retail space. In the 1980s it became part of the Ocean Centre and Harbour City mixed-use development, developed by the Wharf company (Figure 4.1). In Central, The Landmark on Des Voeux Road introduced the form of atrium to the Hong Kong mall, forming the centerpiece between Edinburgh and Gloucester towers.[4] Exits of the Central MTR station thread into The Landmark and adjacent commercial buildings, while Harbour City is the only major mall complex without a direct link to the MTR system. Instead, the Star Ferry piers in front of Ocean Terminal and the China ferry terminal mark the southern end of Harbour City, which makes the mall a direct destination for mainland travelers.

The third of the first three big malls, Pacific Place, opened in Admiralty in 1988 on Queensway across from the Admiralty MTR station. It was the first major mall outside the core areas of Central and Tsim Sha Tsui. Built on the site of British military barracks occupied by Japanese forces during the war, the area was historically "bad luck" for residential investment. Swire Properties bought the site at auction and developed it in stages. The Pacific Place office towers, residential apartments, and hotels opened up the hill above the mall in the early 1990s. When the development was completed, Pacific Place mall linked Queensway via a cascade of covered outdoor escalators with Hong Kong Park on the island's mid-slope.

The iconic new malls of the 1990s, Times Square and Festival Walk, were built close to residential areas. In 1994, Wharf opened Times Square in Causeway Bay on the site of the Hong Kong Tramways depot. Rather than horizontal in form like Ocean Terminal and Pacific Place, the Times Square project, accompanied by two office towers, introduced the vertical mall concept. The success of Times Square intensified commercialization and has contributed to making Causeway Bay the highest rent retail district in the world. In 2012, commercial rents in Causeway Bay surpassed those on Fifth Avenue in New York City.[5] As properties changed hands in the district, rents rose building by building. Causeway Bay's local street front shops have incrementally given way to international brands. In 2013 Cheung Kee Grocery Store, which operated at 5 Canal Road East around the block from Times Square, closed after 40 years when the building was sold for HK$138 million—394 times higher than the original purchase price of HK$350,000 in 1975.[6]

Festival Walk, a major horizontal mall and mixed-use commercial development, opened in an established residential area at a distance from urban cores in 1998. It occupies a narrow site alongside the Kowloon Tong MTR station, the first station after the Lion Rock Tunnel on the Kowloon side, and a juncture with the East Rail Line serving the China boundary. (Figure 4.2) Its location has banked on Kowloon Tong's high-cost residential neighborhoods, in a historic planned "garden city," and youth population from nearby schools, including two universities and multiple private schools, to generate regular patronage. Its pivotal position has also served the New Territories and mainland visitors. Its iconicity owes to visuality of its atrium design, flooded by natural light and crisscrossed by escalators, and its ice rink, which sits at the base of a multistory wall of windows with views to the Lion Rock ridgeline.

Festival Walk's Chinese name Yau Yat Sing 又一城 (another city) appears prominently on the façade. It plays off the historical name of the area, Yau Yat Tsuen 又一村 (another village). Under the flight path of Kai Tak airport, the area necessarily remained low and medium rise density. Urbanization of the "village" intensified in the 1990s with the planned development of the new airport on Lantau. Opening four months after the July 1998 closing of Kai Tak, Festival Walk marked a new period of high-rent residential development in Kowloon Tong.[7] However, in contrast to the post–Kai Tak lifting of building height restrictions for Kowloon in general, in 2006 the Town Planning Board placed new restrictions on Kowloon Tong to limit residential construction to 13 stories, which property interests continue to protest.[8] In 2011 Swire Properties sold Festival Walk, which generated liquidity for its five mixed-use development projects in major cities of China.[9]

Urban Redevelopment: Langham Place, apm, and K11

Langham Place mall in Mong Kok opened its doors in December 2004 before shops were fully installed. Behind a trio of elderly women who had come in from the nearby wet market, I wandered in and followed them up to the fourth floor and stepped on to the 42-meter escalator.[10] On the eighth floor landing, we stood together looking out over the 60-meter-glass atrium. (Figure 4.3) They pointed at buildings outside in the direction of the market beyond Shanghai Street. By putting the surrounding city on display, the glass-walled atrium set a new aesthetic standard for mall space.

Development of Langham Place, a 15-story vertical mall, 59-story office tower, and 45-story hotel, was a major project of the Hong Kong Urban Renewal Authority (URA). The project site, adjacent to the Mong Kok MTR station, restructured urban space by eliminating Hong Lo Street, the site of Mong Kok's historic bird market, and demolishing the homes of

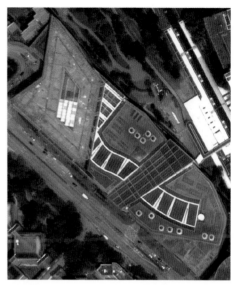

Figure 4.2
Festival Walk, Kowloon Tong. Google Earth, 2013

some 6,000 flat owners and tenants who received compensation to relocate.[11] Spatial restructuring relocated the bird market to a new themed Chinese garden in Prince Edward, and the Langham Place office tower rose to dwarf adjacent low-rise buildings and increase commercial rents. Co-developed with Great Eagle Group, it also symbolized the capacity of government and the property industry to capitalize urban upgrading. Under development for 16 years, with challenges to land resumption and assembling the site, the project generated interest in conserving local neighborhoods and historical market environments.[12]

By the 2000s, the sheer number of malls in Hong Kong pressured new malls to achieve distinction and names started to reflect the branding trend for abbreviations, acronyms, and memes. Still, when the Hong Kong Post issued the special set "special attractions of the 18 districts in Hong Kong" in 2006, most people were caught unaware to find "apm" depicted on the Kwun Tong stamp. (Figure 4.4) Another vertical mall, apm opened in 2005 in the Millennium City 5 mixed-used commercial development located opposite Kwun Tong MTR station and above a long-distance bus station serving the China border and intermediate cities in the Pearl River Delta. The brand "apm," developed by Sun Hung

Figure 4.3
Langham Place, Mong Kok. Google Earth, 2013

Kai Properties (SHKP), condensed a.m.–p.m. to signify day and night or extended retail hours up to midnight, and early morning for restaurants and entertainment. It targets the strategic under-35 demographic and cultivates it through celebrity and art-retail crossover events.[13] The mall's aesthetic, with digital screens in the atrium, evokes scenes of Shibuya, Hongdae, and Ximending, the Asian transnational consumer landscapes of teenagers and 20-something travelers. However, the brand itself was not innovative *per se* since it rode the district's postindustrial vibe as a scene of rock music and art studio space.[14]

The historical built environment of Kwun Tong, dominated by industrial buildings and public housing, symbolizes Hong Kong's manufacturing past. A district of Kowloon East, and not far from the Kai Tak airport site, Kwun Tong started de-industrializing with the relocation of garment and assembly industries to Mainland China. Yet the Millennium 5 mixed-use development does not represent a standard story of gentrification, as in New York or London, where real estate investment follows "creative pioneers" into

marginal areas. Planning for new commercial buildings in Kwun Tong started in the 1990s after the Land Development Corporation, precursor to the URA, marked the area for redevelopment.[15] SHKP's construction of Millennium City 1, 2 and 3 commercial office buildings preceded the Millennium City 5 mixed-use project. The process demonstrates how property developers closely track and anticipate government planning decisions. In restructuring from manufacturing to commercial use, Kwun Tong rents increased at more extreme rates than those in Causeway Bay: from HK$800 ft^2 in the early 2000s to HK$7,500 ft^2 by 2013, an increase over 800 percent.[16]

The K11 mall in Tsim Sha Tsui occupies the base of a podium for a 67-story high-rise mixed-use tower, which occupies a full block in the middle of a historically low-rise area. Because the tower structure effectively arcs over a plaza at the ground level which opens to the street, the design reins in the spatial impact of the outsize, pre-demand structure. Similar to other redevelopment projects, the Land Development Corporation originally targeted the area. On Hanoi Road at Mody Road in Tsim Sha Tsui, a dense commercial district, the project removed 20 buildings and relocated local residents.[17] The URA completed the project in joint venture with New World Development, while the MTR completed the new Tsim Sha Tsui East station under Mody Road.

Opened in 2009, K11's idiosyncratic name (corresponding to the site's lot number on the URA's Kowloon list) has no intrinsic relationship to the brand, "the world's first art mall." The brand riffs on the contemporary art trend in Hong Kong and its role as the center of the Chinese art trade, and the mall space/gallery features artworks chosen by the developer. The name of the tower, the Masterpiece, the second tallest residential building in Hong Kong, continues the art theme yet challenges definition. The tower has intensified public debate over light pollution, since the "bright white glaring strips [of the Masterpiece] can be seen as far away as Mui Wo,"[18] a coastal settlement on Lantau. The original public plan for the site, "to turn the rundown neighborhood into a commercial block with public open space and underground parking" did not permit residential development, but the project won a number of exceptions.[19] When residential sales commenced, the smallest flat in the project, an 816 square feet one-bedroom flat, set a record price for its size at $HK24.5 million.

Mega-Development: IFC Mall and Elements

The malls in Hong Kong's two landmark harbor developments—the International Finance Centre (IFC) on Hong Kong Island and the Union Square development at West Kowloon—are consumption spaces of mega-projects. With the completion of the 88-story IFC Two, the IFC Mall opened in the podium structure above the Hong Kong MTR/Airport Express station. ("IFC" names the integrated development, its two office towers, IFC One and IFC Two, and the mall.) In 2007 Elements opened in the podium above the Kowloon MTR/Airport Express station, which is dominated by the tallest building in Hong Kong, the 118-story International Commerce Centre (ICC). Both the IFC and Union Square occupy land reclamations developed with the new airport, at Chek Lap Kok on Lantau. They channel the Tung Chung MTR and Airport Express rail lines into the urban core, making the Kowloon and Hong Kong stations airport satellites: at either station it is possible to complete airline and baggage check-in and then go shopping.

The sense of place in IFC Mall is about mobility and connecting. IFC Mall links via elevated walkways to the Hong Kong General Post Office, the Hong Kong Island ferry piers, the Central-Mid-Levels escalator and also to the Macao ferry terminal. Yet its location, seaward of Central's traditional core district and west of the historic Star Ferry piers, contributed to resituating places of meeting and gathering and "downtown" shopping in the daily life of the city. In the consumer space of the mall, the flagship Lane Crawford store, founded in Hong Kong in 1850, symbolizes these shifts. Lane Crawford departed its historic location in the retail heart of Queen's Road Central for the IFC, which impacted Queen's Road while lending legitimacy to the IFC as a new urban center. In contrast, it is impossible to imagine, for example, Saks Fifth Avenue in Manhattan moving from Fifth Avenue to South Street Seaport or Harrods moving from Knightsbridge in London to Canary Wharf.

As part of a mixed-use development, Elements at Union Square serves as a consumer enclave for a veritable new town. Union Square covers 33.5 acres: in addition to the ICC and two luxury hotels, it has 15 residential towers which together contain more than 8,000 flats and serviced apartments. The mall has the largest cinema in Hong Kong. The Elements brand adopts the Chinese traditional *wuxing* 五行 or five elements—

Figure 4.4
Kwun Tong District stamp depicting Lei Yue Mun fishing village, the Tin Hau temple at Cha Kwo Ling, apm, and Millennium City 5. Hong Kong Post, 2006

Figure 4.5
Elements at Union Square, Google Earth, 2013

wood, fire, earth, metal, and water—to label mall zones and categorize selectively placed artworks, similar to K11. Like apm, Elements offers mainland bus service, but upgrades the "ticket office" to a mall shop where passengers view departure times on an LED signboard as if selecting from a menu. In contrast with the IFC, Union Square stands relatively isolated from the surrounding urban fabric as if anticipating the future of the West Kowloon Cultural District and the Express Rail.

The mixed-use developments that house the IFC Mall and Elements restructure the space of the city by allocating and concentrating capital investment, reorienting commercial space, and, in the case of Elements, introducing new high-cost high-rise housing. The reclamation projects that raised the earth for these projects were among the last in a long history of filling in the shores of Victoria Harbour—the reclamations on Hong Kong Island led to the Protection of the Harbour movement.[20] In land-constrained Hong Kong, land reclamation is the alchemy of real estate gold. The malls lie at the center of the investment logic by providing public access to the commercialized cores of new privatized space. The IFC Mall, circling between two office towers and a high-rise harborfront hotel, is the first consumer space many visitors encounter. At the terminus of the Airport Express rail, the IFC delivers a globalizing consumer environment direct from Chek Lap Kok.

Hong Kong in China

Hong Kong companies have been developing housing and commercial properties in the Mainland since the 1980s. By the 2000s, new rounds of redevelopment in the major cities included mixed-use projects featuring branded Hong Kong malls. Swire Properties, for example, has five major mixed-used developments in the Mainland. Wharf has developed a Times Square for Shanghai, Dalian, Wuhan, and Chongqing. In Shanghai alone, Shanghai Times Square, Shanghai IFC, International apm in Shanghai ICC, and Shanghai K11 are new consumer cores of large mixed-use development projects—localizing the Hong Kong mall as the leading consumer destination in the Mainland.

Mixed-use developments by Hong Kong property firms have widely contributed to restructuring

urban environments in China. In Beijing, a government joint venture with SHKP redeveloped the historic market in Wangfujing into a shopping mall and office towers in the 1990s, and then re-branded the mall "Beijing apm" in time for the Olympics. Re-branding "apm" tracks social mobility-in-formation, and also demonstrates the calculus of planned gentrification: when Beijing apm opened, rents in the mall increased 30 to 50 percent.[21] The Shanghai city government targeted the famous Xiangyang market on Huaihai Middle Road for redevelopment and partnered with SHKP to develop the site as the Shanghai International Commerce Center. Unlike the ICC in Hong Kong, Shanghai ICC is a set of mid-rise office buildings and residential towers, and forges the brands of two different SHKP Hong Kong projects, the ICC and apm, to name its mall "International apm." In both cities, mixed-use projects replaced low-cost markets with international branded goods for urban elites. The socio-economic spatial dynamic transforms the urban environment and also contributes to the entrenchment of inequality in urban society.

By 2010, the flow of mainland visitors to Hong Kong surpassed 20 million annually and increased to over 30 million in 2012.[22] This intensive "tourism engagement" characterizes the unfolding relationship between Hong Kong and China and it is taking place through leisure consumerism in the mall. In the process, malls in mixed-use developments in Hong Kong have become common sites of experience for Mainlanders, and have fueled ideas about new property development projects in mainland cities. This relational geography between Hong Kong, Guangzhou, Shanghai, Beijing, Chengdu, and other cities shapes China's evolving urban modernity.[23] In the process, the Hong Kong mall, irrespective of location, is becoming China's leading consumer environment.

NOTES

1 Neil Smith, *Gentrification, the Frontier and the Restructuring of Urban Space* (Boston: Allen & Unwin, 1986).

2 The Individual Visit Scheme first allowed visits by residents of four Guangdong cities and has since expanded to 49 mainland cities; see Individual Visit Scheme, Government of Hong Kong, http://www.tourism.gov.hk/english/visitors/visitors_ind.html.

3 Neil Smith, "Gentrification and the Rent Gap," *Annals of the Association of American Geographers* 77, no. 3 (1987): 462–65.

4 Charlie Q. L. Xue, Luming Ma, and Ka Chuen Hui, "Indoor 'Public' Space: A Study of Atria in Mass Transit Railway (MTR) Complexes of Hong Kong," *Urban Design International* 17 (2012): 87–105.

5 "Hong Kong's Causeway Bay Tops Shop Rent List," *South China Morning Post*, November 16, 2012, http://www.scmp.com/news/hong-kong/article/1083879/hong-kongs-causeway-bay-tops-shop-rent-list.

6 Peggy Sito, "Neighbourhood Shops of Causeway Bay Squeezed Out by Highest Rents in the World," *South China Morning Post*, February 19, 2013, http://www.scmp.com/property/hong-kong-china/article/1153431/neighbourhood-shops-causeway-bay-squeezed-out-highest-rents.

7 "Kowloon Tong's Cachet Pushes Prices to Peak Level," *South China Morning Post*, August 11, 2012, http://www.scmp.com/node/565174.

8 Yvonne Liu, "Planning Board Keeps the Lid on Kowloon Tong despite Protests," *South China Morning Post*, August 10, 2012, http://www.scmp.com/article/556627/planning-board-keeps-lid-kowloon-tong-despite-protests.

9 Kevin Wong, "Swire Agrees to Sell Festival Walk Shopping Mall for $2.4 Billion," Bloomberg.com, July 29, 2011, http://www.bloomberg.com/news/2011-07-28/swire-pacific-agrees-to-sell-festival-walk-shopping-mall-for-2-4-billion.html.

10 ARUP, Langham Place, 2012, http://www.arup.com/Home/Projects/Langham_Places_HK.

11 "Langham Place Kick-Starts Regeneration of Mong Kok," Urban Renewal Authority, Government of Hong Kong, January 25, 2005, http://www.ura.org.hk/en/media/press-release/2005/20050125.aspx.

12 See, for example, Marissa Yiu, "Politics of the Light Object: Transformative Architectural Installations," *Journal of Architectural Education* 63, no. 1 (2009): 107–19.

13 Kara K. W. Chan documents celebrity events at Kwun Tong apm in *Youth and Consumption* (Hong Kong: City University of Hong Kong Press, 2010), 88–95.

14 Ling Wing-sze, "Arts hub," *South China Morning Post*, July 19, 2012, http://www.scmp.com/article/642818/arts-hub.

15 David Adams and E. M. Hastings, "Urban Renewal in Hong Kong: Transition from Development Corporation to Renewal Authority," *Land Use Policy* 16, no. 3 (2001): 245–58; and "Kwun Tong Town Center Project," Hong Kong Urban Redevelopment Authority, 2012, http://www.ura.org.hk/en/projects/redevelopment/kwun-tong-town-center-project.aspx.

16 Sandy Li, "HK$100m Facelift for Mall to Prepare for CBD2," *South China Morning Post*, August 15, 2012, http://www.scmp.com/article/984920/hk100m-facelift-mall-prepare-cbd2.

17 "Hanoi Road Project (The Masterpiece)," Hong Kong Urban Redevelopment Authority, http://www.ura.org.hk/en/projects/redevelopment/tsim-sha-tsui/hanoi-road-project-the-masterpiece.aspx.

18 Cheung Chi-fai and Ng Kang-chung, "Light-Pollution Complaints Spread in Tsim Sha Tsui," *South China Morning Post*, February 21, 2011, http://www.scmp.com/article/738729/light-pollution-complaints-spread-tsim-sha-tsui.

19 "How the Masterpiece Came to Feature in a Changing Landscape," *South China Morning Post*, February 17, 2010, http://www.skyscrapercity.com/showthread.php?t=275877&page=53.

20 Mee Kam Ng, "World City Formation under an Executive-Led Government: The Politics of Harbor Reclamation in Hong Kong," *Town Planning Review* 77, no. 3 (2006): 311–37.

21 Raymond Wang, "SHKP Lands Nike in Race to Reprise Mall Success," *The Standard* [Hong Kong], June 8, 2007, http://www.thestandard.com.hk/archive_news_detail.asp?pp_cat=1&art_id=46332&sid=13969203&con_type=1&archive_d_str=20070608.

22 Immigration Department, *Annual Report 2011* and *Annual Report 2012* (Hong Kong: Government of Hong Kong).

23 On the regional context of consumerism in the Hong Kong economy, and in relation to Shanghai, see Carolyn Cartier, "Production/Consumption and the Chinese City/Region," *Urban Geography* 30, no. 4 (2009): 368–90.

5. Mall Cities in Hong Kong

CHUNGKING MANSIONS

Gordon Mathews

Chungking Mansions as an Exception

I f a mall city may be defined as an urban typology characterized by a set of residential or office towers standing on a podium shopping mall, often in close proximity to mass transit, then Chungking Mansions is a standard exemplar of this typology, along with many other examples, from K11, just around the corner from Chungking Mansions, to Pacific Place in Admiralty, to Langham Place in Mong Kok. But Chungking Mansions is remarkably different from these other examples in how it has evolved over its history and in what it represents today.

Chungking Mansions is probably the most globalized building in the world—I have counted 130 different nationalities in its guesthouse logs. Some large hotels may perhaps rival this total in the diversity of their clientele; but in Chungking Mansions, people of different nationalities typically must interact with one another, in that the tiny spaces in the crowded elevators, where you may become uncomfortably intimate with people of half-a-dozen different nationalities, and the narrow corridors of its ground floor aisles, mean that aloofness is all but impossible. For those who work in Chungking Mansions, the businesses on the ground and first floors contain so many different types of people in their diversity of shops that cross-cultural interaction of various sorts is all but inevitable: in Chungking Mansions, it is all but impossible not to become cosmopolitan, at least in the diversity of one's associations. Chungking Mansions's architecture— its guesthouses, restaurants, and residences

on three tower blocks atop a podium shopping mall that all who leave the building must pass through—is partly what creates its globalism. But if this is the case in Chungking Mansions, why is it not true for the other podium-style structures mentioned above?

Other podium structures in Hong Kong, such as Pacific Place or K11, typically have businesses in which Hong Kong Chinese merchants deal with Hong Kong Chinese or sometimes Western customers, with a smattering of additional nationalities, such as Filipinos and Indonesians. Chungking Mansions, on the other hand, typically involves Pakistani, Indian, African, or mainland Chinese merchants who may deal with customers from all over the world. All of urban Hong Kong is potentially international, with people from all over the world at least possibly appearing at the door of any business throughout the city. But in Chungking Mansions this is not a possibility but an inevitability. Except for the one Chinese restaurant on the building's first floor, and a few South Asian restaurants on upper floors catering to a Hong Kong clientele, the idea of a Chungking Mansions business catering to a dozen Hong Kong Chinese customers in a row is unthinkable. In the international cavalcade of Chungking Mansions, Hong Kong Chinese have long been one cultural group that you are not very likely to encounter.

Why is this the case? Chungking Mansions is located on some of the most expensive property on earth, catty-corner to the Peninsula, by some accounts Hong Kong's best hotel, and within a hundred meters or so of Hong Kong's newest and glitziest shopping malls, K11 and iSQUARE. But within Chungking Mansions itself, the economic rules that apply to the rest of Tsim Sha Tsui do not fit. A guesthouse in Chungking Mansions that raised its prices might go out of business, as several have; a phone stall that sells new, high-end phones may also be in danger of going out of business, as several have. In Chungking Mansions, the dominant clientele for most businesses are developing-world traders, most often from South Asia and sub-Saharan Africa. In a Hong Kong of ever-glitzier malls and ever-pricier housing developments, Chungking Mansions thus stands as a remarkable exception. Cheap prices—among the cheapest in Hong Kong for guesthouse rooms, restaurant meals, mobile phones, and computers—are what enable the building to continue to make profits for its hundreds of property owners. The reason why this is the case lies in Chungking Mansions's unique history, unlike any other building in Hong Kong.

Chungking Mansions's History

Chungking Mansions was opened in 1962, and was initially advertised as a luxury building: certainly its height of 17 stories, towering above other buildings in Tsim Sha Tsui at the time, indicated its high status along with its high elevation. For reasons I have not been able to fully disentangle, however, it rapidly lost its luxury status. It was built rather cheaply as compared to later buildings in Tsim Sha Tsui, but this seems to have been less a function of Chungking Mansions in particular than of Tsim Sha Tsui and Hong Kong as a whole, which in that era was still quite poor as compared to two and three decades later. Chungking Mansions from its very start had no unified ownership structure, but this was true of many Hong Kong buildings in that era. Perhaps one key to understanding Chungking Mansions's rapid decline lay in the presence of South Asians in the building; in a Hong Kong in which there was widespread racial discrimination against South Asians, this may have been an initial kiss of death. This racism was unwittingly confirmed by a woman I interviewed, who had grown up in Chungking Mansions: "Early on, it was very nice. It was a little later that the reputation went down. Indians came, and so on." It is an unsettling thought that the very presence of South Asians may have doomed the building's reputation in the eyes of many of Hong Kong's Chinese ethnic majority, but perhaps this was

the case. Within a few years after the building's construction, it was already a haven for sex workers soliciting American GIs on rest and relief from Vietnam;[1] residents of the building in the late 1960s have described to me the presence of various brothels.

The fact that Chungking Mansions lacked a unified ownership structure gave its resident owners freedom to do what they wanted with their apartments. In the 1970s, this came to mean making them into guesthouses. Typically a mainland family would emigrate to Hong Kong in the late 1960s or 1970s and move into Chungking Mansions, because even though it was in a central location, it was also relatively cheap, cheaper than most other lodgings in Hong Kong. They would then eventually come to realize that much money could be made by vacating their premises and converting their home into a guesthouse. Even a guesthouse of five to six rooms charging rock-bottom prices could offer a very good living as compared to other forms of employment in Hong Kong. One young man who grew up in Chungking Mansions criticized me several years ago for what he had heard of my research: "You focus on the Indians and Africans but leave out people like my relatives, who came from Shanghai to Hong Kong, bought up properties in Chungking Mansions, turned them into guesthouses, and eventually leased them to Indian managers. They made a success of their lives. That's really important!" Indeed it is—this is a key part of Chungking Mansions's history. Chungking Mansions enabled significant numbers of mainland immigrants to Hong Kong to live out the dream of making a better life for their family and children.[2]

Guests in this era were not primarily African and South Asian traders—that came only later, in the 1990s and 2000s. Instead they were predominantly backpackers from Western Europe, Australia, the United States, and Japan. The *Lonely Planet* guides played a major role in this process. One of Tony Wheeler's initial guides to the region was *Southeast Asia on a Shoestring*, first published in 1975; its 1981 edition proclaimed: "There's a magic word for cheap accommodations in Hong Kong—*Chungking Mansions.*"[3] The *Lonely Planet* boom continued into the 1980s and 1990s, and provided Chungking Mansions with tens of thousands of temporary guests over the years.[4]

This construction of so many guesthouses had a very significant effect on the building's infrastructure. A guesthouse needs far more electricity than does a private residence, in that each room requires its own television, air conditioner, and telephone. The presence of so many guesthouses also led to increasing numbers of restaurants in the building. Together these factors created both great fire hazards and massive pressures on the building's electrical grid. After a fire in 1988 killed a Danish tourist, debate began to rage about Chungking Mansions in Hong Kong mass media.[5] In Chungking Mansions, "A Disaster Lies Waiting," one columnist fulminated: "The Hong Kong Tourist Association boasts to visitors that wonders never cease; neither does the stench from the illegal structures of Chungking Mansions . . . Will the authorities leap into action only when catastrophe happens?"[6]

In 1993, power in the building went out for a full ten days. The ensuing outcry led to a massive reduction of guesthouses:[7] "Most of the 240 guesthouses in Chungking Mansions had to be closed." Within a year after the blackout, thanks to its new owners' association chair Lam Wai-lung, a new power transformer was installed,[8] decreasing the risk of fire, and guesthouses were being refurbished or newly constructed in the building, to meet its ongoing demand.

Mrs. Lam has continued as the owners' association chairperson over most of the past eighteen years, and has done a remarkable job in refurbishing the building: the old, balky elevators were replaced, security guards were hired, and some 200 CCTV cameras were placed throughout the building. These steps, while welcomed by almost everyone, have not had much effect on Chungking Mansions's basic trade: "Chungking Mansions' Facelift Only Skin Deep," a skeptical *South China Morning Post* headline read.[9] While crime seems to have lessened in the building in recent years,[10] Chungking Mansions's basic trade, of developing-world traders buying cheap China-made goods to send back to Africa and elsewhere, remains strong. Rents have significantly risen in the building, but because its owners generally seem to realize that the path to profit is to keep prices low, they have done exactly that—traders complain about prices, but they still come. The ethnic composition of

Figure 5.2
Chungking Mansions's entrance

Figure 5.3
Business scene, Chungking Mansions

Figure 5.4
A view down one of Chungking Mansions's light wells

the building has shifted markedly over the past twenty years, particularly with a huge increase in sub-Saharan African traders over the past fifteen years, drawn by the industrial might of South China, for which most could easily get visas in Chungking Mansions. The peak period of African traders was 2005–2010, with numbers today somewhat less; at present, the biggest new influx is that of mainland Chinese tourists, drawn by cheap guesthouse prices now that many can individually travel into Hong Kong. There is also, over the past several years, an increase in Hong Kong people themselves coming to the building, as I will shortly discuss.

Chungking Mansions's Present and Future

Despite the building's recent transformations, it does not appear much different than it did in the past to most casual observers; and just as its appearance is largely unchanged, so too (at least until very recently, perhaps) is its reputation. As one commentator wrote, "Having stayed in Chungking Mansions is a badge of honor among backpackers—it's a legendary waystation among worldwide wanderers who love to spin tales of squalor endured."[11] This bad reputation continues today—a Google search of the building turns up innumerable references to the phrase "the infamous Chungking Mansions." In fact, the building is a perfectly reasonable place to stay today: I have spent the night in most of Chungking Mansions's 90 or so guesthouses, and have found the overwhelming majority of rooms to be quite clean and comfortable, albeit very small and basic. I have also found virtually all of the 30 or so South Asian restaurants spread throughout the building to be quite good. Fire danger in the building seems to be stabilized, with centralized fire equipment in the building; and I have never been robbed during the four years of research I conducted in the building. All in all, it is a reasonably salubrious place; but its poor reputation, the product of its history, continues to shadow it.

One reason for its poor reputation over the years is directly related to its architecture as a "mall city." Chungking Mansions's five elevators ascend to three large tower blocks: A elevator going to the first block, B and C elevators going to the second block, and D and E elevators going to the third block. If you take an elevator up one block, you cannot get to the other blocks except by returning to the ground floor; and even within a given block, one elevator is blocked off from the other. It is thus very easy to vanish in Chungking Mansions; if, for example, police seek to catch an asylum seeker illegally working on an upper floor, it will take police ten or more minutes to reach that upper floor, and by that time he or she will have long since been tipped off by friends from below, and will have slipped off into the anonymous crowd. Architectural features such as these are not an issue in many other mall cities in Hong Kong—I doubt that many miscreants vanish in K11 or Taikoo Shing—but definitely contributes to Chungking Mansions's reputation as a "maze" and a "criminals' paradise," just because one can so easily disappear in the building (and this same feature also makes it difficult for paramedics and firemen to access the building—they too are at the mercy of a single leisurely elevator, or else dauntingly long staircases, if they seek to access an upper floor). Illegal workers, of whom there are many, are in my view a very good thing for Chungking Mansions, for they enable prices to remain low and Chungking Mansions's global nature to continue; no Hong Kong person would work for the wages that these mostly South Asian workers are paid. But this does contribute to Chungking Mansions's ongoing shady reputation.

One might ask why Chungking Mansions has never been demolished, given its shady reputation, and given the massive increase in real estate prices in Tsim Sha Tsui over the years. The land is extraordinarily valuable, and becoming ever more so. But as a real estate reporter wrote two decades ago, "To try to demolish Chungking Mansions and rebuild on the site would be a developer's nightmare, with up to 600 separate properties involved. 'I can't imagine that any developer would want to become involved with it,' an agent said."[12] In order for a building to be demolished, a large percentage of owners—and there are some 920 ownership shares—must agree to a building's demolition before it can be demolished, and why would they? "Even in its current condition, the building is a gold mine for its owners," one government minister commented,[13] and indeed it still is, not necessarily for all of its businesses, but for many.[14] Another authority commented on how the building "should be looked after by the Urban

Renewal Authority,"[15] which would tear it down to put in a grand new megastructure in its place. However, the Urban Renewal Authority must be able to make a profit on the buildings it replaces, and typically does so by tearing down a building of a few stories and putting up a skyscraper in its place. Since Chungking Mansions is already so tall, no rebuilding could much increase its existing floor space, and thus the Urban Renewal Authority can find better pickings elsewhere. There have been developments in the building, such as Chungking Express,[16] an area of comparatively upmarket stores not accessible from Chungking Mansions proper, but only from an escalator on Nathan Road, and more recently, Woodlands; few who enter these ever think of them as part of Chungking Mansions. For Chungking Mansions proper—those businesses accessed through the entrance to Chungking Mansions—these kinds of developments are all but unimaginable. Although anything might happen in the coming years, Chungking Mansions continues into the foreseeable future as an island of the developing world perched in the midst of some of Hong Kong's most expensive real estate.

Figure 5.5
Afternoon bustle, Chungking Mansions

The elaborate array of factors I have discussed has led Chungking Mansions to become what it is. The lack of ownership structure led to guesthouses being built, since no one could dictate to individual apartment owners what they should do with the places they owned. The *Lonely Planet* guides in their recommendations of Chungking Mansions were the result of this emergence of guesthouses, and also led to their proliferation. This led to the building's increasing infrastructural overload, and to the building becoming more dangerous; this also kept prices extremely low, with profits remaining high for landlords. By the 1990s, with the emergence of China as the world's factory for cheap goods, the developed-world *Lonely Planet* backpackers eventually gave way to developing-world traders, who, like the backpackers, had little money for expensive accommodations and meals. This is why Chungking Mansions became a center of globalization, and also why Chungking Mansions has emerged as the building it has: its unique history has made it utterly different from other "mall city"-style developments in Hong Kong.

How long Chungking Mansions will continue in its unique contemporary configuration—as "the most

Figure 5.6
Goods bound for Africa

Figure 5.7
Ghanaian merchant outside his shop

globalized building in the world"—is anyone's guess. At present, far more African traders are in Guangzhou than in Hong Kong, due to the latter's tightened immigration procedures, apparently because of fears of increasing numbers of asylum seekers; this is one threat to Chungking Mansions's globalized status. A second threat relates to the increasing value of the land upon which Chungking Mansions is located: will a developer offer such a good price as to persuade the multiplicity of owners of Chungking Mansions to sell? As one owner of a guesthouse exclaimed to me about this prospect, "After all, no one hates money!" A third threat to Chungking Mansions relates to the building itself: will rising rents at some point lead to significantly higher prices for accommodations, food, and goods, rising beyond the reach of developing-world traders, and leading them to stop coming? Might Chungking Mansions eventually become just one more Hong Kong Chinese mall? This third threat is one that I myself may in a small way have contributed to through my own book on Chungking Mansions.[17] This book gathered significant popular attention in Hong Kong, not necessarily because it was particularly good, but because it was published at a time when Hongkongers sought to emphasize the "non-Chineseness" of Hong Kong—of which Chungking Mansions was seen as the primary example. Today, Hong Kong secondary school students, of the type who used to be afraid to even enter the building, go on tours of the place and sometimes spend the night there; Chungking Mansions has become increasingly featured as "the place to go in Hong Kong to find out about globalization." This very fact, if developing-world traders become priced out of the market, may become the reason why it no longer is "the place to go in Hong Kong to find out about globalization."

If this happens, it would simply mark one more transformation of a building that has already seen multiple transformations over its history. But—although the owners of the building are very smart, and may know very well how much to push up prices just enough to avoid losing their developing-world customer base—Chungking Mansions's future as "the most globalized building in the world" seems a little hazy. My guess is that the building will still be around ten or fifteen years from now, not fundamentally different from what it is today. But in case I am wrong, visit now, before it is too late.

NOTES

1 Exactly this scene is described in Xu Xi, *Chinese Walls/Daughters of Hui*, Second Edition (Hong Kong: Chameleon Press, 2002).

2 This young man, like almost all the offspring of the families from the Mainland who came to own guesthouses in Chungking Mansions, wanted nothing to do with the building—his dream was to become a well-educated Hong Kong professional, far higher on the class level than his parents ever were. In this, again, he is fulfilling his parents' dream in being successful in life far beyond what they could achieve.

3 Anthony Ian Wheeler, *Southeast Asia on a Shoestring* (Victoria AU: Lonely Planet Publications, 1981), 47 (italics in original).

4 My book on Chungking Mansions, *Ghetto at the Center of the World* (2011), attracted far more mainstream media attention than any of my earlier books. I initially wondered why this was the case, until I realized that some of the book review editors of prominent newspapers and magazines in the United States, Europe, and Australia, now in their fifties, were backpackers thirty years earlier, of the type that had stayed in Chungking Mansions; their interest in the book may have stemmed from the experiences of their youth.

5 For example, "High-Rise Menace Needs Urgent Action by Government," *Hong Kong Standard*, August 30, 1988.

6 Kevin Sinclair, "A Disaster Lies Waiting," *South China Morning Post*, September 22, 1997.

7 Patrick Yeung, "Tourists Left Homeless by Chungking Closures," *South China Morning Post*, September 2, 1993.

8 Brendan Delfino, "Facelift for Eyesore of Golden Mile," *South China Morning Post*, May 28, 1994.

9 Chandra Wong, "Chungking Mansions' Facelift Only Skin Deep," April 29, 2005.

10 The biggest reason for the apparent decrease in crime in Chungking Mansions is not the CCTV cameras, but rather the departure of the fifty or so Nepalese heroin addicts who used to live in cardboard shacks on the sidewalks surrounding Chungking Mansions. They have followed an NGO to the neighborhood of Yau Ma Tei. Much of the petty crime around the building, such as pickpocketing, was committed by some of these addicts.

11 Gary A. Warner, "Hong Kong High Rise: Is Hong Kong a Backpacker's Dream or a Skyscraper of Squalor?", *Orange County Register*, May 20, 2001.

12 "Developers Steer Clear of Chungking," *South China Morning Post*, June 20, 1990

13 Joshua Fellman, "Eason Calls for Faster Approvals," *Hong Kong Standard*, August 4, 1993.

14 In 2006–2009, phone stalls were the most profitable business in Chungking Mansions, but today this is no longer the case. This boom was because these were the years in which copy and knock-off phones were most well-made, due to innovations of the Taiwanese phone-chip designer Media Tek. See Jessica Lin Yi-Chien, *Fake Stuff: China and the Rise of Counterfeit Goods* (New York: Routledge, 2001), 17. Today guesthouses tend to be the most profitable. I have heard that Media Tek has been hard at work developing motherboards for knock-off smart phones, leading, perhaps, to an eventual resurgence of phone stalls.

15 Quoted in Supapohn Kanwerayotin, "Property Suite: Concrete Plans for Change," *Far Eastern Economic Review*, April 26, 2001.

16 See Peggy Sito, "Investors Crowd into Chungking," *South China Morning Post*, November 24, 2004.

17 Gordon Mathews, *Ghetto at the Center of the World: Chungking Mansions, Hong Kong* (Chicago: University of Chicago Press, 2011).

Figure 5.8
A Muslim seeker and teacher

Figure 6.1
King Wah Centre, one of the many older shopping malls in Hong Kong that is about to be demolished to make way for a more upscale shopping center, 2013 (source: *Apple Daily*, February 27, 2014)

6. NARRATING THE MALL CITY

Cecilia L. Chu

In her discussion of Hong Kong's mall culture, Janet Ng notes that Hong Kong's omnipresent shopping malls are not only vessels of capitalist development, but also local places where people are acculturated in everyday life.[1] This can be seen, for example, in many literary works that focus on the construction of memories around various objects and spaces of consumption, memories that elicit strong sentiments amongst those who shared these experiences.[2] These kinds of narratives have become more pronounced in recent years, with the growing nostalgia of "old Hong Kong" coming to encompass some of the older shopping malls that are under threat of demolition or significant makeover in order to attract tourists and multinational retail chains[3] (Figure 6.1). This situation has prompted widespread criticisms of the profit-making mentality of landlords and developers on the one hand, and the failure of the government to protect the interests of Hong Kong citizens and local businesses on the other.

The mourning for the loss of older shopping malls and local retailers has rapidly transformed these places of consumerism—many of which were once charged for having destroyed the older urban fabrics themselves—into "symbols of community" worthy of protection. This situation offers a new twist on the familiar critique of consumerist culture for segregating individuals from community life.[4] Although resistance against urban renewal projects also tends to solidify collective action elsewhere, the narratives

surrounding Hong Kong's shopping malls and their associated "cherished local way of life" also underscore the specificity of histories and spatial practices. What then, are the historical processes that shaped the relations between the residents of this "mall city" and the urban environment? What kinds of social imaginaries have Hong Kong's shopping malls helped engender in the past, and what memories have been invoked and mobilized in the present in the attempt to protect these places from further transformation?

In the following, I consider these questions by examining the development of one of Hong Kong's iconic shopping malls, the New Town Plaza in Sha Tin. Completed in 1984, the New Town Plaza has over the years become recognized as key to the success of Sha Tin's new town development. Although many of the plaza's physical features were reminiscent of those of other shopping centers, to many Sha Tin residents it was a special place to which they had developed strong attachments. However, this sentiment began to change after 2005, when the plaza underwent a series of renovations that resulted in the loss of much of its original character and the eventual closure of many long-time retail shops that could not afford the escalating rent. While local residents lamented that they can no longer relate to the mall in the way they did in the past, these changes also ushered in a series of "bottom-up" initiatives to revive the sense of place and "community spirit." These initiatives, along with those that have proliferated in other neighborhoods across the city, illustrate the widening contestations over urban renewal and conservation in an economy increasingly predicated on market optimization amidst ongoing political change.[5]

The New Town and the Mall: A Symbiotic Development

The completion of the New Town Plaza in 1984 was arguably a historical moment in Hong Kong's urban development. Although not the first shopping center built as an integral part of a housing estate, it was by far the largest and the most spectacular, boasting an unprecedented one million square feet of retail space that also included a flagship Japanese department store, the Yaohan (八佰伴).[6] As noted by Anthony Yeh, the New Town Plaza was an early test case of "comprehensive planning," which was adopted by the Hong Kong government in 1972.[7] The goal was to provide much-needed housing for the working populations in the then still rural New Territories. Under this arrangement, the British new town planning concepts of "self-containment" and "balanced development" were adopted, the aim being to provide employment opportunities as well as shopping, recreational, and community facilities for the new residents. Although the goal of "self-containment" was never fully realized due to inadequate employment in these areas, a large contingent of the members of the working class voluntarily moved to the new towns, not least due to the attractiveness of the shopping and other modern amenities.[8] The development of Sha Tin also came to represent the successful cooperation between town planners and private developers, with the latter assuming the responsibility for managing many public areas that connect the mall and other community spaces. With its central location and direct connection to major transit links, the New Town Plaza also became seen as the very heart of Sha Tin new town itself (Figures 6.2 and 6.3).

While government planners often proclaim the New Town Plaza as a successful example of town planning, the developer of the mall, Sun Hung Kai Properties, refers to this development as a heroic move spearheaded by the company. The idea of building a megamall in a newly developed urban area in the early 1980s was a huge gamble, on the account of a company representative, as the

project risked failure if it was unable to bring in enough shoppers to the mall.[9] To ensure success, the company proposed two strategies. The first was to secure the lease of a flagship department store (which it managed to do after hard negotiations with the Japanese retailer Yaohan). And the second was to build a large car park for encouraging out-of-town shoppers to come to Sha Tin. In the beginning, the car park proposal was repeatedly rejected by the government for the reason that it went against the fundamental objective of new town development; that is, it must first and foremost serve the interests of the local community.[10] After many months of negotiations, the two parties finally made a compromise: Sun Hung Kai would be allowed to build an underground car park on the condition that it would also provide additional community facilities in the mall, including a bowling arena, a skating rink, and billiard rooms that catered primarily to Sha Tin's residents. The arrangement was seen as a "win-win" solution for all. For the government, the new provisions would ensure the comprehensiveness of new town planning without spending additional public money. At the same time, Sun Hung Kai received praise for its "ethical commitment" to doing something beneficial and meaningful for the community—a move that was not usually expected from profit-making developers. And certainly for many local residents, the new facilities were welcome features that made them proud of living in Sha Tin.

Perhaps to the surprise of even the developer, the New Town Plaza rapidly emerged as the most popular mall in the city. Throughout the 1980s and 1990s, it was the most visited shopping center not only in Hong Kong but also in the world, with an average of 150,000 visitors per day and reaching 200,000 in the weekends.[11] While the high number was boosted by the mall being a major thoroughfare connecting different public spaces, Sun Hung Kai also invested heavily in the plaza's architectural design in the attempt to draw in more shoppers. These include providing attractive features in the open areas to create memorable experiences for the visiting crowds. Among the most well-known was the Music Fountain (音樂噴泉) in the mall's central lobby, the first automated musical fountain installed in Hong Kong (Figure 6.4). Another highly praised design was the spectacular atrium constructed

Figure 6.2
The New Town Plaza and its adjacent community facilities, Sha Tin.
Courtesy of Wikipedia user—Wing1990hk

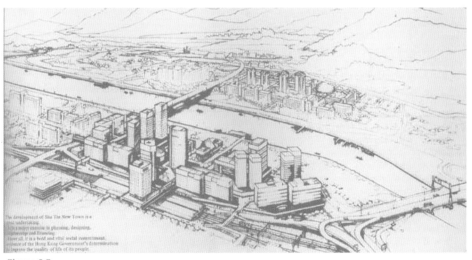

Figure 6.3
A rendering of the proposed New Town Plaza in 1984.
(source: 新沙田月刊, April 10, 1984)

with curved glass panels, which again was the first in the city and became a precedent for many that followed (Figure 6.5). According to a representative of Sun Hung Kai, all of these elements were built using the most advanced technologies and followed the most up-to-date design trends in the world. And these had been proved to be tremendously successful not only in boosting the popularity and prestige of the New Town Plaza, but also became spectacular symbols of a modernizing, flourishing commercial culture that characterized Hong Kong in the last quarter of the twentieth century.

As mentioned earlier, the strong sense of community ties assumed by Sha Tin's residents and their collective sentiment toward the New Town Plaza seems to have defied the familiar critique of consumerist culture for atomizing individuals from social life. But as Tai-lok Lui has noted, it is important to distinguish Hong Kong's "malling process" from those of other places such as North America, where the development of shopping centers was closely associated with increased automobile ownership and suburbanization.[12] The New Town Plaza and other shopping malls in the new towns were all built as an integral part of large housing estates and were promoted from the beginning as "community development" (Figure 6.5). A key focus was on providing ample spaces for collective activities, including shopping, recreation, and other forms of entertainment, all of which being assumed to play significant roles in strengthening the sense of belonging amongst the new town residents. It was also in this context that mass consumption in Hong Kong became full-fledged. Indeed, Sun Hung Kai had from early on noticed the demographic change in Sha Tin, where a majority of the households were no longer members of the "poor working class."[13] Rather, after having benefited from the rapid economic growth in the 1970s and 1980s, they now made up an expanding middle-income group that were motivated to consume and to improve their standards of living. The need to appeal to these people also means that consumer goods must remain affordable for the masses and cater for popular taste. The arrangement of retail spaces and design of the mall itself also closely followed this direction. The idea was to provide a modern, attractive, yet highly accessible shopping environment where different members of new town families were able to find something they desired and through which imagined a better future on their own terms.

In recalling his experience growing up in Sha Tin, one resident, now in his mid-30s, contended that the New Town Plaza was undoubtedly an important place that defined his childhood years.[14] The fact that the mall was connected to major public amenities, including the city hall, the public library, and the large park and garden along Sha Tin's waterfront made it not only a popular meeting point but also a central place for socializing. The resident also revealed that although he did not have much money to spend in the past, he would often linger at various places of the mall, such as the McDonald restaurant, where he would meet up with his classmates for drinks and chats after school hours. Another favorite spot of his was the Commercial Press bookstore (商務印書館), where he had spent endless hours browsing the latest books and popular magazines. Like many others, he would also sometimes go to the mall for people watching, or simply to enjoy the air-conditioned interior during hot summer days. Indeed, similar narratives surrounding the New Town Plaza have also been told by many Sha Tin residents. Although it was a space of consumption geared toward profit-making, the mall was also something more to its users, who inscribed different meanings and values to the place in ways that made sense to them.

A New Mall in the New Millennium

As with many narratives of places undergoing rapid change, these fond memories of the New Town Plaza have become more pronounced in recent years, when the management of the mall embarked on a series of expensive renovations that resulted in the loss of much of the building's original character (Figure 6.6).[15] The decision, which was made in the early 2000s after a prolonged economic downturn, was predicated on the need to adapt to a changing economy in which mass consumption was no longer the dominant business model. With affluence increasingly concentrating on a narrow segment of the population, it was believed that the creation of a niche market catered for the more wealthy would allow retailers and mall owners to gain more profits. While this has been a general trend in other parts of the world, the prospects of transforming Hong Kong's shopping malls into a more upscale environment were also boosted by a rapid increase of wealthy mainland Chinese tourists in recent years. This growth was an effect of a government scheme initiated in 2003 in the attempt to shore up the economy through tourism. Since then the scheme has ushered in hundreds of thousands of mainland visitors.[16] Although this influx has brought sizable revenue to businesses and the government, it also led to escalating rent and closures of many long-time local shops that were unable to compete with the more well-capitalized international retail chains. The situation incited discontent from many ordinary Hong Kong citizens, who lamented that the local environment and "Hong Kong's way of life" are under threat in an economy increasingly subsumed to the logic of the market on the one hand, and to the "invasion" of wealthy mainland consumers on the other.

Amongst the many changes made to the New Town Plaza in the renovation, one that prompted the most criticism was the removal of the iconic Musical Fountain from the mall's central lobby. While the management saw it to be an outdated feature that no longer fit with contemporary design trends, many Sha Tin residents felt that the removal represented a huge loss of something that had long defined their sense of place and collective memories. Another more recent change that instigated an outcry was the relocation of the Commercial Press bookstore, which could no longer afford the high rent after the renovation[17] (Figure 6.7). In view of this and the continual exodus of other long-time retailers, a number of residents initiated a campaign, "Help New Town Plaza," with the goal to prevent the building from further changes (Figure 6.7). While it remains unclear to what extent this campaign will have implications on the ongoing transformation of the mall, it has helped raise awareness of the significance of the New Town Plaza and interests in the Sha Tin community itself. This can be seen, for example, in the emergence of several local tours last year that took visitors to explore different parts of the town. These tours were guided by young people who grew up in the area, the so-called "Shantinites," who were keen to promote the uniqueness of their neighborhoods, including the residential estates, popular eateries, and

Figure 6.4
The Musical Fountain, an iconic feature of the New Town Plaza (source: *House News*, October 27, 2012)

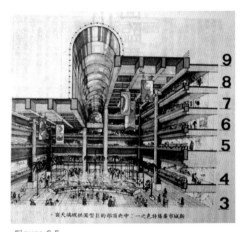

Figure 6.5
A perspective drawing of the New Town Plaza in 1984 showing the mall's central atrium (source: 新沙田月刊, April 10, 1984)

other "local heritage" that are not well known to outsiders and even to some of the residents living here.[18] These activities have also helped draw direct attention to the wider context beyond the New Town Plaza, whist in the process enable a better understanding of the relationship between the mall and the new town.

It should be noted here that these initiatives were not isolated instants confined to one district, but part and parcel of a wider struggle of local communities against urban renewal projects across Hong Kong in recent years. As I have discussed elsewhere, these contestations were themselves closely tied to larger processes of economic and political change in the territory, particularly those after the Asian financial crisis that coincided with the change of Hong Kong's sovereignty in 1997.[19] The slow progress in the push for democratic reform, the accelerating privatization of public assets, and increased reliance on mainland visitors for shoring up the economy have all contributed to a growing pessimism amongst Hong Kong citizens about the territory's urban future. At the same time, the desire to preserve "Hong Kong's way of life" amidst ongoing integration with Mainland China has been fueling a new series of grassroots-led activities that encourage people to rediscover the city's neighborhoods and their histories. A common emphasis running through these activities is "community ties and cohesion," which have been widely hailed to have aided Hong Kong's past economic success and defined the collective memories of many working-class families, including a large contingent of those living in the new towns.

It is within this context that the New Town Plaza, along with other familiar places and objects of consumption, became seen as testimonies of the "success story" of Hong Kong—a story that centers on the themes of upward mobility, modernization, and mass consumption. It is important, however, to note that while these themes remain central to many narratives about Hong Kong's past, there has been a shift of emphasis on the roles assumed by the key actors over time. As this essay has shown, the development of the New Town Plaza has long been hailed by the government as an ingenious case of good town planning and by the developer as a heroic undertaking of private enterprise. In both of these narratives, "community development" has been repeatedly invoked to underscore the "ethical commitment" of officials and the developer to serve the interests of new town residents. Although few may challenge these claims when looking back in history, they have now, ironically, become the rationale for resistance against new forms of development in the present, whereas the government, developers, and big corporations are being accused to be "colluding" with each other to maximize revenue at the expense of the welfare of ordinary citizens. And there is, indeed, no better case to illustrate these dynamics than the transformation of the New Town Plaza— the exemplar of Hong Kong's consumerist culture and a cherished symbol of "community development."

Figure 6.6
An interior view of the New Town Plaza after the rennovation.
Courtesy of Wikipedia user—Wing1990hk

Figure 6.7
An article that discussed the recent protests against the transformation of the New Town Plaza.
(source: *Hong Kong Economic Journal*, October 15, 2012)

NOTES

1 Janet Ng, *Paradigm City: Space, Culture and Capitalism in Hong Kong* (New York: Sunny Press, 2009).

2 Ibid., 95–96.

3 The phenomena can be observed in many recent articles in Hong Kong's local Chinese newspapers. For an example showing the nostalgic sentiment about the city's old shopping malls, see 陳裕匡，"我與瓊華中心一起成長" [Chan Yu Hong, "I grew up with King Wah Centre"], *House News*, February 12, 2013.

4 For a discussion on Hong Kong's "malling process," see Tai-lok Lui, "The Malling of Hong Kong," in Gordon Mathews and Tai-lok Lui (eds.), *Consuming Hong Kong* (Hong Kong: Hong Kong University Press, 2001), 25.

5 See Cecilia Chu, "People Power as Exception: Three Controversies Over Privatization in Post-handover Hong Kong," *Urban Studies* 47, no. 8 (July 2010): 1773–92.

6 For a discussion on the expansion of Yaohan in Hong Kong, see Lonny E. Carlile, "The Yaohan Group: Model or Maverick among Japanese Retailers in China?" in Kerrie L. MacPherson (ed.), *Asian Department Stores* (Hawai'i: University of Hawai'i Press, 1998), 233–52.

7 Anthony Yeh, "Public Housing and New Town Development," in Yue-man Yeung and Timothy K. Y. Wong (eds.), *Fifty Years of Housing in Hong Kong: A Golden Jubilee and Appraisal* (Hong Kong: The Chinese University Press, 2003), 87–90.

8 Between 1976 and 1986, almost 80% of the growth took place in the new towns, and the number of people living there had increased by an average of about 150%. See Yeh, "Public Housing and New Town Development," 91–92.

9 "人物專訪：新市鎮創建里程碑：訪問陳啟銘先生" [Interview with Mr. Chan Kai Ming], http://www.shatin.hk (accessed May 25, 2013).

10 Ibid.

11 張雅琳，"從「歡迎光臨」到「窮人免進」，新不如舊的沙田新城市廣場？" 嶺南大學文化研究系碩士論文 [Jacqueline Cheung, "From 'welcome, everyone' to 'sorry, not for the poor': our good old New Town Plaza is going to be missed"], 2011.

12 Lui, "The Malling of Hong Kong," 25. For a discussion on the development of shopping malls in North America, see Margaret Crawford, "The World in a Shopping Mall," in Michael Sorkin (ed.), *Variations on a Theme Park: The New American City and the End of Public Space* (New York: Hill and Wang, 1992), 3–30.

13 Also see Lui's discussion on the changing demographic in the new towns, "The Malling of Hong Kong," 39.

14 Private interview with a Sha Tin resident, 2013.

15 For a discussion on the transformation of the New Town Plaza and related personal reflections on these changes in Chinese, see "新城市廣場的變臉與光復" [Reclaiming New Town Plaza], *House News*, October 17, 2012; 明永昌，"一个商场的故事" [Ming Wing Cheong, "The story of a shopping center"], 聯合早報 *Lianhe Zaobao*, October 30, 2012; 阿果，"是新城市廣場，也是香港故事" [Kenny Leung, "The New Town Plaza and the Hong Kong story"], 港文集 [Hong Kong essays], http://hktext.blogspot.hk, October 14, 2012; 張雅琳，"從「歡迎光臨」到「窮人免進」，新不如舊的沙田新城市廣場？" [Jacqueline Cheung, "From 'welcome, everyone' to 'sorry, not for the poor': our good old New Town Plaza is going to be missed"], 2011.

16 In the attempt to boost Hong Kong's sagging economy, the government introduced the "Individual Visit Scheme" in 2003, making it easier for more mainland Chinese tourists to visit the city.

17 This relocation of the bookstore, which occurred in late 2012, has incited great reactions from the Sha Tin community and heated discussions in the Chinese media. For example, see, "「商務」結業哀新市鎮變質：沙田爆發另類光復運動" ["Closure of the Commercial Press and the reclaiming of Sha Tin"], *Hong Kong Economic Journal*, October 15, 2012.

18 "一樓一古：沙田友苦笑，家變" ["Stories of Sha Tin"], *Apple Daily*, February 20, 2013. For an example of these tours, see http://cache.org.hk/word/shatin.pdf.

19 Cecilia Chu, "Heritage of Disappearance: Shekkipmei and Collective Memories in Post-handover Hong Kong," *Traditional Dwellings and Settlements Review* 18, no. 2 (2007).

7. IT MAKES A VILLAGE

Jonathan D. Solomon

Hong Kong defies simple solutions.[1] The official slogan, "Asia's World City," suggests a bland and artificial peace with its complex history: junk boats floating serenely past skyscrapers. In fact, Hong Kong's transition from a British colony to a global city is characterized by rougher waters. "Asia's World City" has the right idea: As a postcolonial-global city, it is precisely Hong Kong's relationship to the rest of the world that defines its character and its qualities today, from its unique political and cultural institutions to its continued economic rise. Hong Kong, in contrast to other post-colonial cities such as New Delhi, Penang, or Jakarta, is able to achieve cosmopolitan or extra-national status as a world city because of its ability to forge and maintain strong links between local and global populations. It is in the nature of "Asia," "World," and "City" where the smooth and homogeneous marketing tool diverges from a segmented and heterogeneous reality. Recent cases, from September 2012 protests against the adoption of a curriculum sympathetic to the Communist Party in Hong Kong schools to the months of street protests and encampments by pro-democracy supporters, demonstrate points of conflict in a society contending with increasing stratification. Borders between culture, class, and economy, and the systems for connecting across them figure largely in Hong Kong's formulation of itself as a global city today. How do such systems for connection manifest in built form? The answer may be surprising: shopping malls.

Despite its long colonial history, Hong Kong bears almost no physical trace of its past. A rapacious development environment and general antipathy towards history under both British and Chinese rule conspired to eliminate all but the faintest trace of the colonial city. Most visibly, the site of Murray House, an 1846 barracks later used as a government office, was vacated in 1982 (the building was eventually reconstructed on the south of the island) to make way for the Bank of China Tower. The Murray Barrack Parade Ground became the site of the Hong Kong Hilton Hotel in 1961, and was cleared in 1995 to make way for a commercial office tower. In 2006, the 1957 Edinburgh Place Ferry Pier, from which the Star Ferry had operated, was demolished to make way for an at-grade highway amid protest that it should be conserved as a part of the city's cultural heritage. Such examples demonstrate the ease with which Hong Kong has historically been willing to replace buildings and fabric rich in historical symbolism, and thus in links to the past, with the accoutrements of globalism. Ironically, it is one of the most conspicuously generic of urban typologies, the shopping mall, which ultimately provides Hong Kong with the functional infrastructure for connecting between global and local communities within its borders. In place of symbolic links to its past that could provide the basis of a collective memory, shopping malls provide functional links in the city that bring diverse cultures into propinquity. This unlikely role for a building form widely considered to be fundamentally anti-urban is a unique characteristic of Hong Kong urbanism.

Buying Space: ACP and the Apotheosis of the Hong Kong Mall

As British colonial rule in Hong Kong waned, a framework document was drawn up for the future of the city as an interconnected global

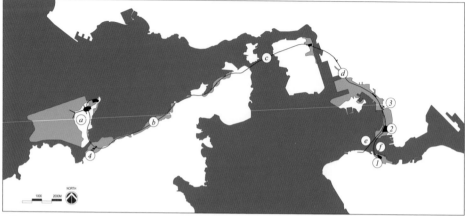

Figure 7.1
The Airport Core Program, a US$20-billion public works project for
Hong Kong's new international airport, including bridges, tunnels
and highways, rail links, and extensive land reclamation works. 1. IFC
Mall; 2. Elements Mall; 3. Olympic City Mall; 4. Citygate Mall; a. Hong
Kong International Airport; b. North Lantau Expressway; c. Tsing Ma
Bridge; d. Western Kowloon Corridor; e. Western Harbour Crossing;
f. Airport Express Rail. Image: Jonathan D. Solomon

metropolis. Dubbed Metroplan, the first goal
of the framework was to enhance Hong Kong's
role as an international port and airport. Then
referred to as PADS, a Port and Airport Design
Strategy was closely linked with Metroplan,
with new development parcels planned along
the infrastructure being built to facilitate access
to a new airport planned on reclaimed land
on outlying Lantau Island. The vision of these
developments was clearly laid out in Metroplan;
they were to be dense, multiuse communities
separated from the older city grid but knitted
together by three-dimensional circulation
networks.[2]

PADS was ultimately realized as a US$20-billion
public works project called the Airport Core
Program, or ACP. The project comprises ten
major infrastructure projects along 34 kilometers
that connect the city to the world, including
highways, bridges and tunnels, high speed rail,
a new international airport, and prodigious
land reclamation for development in the urban
core and suburban fringe (Figure 7.1).[3] The Mass
Transit Railway Corporation (MTRC), owner and
operator of Hong Kong's intracity rail network,
was a major player in the planning of the project

and a developer of the properties located over
new rail stations. MTRC had utilized the form of
the podium mall to maximize the development
potential of its other land holdings under
Hong Kong's unique constraints.[4] The three-
dimensional planning approach and integrated
podium became the model for the new
properties, fulfilling part of Metroplan's vision.[5]

This essay demonstrates how podium shopping
malls that connect between Hong Kong's
global and local infrastructures create unique
communities.

Manuel Castells argues that infrastructure
projects serving high valued spaces to
international users constitute a form of neo-
colonialism, by which economic dominance
replaces political dominance.[6] Graham and
Marvin have called such projects "Glo-cal Bypass,"
infrastructure designed to allow the empowered
international business class to bypass local
context. Glo-cal Bypass is intended to create
redundant and resilient solutions to "connect
local segments of cities to other valued segments
in different parts of the globe." Often involving
major physical planning schemes that circumvent

existing fabric, Glo-cal Bypass connects selected users and bypasses others, creating spatial and social stratification and establishing and reinforcing hierarchies.[7] The podium shopping mall has the potential to reinforce or subvert the Glo-cal Bypass in proportion to its degree of engagement in local fabric. This integrated model describes yet another outcome, for which we could use the term "Global Villages" as outlined by Marshall McLuhan: a space of discontinuity and division developed out of increased connectivity.[8] Not necessarily leading to greater cohesiveness or tranquillity, Global Village describes not a utopian ideal, but a contested space, a fractious and messy community in which inequality is not so much eliminated as confronted.

Taken in its entirety, the ACP suggests a Glo-cal Bypass. By building new single-purpose rail lines and redundant roadways, it creates a new infrastructure for international and global travel that bypasses existing local networks. By creating integrated, high-end living, working, shopping, and entertainment spaces it provides resilient infrastructure to target valued users. By allowing international personnel to live in a contained and privileged environment it creates spatial and social stratification and establishes and reinforces hierarchies. However, when it is appropriately networked to surrounding local social fabric, the podium shopping mall has the capacity to transform the Glo-cal Bypass into Global Village by creating intensive pedestrian links with local context and, facilitated by these links, allow the piggybacking of global infrastructure with entrepreneurial local uses. The first breaks spatial hierarchies and the second breaks social hierarchies.

Two malls on the ACP form the basis of a comparison between a Glo-cal Bypass and a Global Village (Figures 7.2 and 7.3). Facing one another across Victoria Harbour, the International Finance Centre (IFC) and the Union Square development are home to Hong Kong's two tallest buildings, and two of the city's most prominent malls, the IFC Mall and Elements Mall. Built explicitly to facilitate the transition from a colony to a global city, both are elite shopping malls associated with international travel and serve a global clientele. Yet due to its physical networking IFC establishes a Global Village

among the local spaces of Central, while in its present isolation Elements remains a Glo-cal Bypass insulated from older fabric. Both sites are in dynamic transition: adjacent to the IFC, a new park is being built on 18ha of reclaimed land in Victoria Harbour. Two major developments: the terminus of the Express Rail link to Shenzhen, Guangzhou, and points in China and the West Kowloon Cultural District are under construction adjacent to Elements Mall. How well the planning of these new projects in West Kowloon integrates the shopping mall with the city will determine whether it will become a Global Village.

The Glo-cal Bypass

Located at the Southwest tip of the West Kowloon, a 334-hectare area reclaimed from Victoria Harbour as a part of the Airport Core Program, Elements Mall forms the podium of a megablock complex called Union Square. The mall is topped by some of Hong Kong's tallest residential and commercial towers and several international hotels, and surrounded by building sites that will one day hold the world's largest performing arts complex and the Hong Kong terminus of China's new high speed rail network, with service to Shenzhen expected to take only 12 minutes and Guangzhou 48. While the eventual development of these parcels—still construction sites at the time of this writing—may yield greater pedestrian connectivity, Union Square is currently isolated from all foot traffic from outside (Figure 7.4).

Easy to access from global networks, Elements is harder to reach by local networks, and nearly impossible to approach on foot (Figures 7.5 and 7.7). The complex does include a single bus terminus and several integrated taxi stands. A direct link to the Airport Express and Tung Chung Mass Transit Railway (MTR), the trunk lines of the ACP, forms an atrium that is the central architectural feature of the mall. A link by footbridge joins the mall to the Austin Road station of the city's commuter rail, the West Rail line to the New Territories. Efficient connections to the airport are supplemented by bus service across the border with Mainland China, including check-in services and direct routes to Shenzhen's Bao'an International Airport. As a result, the mall has become a destination of choice for mainland tourists who utilize direct links to benefit from

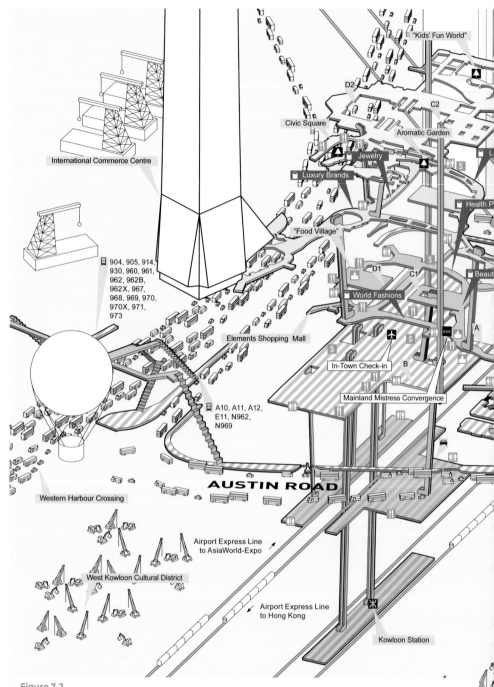

International Commerce Centre

"Kids' Fun World"

D2

C2

Civic Square

Aromatic Garden

Jewelry

Luxury Brands

Health P

"Food Village"

904, 905, 914, 930, 960, 961, 962, 962B, 962X, 967, 968, 969, 970, 970X, 971, 973

D1

C1

Beaut

World Fashions

A

Elements Shopping Mall

In-Town Check-in

B

A10, A11, A12, E11, N962, N969

Mainland Mistress Convergence

Western Harbour Crossing

AUSTIN ROAD

Airport Express Line to AsiaWorld-Expo

West Kowloon Cultural District

Airport Express Line to Hong Kong

Kowloon Station

Figure 7.2
The Glo-cal Bypass: smoothly connected to the international airport and cross-boundary trains to Mainland China, Elements Mall is hard to reach from adjacent Kowloon. Future footbridges could change this, creating links to the city and fostering a Global Village. Drawing by Adam Frampton, Jonathan D. Solomon, and Clara Wong

K1(1)

Tower 1

"The Grand" (Cinema)

B5

Tower 2

B1

Tower 3

B2

Books

Border Coach Terminus

26, 77M

West Kowloon Terminus

Commuter Convergence

A

"The Rink"

8, 11, 203E, 215X,
270A, 281A

D1,

D2

F

Austin Station

West Rail Line
to Nam Cheong

West Rail Line
to East Tsim Sha Tsui

Shuttle Platforms

Long Haul Platforms

Express Rail Link

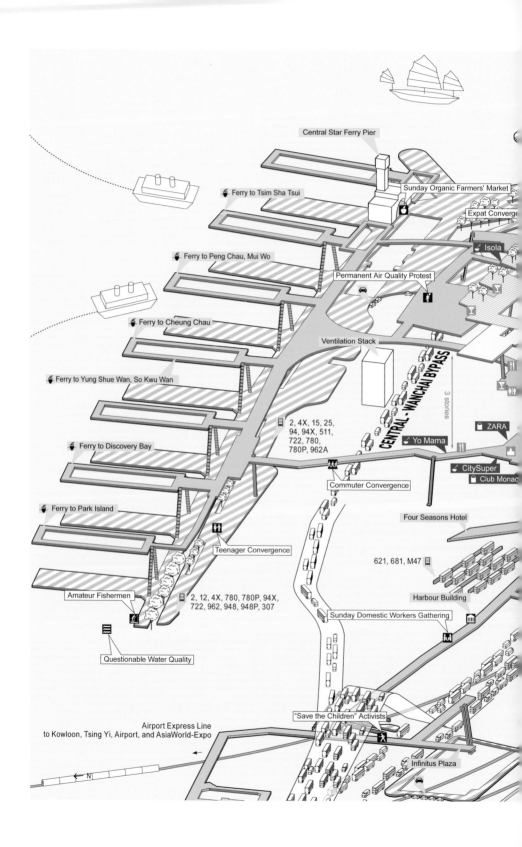

Central Star Ferry Pier

Ferry to Tsim Sha Tsui

Sunday Organic Farmers' Market

Expat Convergence

Isola

Ferry to Peng Chau, Mui Wo

Permanent Air Quality Protest

Ferry to Cheung Chau

Ventilation Stack

Ferry to Yung Shue Wan, So Kwu Wan

CENTRAL - WANCHAI BYPASS

3 stories

ZARA

2, 4X, 15, 25, 94, 94X, 511, 722, 780, 780P, 962A

Yo Mama

Ferry to Discovery Bay

CitySuper

Club Monaco

Commuter Convergence

Four Seasons Hotel

Ferry to Park Island

621, 681, M47

Teenager Convergence

Amateur Fishermen

2, 12, 4X, 780, 780P, 94X, 722, 962, 948, 948P, 307

Harbour Building

Sunday Domestic Workers Gathering

Questionable Water Quality

"Save the Children" Activists

Airport Express Line
to Kowloon, Tsing Yi, Airport, and AsiaWorld-Expo

Infinitus Plaza

← N

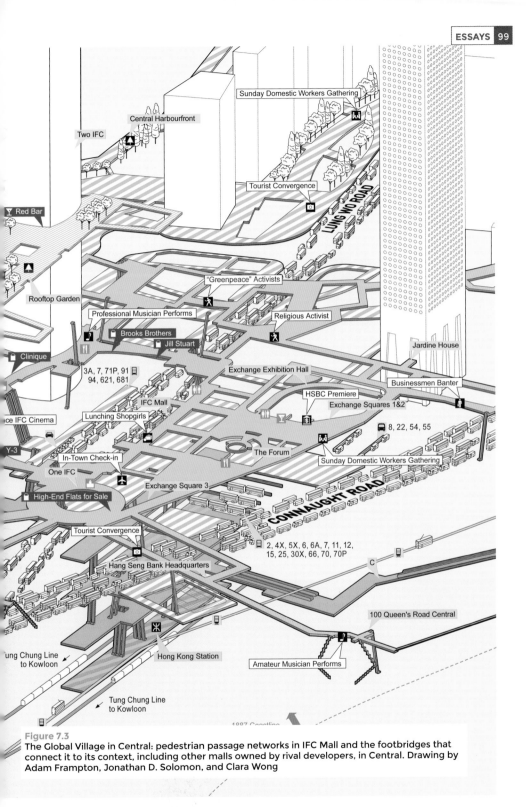

Figure 7.3
The Global Village in Central: pedestrian passage networks in IFC Mall and the footbridges that connect it to its context, including other malls owned by rival developers, in Central. Drawing by Adam Frampton, Jonathan D. Solomon, and Clara Wong

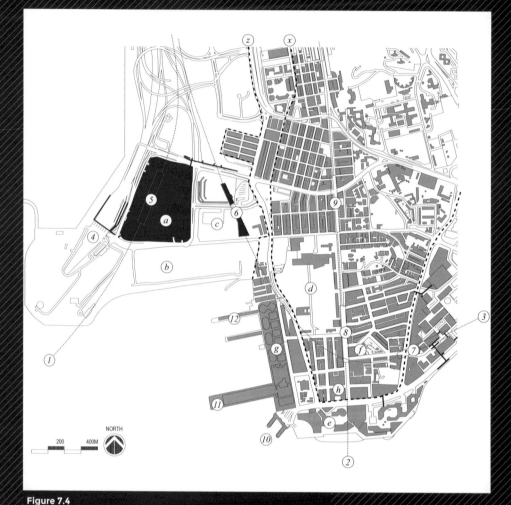

Figure 7.4
Tsim Sha Tsui, Jordan, and West Kowloon: the vicinity of Elements
Mall, demonstrating its current isolation. 1. Airport Express Rail
and MTR Tung Chung Line; 2. MTR Tsuen Wan Line; 3. West Rail
Commuter Line; 4. Western Harbour Crossing; 5. Kowloon Station;
6. Austin Station; 7. East Tsim Sha Tsui Station; 8. Tsim Sha Tsui
Station; 9. Jordan Station; 10. Star Ferry Pier; 11. Ocean Terminal;
12. China Ferries Pier; a. Elements Mall and the Union Square
development; b. Site of the future West Kowloon Cultural District;
c. Site of the future Express Rail terminus; d. Kowloon Park; e.
Hong Kong Cultural Centre; f. Chungking Mansions; g. Gateway
and Harbour City Malls; h. Peninsula Hotel; x. original shoreline;
z. pre-ACP shoreline. Image: Jonathan D. Solomon

reduced tariffs on luxury goods without the discomfort of mixing with the local culture, and for expatriate business people who enjoy its smooth integration with the airport.[9]

Despite its global connectivity Elements is locally isolated, access on foot to the nearest MTR station on the urban network, in Jordan, is not practical. A single public entrance at street level is located at the eastern tip of the complex. Of eight planned, two pedestrian footbridges currently connect beyond the superblock: one westward to a bus station at the entrance to the Western Harbour Crossing, the other eastward to a park at the border of the nearest populated neighborhood.[10] The residential properties treat the elevated podium as a new ground level, and do not engage the public street. Residential rents in the complex are in the city's top bracket, while those in the Kowloon neighborhoods to the east are in its lower range.

The Union Square development was designed as an integrated three-dimensional city with Elements Mall serving to connect the various transport, residential, and commercial programs. Nearly all the facilities necessary for daily life, including grocery stores, convenience stores, cinema, and even a school, are available in the mall.[11] It has a high degree of global and internal connectivity, but it simply is not on the way to or from anywhere by foot. In these ways, Union Square is currently a Glo-cal Bypass: an enclave community for the privileged sector, it is globally connected but locally isolated. Integral and resilient, it is both spatially and socially stratified, reinforcing hierarchies in the city. As the connectivity of the complex increases with new construction, however, it may well begin to behave as a Global Village.

The Global Village

The IFC complex is already both globally connected and well integrated into a local context. IFC Mall has direct pedestrian connections to ferries, buses, minibuses, taxis, and two urban lines on the MTR, as well as the Airport Express Rail. Pedestrian footbridges lead to corporate lobbies, hotels, other shopping malls, and adjacent urban fabric. Two major bus terminals serve the complex and access to numerous taxi stands is available. IFC is also a

Figure 7.5
The main entrance to Elements Mall: an atrium linking to the Airport Express Rail. Image: Jonathan D. Solomon

Figure 7.6
The Union Square development, adjacent to the construction sites that separate it from Kowloon. Image: Cyrus Penarroyo

Figure 7.7
View of the "second ground" created on the roof of Elements Mall, serving the surrounding towers but disconnected from the city. Image: Jonathan D. Solomon

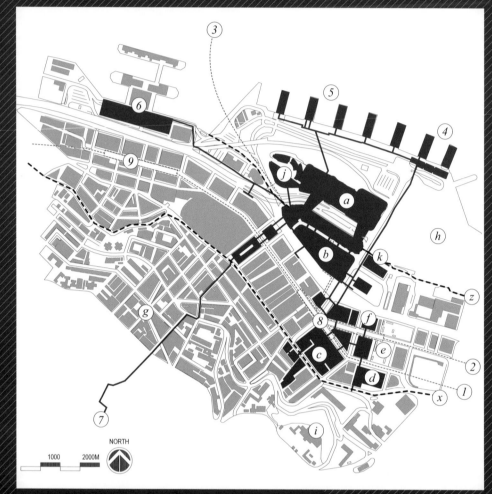

Figure 7.8
Public passage networks in Central district that connect to the
IFC Mall, demonstrating its integration with the city. 1. MTR Island
Line; 2. MTR Tsuen Wan Line; 3. Airport Express Rail and MTR Tung
Chung Line; 4. Star Ferry Pier; 5. Central Ferry Piers; 6. Macau Ferry
Pier; 7. Central and Mid-Levels Escalator; 8. Central Station;
9. Sheung Wan Station; a. IFC Mall and IFC Towers 1 and 2;
b. Exchange Square and the Hong Kong Stock Exchange;
c. Landmark Mall; d. HSBC building; e. Statue Square; f. Mandarin
Oriental Hotel; g. Soho neighborhood; h. Central Reclamation
Phase III; i. Chief Executive's residence; j. Four Seasons Hotel;
k. General Post Office; x. original shoreline; z. pre–ACP shoreline.
Image: Jonathan D. Solomon

part of the network that connects several major ferry lines, including the famous Star Ferry to Kowloon, with the CBD. IFC's major medium of connectivity is intermodal foot traffic. The form of the mall was conceived of early by designers as being fully integrated with public intermodal passage (Figure 7.8).[12] It is common for office workers to pass through the mall as a part of their morning commute from outlying island communities to other parts of the city, or for locals coming to Hong Kong Island on the Star Ferry from Kowloon to use it as an air-conditioned shortcut into the city. Despite being situated on reclaimed land and separated from the older social fabric of the city by a high-speed traffic artery, IFC manages not only to connect to, but to integrate with a neighborhood that is among the most diverse in Hong Kong in terms of the age, scale, and use of its buildings, as well as the ethnicity and class of its population.

IFC enjoys a high degree of connectivity with a unique pedestrian network already in place at the time of its construction, the footbridges and other public passageways that join office lobbies and smaller shopping malls in Central. Unlike the IFC Mall itself or Elements, which, while developed by different interests in a number of parcels, were conceived of through a masterplanning exercise that was ultimately government-led, the network of shopping centers and connecting bridges in Central grew piecemeal as a result of developer's desire to link smaller, scattered properties into a more coherent whole.[13] Unlike newly reclaimed sites throughout the territory, where pedestrian connectivity could be achieved through megablock complexes under a single developer, the footbridge network in Central contends with a legacy of the colonial fabric: small plot sizes and multiple owners. The new datum, dense and redundant, proved both convenient and commercially successful, with rents on the footbridge level equalling or even doubling those at ground level.[14] IFC was planned to connect to and continue this second ground. Stretching from the Macao ferry terminal in the west to Statue Square in the east, this public passage, where global and local flows cross, also serves as an important social space in the city.

IFC Mall forms a Global Village first by creating intensive pedestrian links with its heterogeneous context, both immediate and distant. The mall's

Figure 7.9
View of the public passage area in IFC Mall. Photo by Cyrus Penarroyo

Figure 7.10
Informal restaurants in an alleyway viewed from elevated walkway connecting through office towers to the IFC Mall. Photo by Cyrus Penarroyo

Figure 7.11
View of the network of pedestrian passageways and open spaces that link IFC Mall to its urban context over roads, parking lots, and bus terminals. Image: Jonathan D. Solomon

Figure 7.12
Foreign domestic workers gather on the footbridges outside of the
IFC Mall and Exchange Square. Photo by Jonathan D. Solomon

unique contribution is its hybridization of interior circulation with urban transportation systems. It connects the city's financial and corporate center not only to the international airport, but also to outlying islands, public transportation hubs, and local urban fabric, in an arrangement that breaks spatial hierarchies. IFC creates a Global Village secondly by facilitating the piggybacking of its globally connected infrastructure with entrepreneurial local uses (Figures 7.10 and 7.11).

The most visible and most overtly political of these uses is the occupation of the Central footbridge network by foreign domestic helpers on Sundays, their government-mandated day off. Descending from the remarkably cramped conditions of the apartments they service and confronted with Hong Kong's utter lack of public open space, this population (mostly Filipino women) encamp in makeshift shelters across the network, leaving narrow passageways for residents, tourists, and shoppers to pass (Figure 7.12). An unambiguous political statement by a service class of their importance to the function of the city, this itinerant public demonstration is in fact the result of a set of very specific local conditions: a culture of hard work and long hours amongst the professional class, and the lack of a large, mobile population within the territory

combine to make an attractive market for domestic laborers from poorer neighbor nations. The city's very small apartments, a result of real geographic constraints and of an overheated housing market, provide little excess space. Every Sunday, a government-mandated day off for the highly regulated domestic helper workforce, sends a population of approximately 280,000 into a city as lacking in traditional gathering spaces—large public parks, monuments, and squares—as it is in informal public open space.

The occupation of public passageways is as much a necessity as it is an opportunity. That the global economy of the IFC Mall and its privileged sector users confronts a micro economy of service industries amongst a disempowered segment of society is no accident, but the result of its diverse network. To the degree that this is integration, it comes in the discontinuity and division formed out of increased connectivity, McLuhan's basis of the Global Village. The social hierarchies that exist between these communities during the week are not so much broken down as brought into confrontation with one another. This is a unique character of the "Global Village" of Hong Kong—it does not seek to remedy the inequity of the city, rather it provides a medium on which those inequalities can share space.

Conclusion

"Global Villages" such as the IFC (and global visions such as those for the future of West Kowloon) have profound potential to mix more and less globally connected segments of the population and resist neo-colonial hierarchies while still creating connections between city and world. The case of the adaptability of a market-driven strategy for creating continuous pedestrian networks to a government-led design solution, and eventually to unintended uses by diverse sectors of the urban population suggests that the model has potential to address matters of social sustainability broadly in Asian cities. In the context of the postcolonial-global city of Hong Kong, it is no surprise that links between local and global networks should exist. What bears interest is that it is the shopping mall, an iconic space of globalization, which should accomplish this function in the city.

NOTES

1 This article originally appeared under the title "It Makes a Village: Hong Kong's Podium Shopping Malls as Global Villages," in Gregory Bracken (ed.), *Aspects of Urbanization in China* (Amsterdam: Amsterdam University Press, 2012). The paper has been updated to reflect the changing context of the two sites analyzed over the past three years, notably the construction of the Central Harbourfront, West Kowloon Cultural District, and Express Rail Terminus. Several images were updated and minor revisions were made to the body of the text. In reflection, this essay takes a more hopeful stance toward the eventual integration of Elements Mall into the fabric of Kowloon than its predecessor.

2 Hong Kong government, Metroplan, the Foundations and the Framework, 1, 9, 14.

3 http://www.info.gov.hk/napco/index.html (accessed April 1, 2012).

4 Stephen S. Y. Lau, R. Giridharan, and S. Ganesen, "Policies for Implementing Multiple Intensive Land Use in Hong Kong," *Journal of Housing and the Built Environment 18* (Dordrecht: Kluwer Academic Publishers, 2003), 365–78.

5 Steven Smith, *Kowloon, Transport Super City* (Hong Kong: Pace Publishing, 1998), 30.

6 Manuel Castells, *The Information Age: Economy, Society and Culture I, The Rise of the Network Society* (Oxford: Blackwell, 1996).

7 Stephen Graham and Simon Marvin, *Splintering Urbanism: Networked Infrastructures, Technological Mobilities, and The Urban Condition* (Oxford: Routledge, 2001), 167.

8 Gerald Emmanuel Stearn, *Mcluhan Hot and Cool* (New York: Penguin Books, 1968), 314.

9 See Max Hirsh and Jonathan D. Solomon, "Does Your Mall Have an Airport?" in *Log 19* (New York: Anyone Corporation, Spring/Summer 2010).

10 Steven Smith, *Kowloon, Transport Super City* (Hong Kong: Pace Publishing, 1998), 30.

11 Ibid., 25.

12 Greg Pearce, *Arup, Hong Kong Station* (Stuttgart: Edition Axel Menges, 2001), 12.

13 Zhang Ziayuan et al., "The Central District of Hong Kong: Architecture and Urbanism of a Laissez Faire City," *A+U Architecture and Urbanism*, no. 322 (July 1997): 3–17.

14 Leslie Lu, "Asian Arcades Project: Progressive Porosity," in *Perspecta 36* (New Haven: The Yale School of Architecture, 2005), 86–89.

Part 2

CATALOG

THE PRESCIENCE OF MALLS

A Glimpse Inside of Hong Kong's Unique "Public" Spaces

Adam Nowek

The atrium is a somewhat recent introduction to Hong Kong's malls. Older malls such as the Golden Shopping Centre simply do not have the room for a space dedicated to social interaction rather than the consumption of goods and services. As malls became to be viewed by visitors as a node of social interaction in a city that lacks a significant public space, crafting an inviting atrium became an important component of mall design in Hong Kong. Hong Kong's mall atria exist in a wide variety of styles. Mei Foo Sun Chuen, for instance, does not actually contain an atrium, but rather an open outdoor space located between various areas of retail spaces. Other atria contain a central element that serves as an attractive point to meet which ultimately becomes a status symbol for both the developers and the mall itself, including art installations (Elements, New Town Plaza), restaurant-cafés (The Landmark, World Wide House), or simply a wide open space (MegaBox, Pacific Place). While each strategy is a completely different means, all of Hong Kong's mall atria seek the same end: to coax visitors to come to the mall to linger for a full social experience in which shopping is a fundamental part.

ATRIUMS

CITYPLAZA

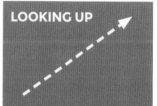

LOOKING UP

CITYWALK

PACIFIC PLACE

amc

ZEN

MEGABOX

LOK FU PLAZA

3

2

IFC

SHUN TAK CENTRE

PARK CENTRAL

IFC

AT THE ATRIUMS

NEW TOWN PLAZA

GRAND CENTURY PLACE

TIMES SQUARE

CHUNGKING MANSIONS

LOOKING DOWN

LANGHAM PLACE

MONKI

IFC

K11

TIMES SQUARE

HARBOUR CITY

NEW TOWN PLAZA

MEGABOX

CITYPLAZA

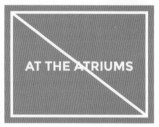

AT THE ATRIUMS

ELEMENTS

THE LANDMARK

SHUN TAK CENTRE

YAN ON BUILDING

LANGHAM PLACE

WORLD-WIDE HOUSE

LOOKING DOWN

GOLDEN SHOPPING CENTRE

TUEN MUN TOWN PLAZA

AT THE ATRIUMS

LANGHAM PLACE

CITYPLAZA

LOK FU PLAZA

PACIFIC PLACE

The size of a mall corridor in Hong Kong is directly correlated to the nature of the city's real estate market: as land prices in Hong Kong are at a premium, a wider network of corridors signifies the luxury of the goods sold within the mall and hints at the socio-economic status of the clientele. Malls containing narrow corridors almost exclusively house retailers that provide more affordable goods and services for a wider segment of the population: Argyle Centre is the proper choice for the penny-pinching fashionista to purchase clothing, Chungking Mansions is the ideal location to bulk buy flimsy mobile phones, while Sino Centre is the top destination for counterfeit copies of K-Pop records and Japanese pornography. The narrow corridors are, above all, a pragmatic design decision due to the limitations of the site, but they ultimately discourage loitering within the space, meaning that retailers need to address the effects of limited corridor capacity on their business. By contrast, many contemporary high-end malls feature much more elaborate and diverse corridor orientations. Harbour City and New Town Plaza differ in their content of high-end retailers, but both are characterized by boulevard-width corridors that prompt visitors to meander slowly past the stores. Other contemporary malls design hallways in different manners for curious effects: for example, K11, a self-branded "art mall," has thinner hallways that prompt movement and browsing, as if the individual were visiting an art gallery or a museum.

CORRIDORS

CHUNGKING MANSIONS

ARGYLE CENTRE

ARGYLE CENTRE

CHUNGKING MANSIONS

CHUNGKING MANSIONS

ELEMENTS

GOLDEN SHOPPING CENTRE

HARBOUR CITY

GRAND CENTURY PLACE

GRAND CENTURY PLACE

NEW TOWN PLAZA

PACIFIC PLACE

PARK CENTRAL

SHUN TAK CENTRE

ARGYLE CENTRE

CITYPLAZA

CHUNGKING MANSIONS

CITYWALK

CORRIDORS

K11

HARBOUR CITY

MEI FOO SUN CHUEN

SINO CENTRE

THE LANDMARK

YAN ON BUILDING

TUEN MUN TOWN PLAZA

WORLD-WIDE HOUSE

In a hyper-dense city such as Hong Kong, developers prefer to maximize the amount of floor space that can be developed on any given site. Hong Kong's resulting mall design typology is vertically stacked retail, with some malls containing the same amount of floors as a mid-rise building. Of the malls featured here, only Chungking Mansions relies on elevators as the primary method of vertical transport, resulting in lengthy queues to use the building's few elevators. The vast majority of Hong Kong's malls have an intricate network of escalators aimed at maximizing the number of visitors to pass by the maximum amount of storefronts. Many of these malls place upward and downward escalators parallel to one another (e.g., Golden Shopping Centre, Tuen Mun Town Plaza), while others invert the escalators, allowing minimal effort for swift passage between multiple floors (e.g., Lok Fu Plaza, Sino Centre). More adventurous vertical transport involves escalators spanning multiple floors, accenting the grandeur of the structure itself: the escalators of Times Square span multiple floors, ascending the atrium in a crisscross shape, while the primary escalator of Langham Place is impressively tall and time-consuming, allowing passengers to take in their surroundings at a leisurely pace. While attractive and interesting visual elements in their own right, these unique escalator configurations additionally serve the purpose of spreading people around as efficiently and as evenly as possible.

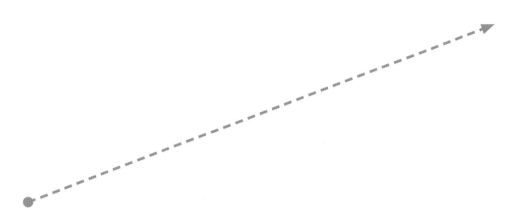

VERTICAL
TRANSPORT

VERTICAL TRANSPORT

NEW TOWN PLAZA

PACIFIC PLACE

PARK CENTRAL

SINO CENTRE

THE LANDMARK

TIMES SQUARE

TUEN MUN TOWN PLAZA

Malls are, first and foremost, sites of consumption. But, considering the lack of grand public spaces in Hong Kong, it might be more accurate to simply refer to the city's malls as leisure centers. Many of these malls contain more typical elements of entertainment programming that are seen in malls in other cities worldwide, such as cinemas or temporary art installations. In some cases, however, malls act as alternative community centers with activities more unconventional within a mall than standard activities such as going to the cinema: both Elements and MegaBox have an ice rink on-site, and frequently host hockey practices and league matches for the predominantly expatriate hockey-playing community, while others incorporate kindergartens into the structure. One of the more prevalent informal activities is photography. Primarily occurring in the high-end malls, friends frequently gather for group photographs by an interesting architectural element (e.g., Times Square's crisscrossing escalators, Langham Place's airy interior), while hobby photographers shoot the temporary art installations seen with the atria and corridors of IFC or Harbour City.

ALTERNATIVE ACTIVITIES

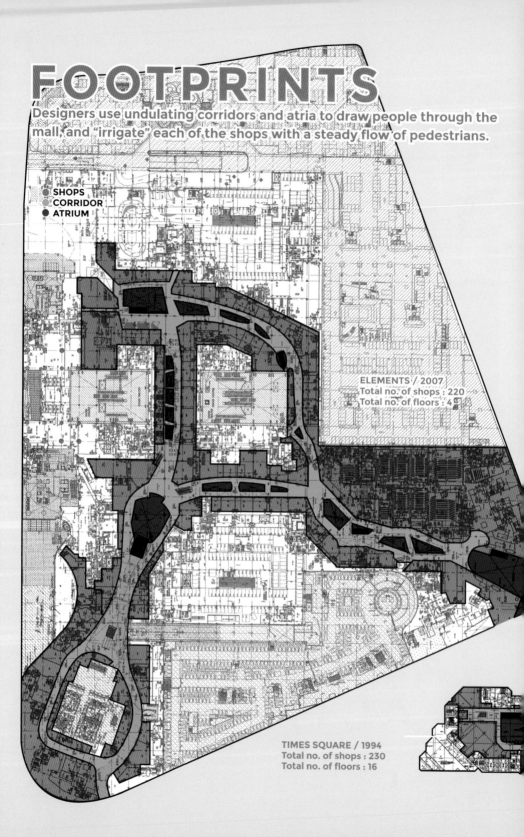

FOOTPRINTS

Designers use undulating corridors and atria to draw people through the mall, and "irrigate" each of the shops with a steady flow of pedestrians.

● SHOPS
● CORRIDOR
● ATRIUM

ELEMENTS / 2007
Total no. of shops : 220
Total no. of floors : 4

TIMES SQUARE / 1994
Total no. of shops : 230
Total no. of floors : 16

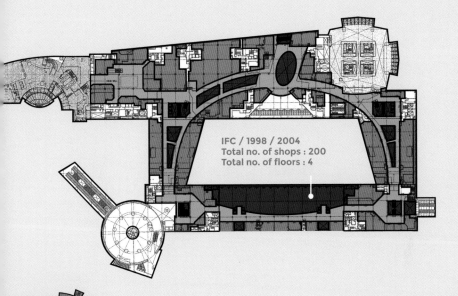

IFC / 1998 / 2004
Total no. of shops : 200
Total no. of floors : 4

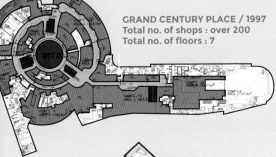

GRAND CENTURY PLACE / 1997
Total no. of shops : over 200
Total no. of floors : 7

MEGABOX / 2007
Total no. of shops : 240
Total no. of floors : 19

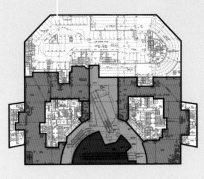

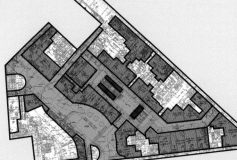

K11 / 2009
Total no. of shops : 80
Total no. of floors : 6

LANGHAM PLACE / 2004
Total no. of shops : around 200
Total no. of floors : 15

CROSS-SECTIONS

In Hong Kong's ever taller malls, atria play a key role to lure people up to the shops on higher floors.

● SHOPS
● CORRIDOR
● ATRIUM

GRAND CENTURY PLACE / 1997
Total no. of shops : over 200
Total no. of floors : 7

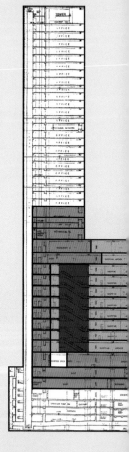

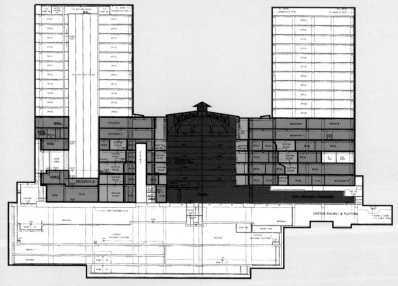

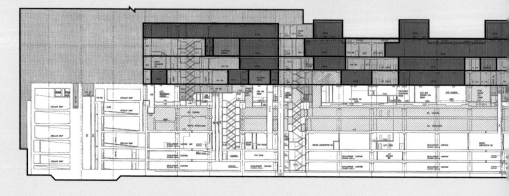

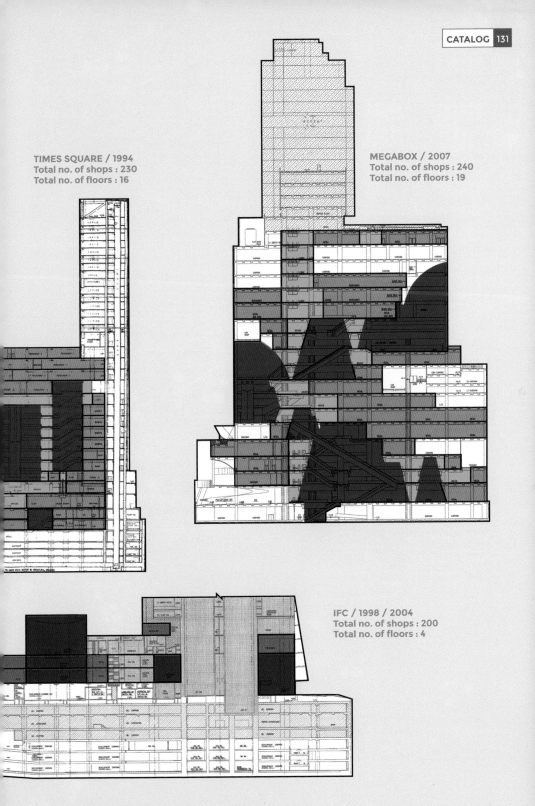

TIMES SQUARE / 1994
Total no. of shops : 230
Total no. of floors : 16

MEGABOX / 2007
Total no. of shops : 240
Total no. of floors : 19

IFC / 1998 / 2004
Total no. of shops : 200
Total no. of floors : 4

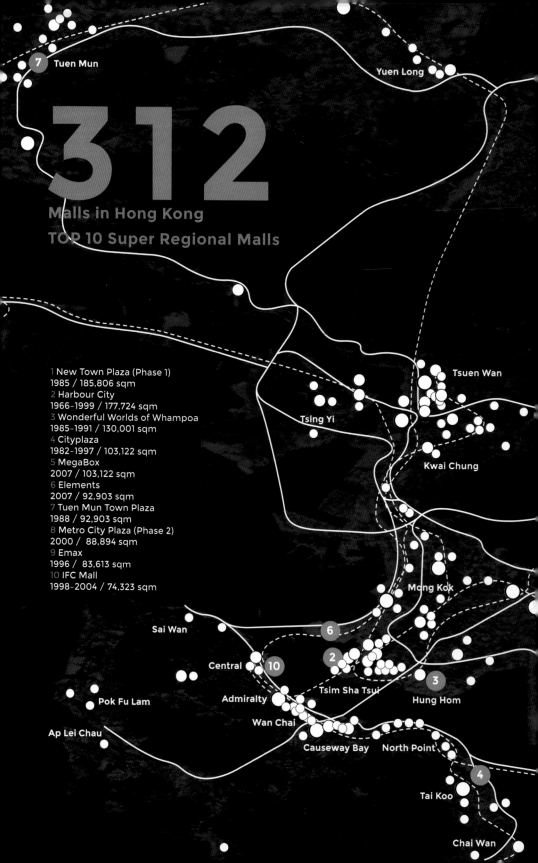

312

Malls in Hong Kong
TOP 10 Super Regional Malls

1 New Town Plaza (Phase 1)
1985 / 185,806 sqm
2 Harbour City
1966-1999 / 177,724 sqm
3 Wonderful Worlds of Whampoa
1985-1991 / 130,001 sqm
4 Cityplaza
1982-1997 / 103,122 sqm
5 MegaBox
2007 / 103,122 sqm
6 Elements
2007 / 92,903 sqm
7 Tuen Mun Town Plaza
1988 / 92,903 sqm
8 Metro City Plaza (Phase 2)
2000 / 88,894 sqm
9 Emax
1996 / 83,613 sqm
10 IFC Mall
1998-2004 / 74,323 sqm

7 Tuen Mun

Yuen Long

Tsuen Wan

Tsing Yi

Kwai Chung

Mong Kok

Sai Wan

6

2

Central

10

3

Tsim Sha Tsui

Hung Hom

Admiralty

Wan Chai

Pok Fu Lam

Ap Lei Chau

Causeway Bay

North Point

4

Tai Koo

Chai Wan

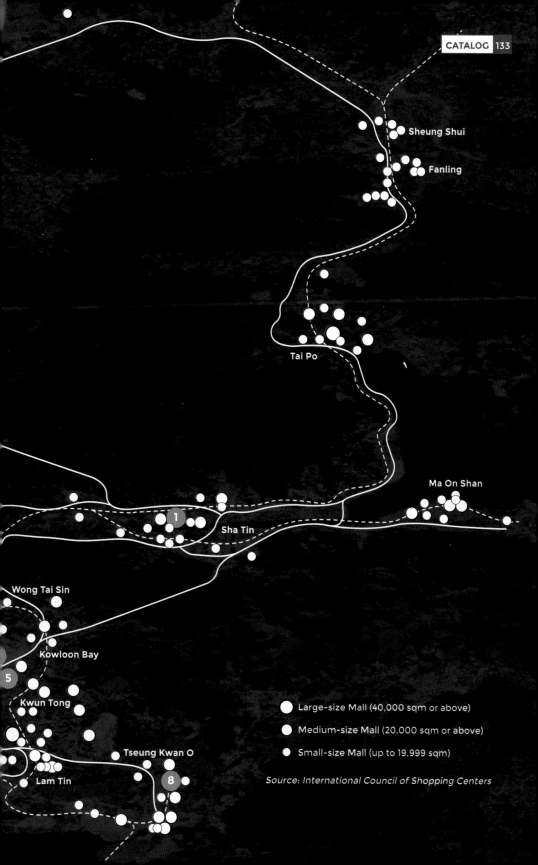

Sheung Shui

Fanling

Tai Po

Ma On Shan

Sha Tin

Wong Tai Sin

Kowloon Bay

Kwun Tong

Tseung Kwan O

Lam Tin

Large-size Mall (40,000 sqm or above)

Medium-size Mall (20,000 sqm or above)

Small-size Mall (up to 19,999 sqm)

Source: International Council of Shopping Centers

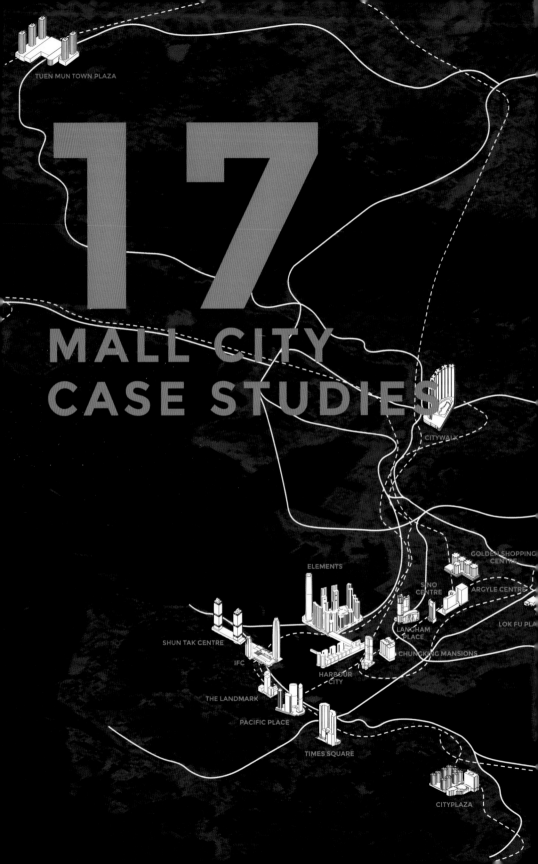

17
MALL CITY
CASE STUDIES

TUEN MUN TOWN PLAZA

CITYWALK

GOLDEN SHOPPING CENTRE

ELEMENTS

SINO CENTRE

ARGYLE CENTRE

LANGHAM PLACE

LOK FU PLA

SHUN TAK CENTRE

IFC

CHUNGKING MANSIONS

HARBOUR CITY

THE LANDMARK

PACIFIC PLACE

TIMES SQUARE

CITYPLAZA

MEGABOX

F.A.R.

Floor area ratio = (total covered area on all floors of all buildings on a certain plot, Gross Floor Area) / (area of the plot)

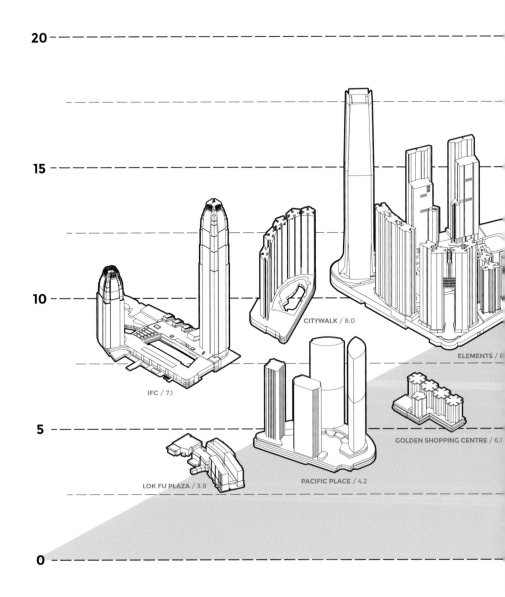

20

15

10

5

0

CITYWALK / 8.0

IFC / 7.1

ELEMENTS / 8

GOLDEN SHOPPING CENTRE / 6.1

LOK FU PLAZA / 3.9

PACIFIC PLACE / 4.2

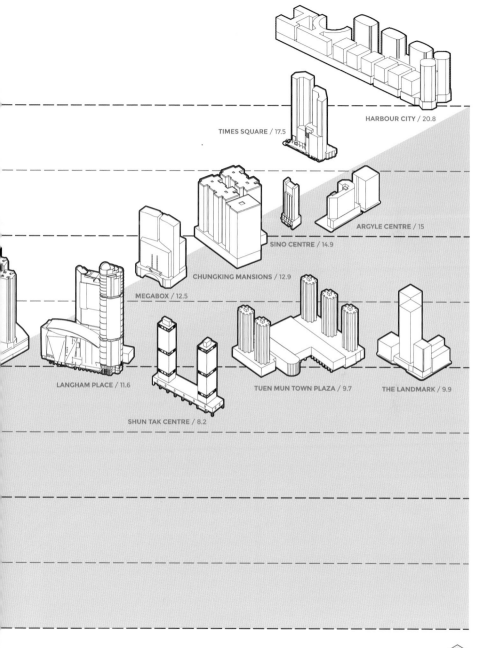

HARBOUR CITY / 20.8

TIMES SQUARE / 17.5

ARGYLE CENTRE / 15

SINO CENTRE / 14.9

CHUNGKING MANSIONS / 12.9

MEGABOX / 12.5

LANGHAM PLACE / 11.6

TUEN MUN TOWN PLAZA / 9.7

THE LANDMARK / 9.9

SHUN TAK CENTRE / 8.2

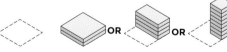

SITE   F.A.R. = 2.0   OR   OR

BLANK WALL RATIO

At Ground Level

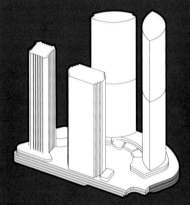

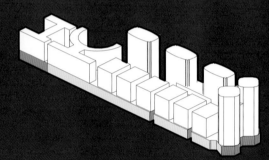

PACIFIC PLACE
11.3%

HARBOUR CITY
37%

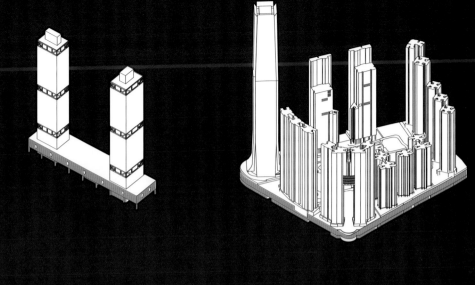

SHUN TAK CENTRE
65%

ELEMENTS
89%

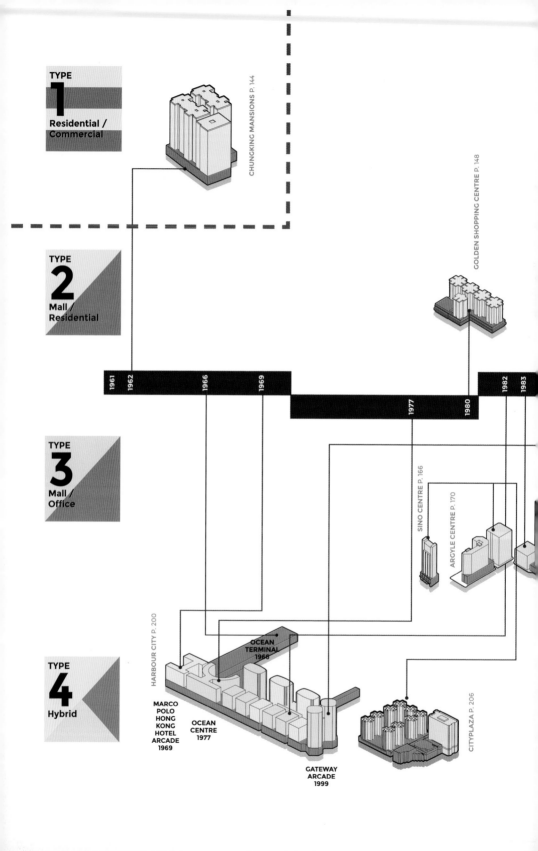

TYPE

1

Residential /
Commercial

CHUNGKING MANSIONS P. 144

GOLDEN SHOPPING CENTRE P. 148

TYPE

2

Mall /
Residential

1961 1962 1966 1969 1977 1980 1982 1983

TYPE

3

Mall /
Office

SINO CENTRE P. 166

ARGYLE CENTRE P. 170

HARBOUR CITY P. 200

OCEAN
TERMINAL
1966

TYPE

4

Hybrid

MARCO
POLO
HONG
KONG
HOTEL
ARCADE
1969

OCEAN
CENTRE
1977

GATEWAY
ARCADE
1999

CITYPLAZA P. 206

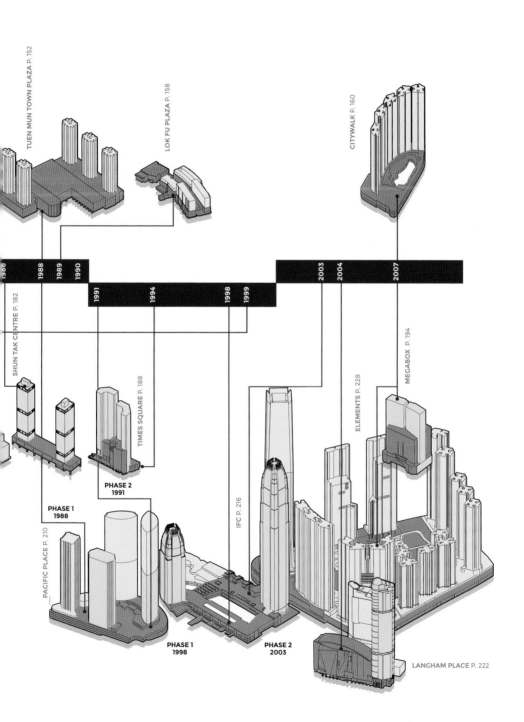

TUEN MUN TOWN PLAZA P. 152

LOK FU PLAZA P. 158

CITYWALK P. 160

SHUN TAK CENTRE P. 182

TIMES SQUARE P. 188

MEGABOX P. 194

ELEMENTS P. 228

PACIFIC PLACE P. 210

IFC P. 216

LANGHAM PLACE P. 222

1988
1989
1990
1991
1994
1998
1999
2003
2004
2007

PHASE 2
1991

PHASE 1
1988

PHASE 1
1998

PHASE 2
2003

TYPE

1

**Residential /
Commercial**

TYPE

2

**Mall /
Residential**

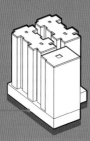

CHUNGKING MANSIONS
P. 144

GOLDEN SHOPPING CENTRE
P. 148

1962

1980

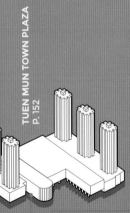

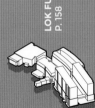

TUEN MUN TOWN PLAZA
P. 152

LOK FU PLAZA
P. 158

CITYWALK
P. 160

1988
1989

2007

The Entire World in
60,923 Square Meters

CHUNGKING MANSIONS

Chungking Mansions was initially a high-end housing project. One of the tallest buildings within Kowloon, it was a place where celebrities would stay. But its luxury status declined quickly, perhaps because of the large presence of South Asians, which were heavily discriminated against.

In the late 1970s Chungking Mansions became a convenient and cheap place to stay for travelers. Owners subdivided their apartments and turned them into guesthouses with tiny rooms for travelers.

But the building's power supply was not designed in anticipation of this larger number of residents, the strained electrical system becoming a fire hazard. In 1988 a fire killed a Danish tourist. Only five years later, an explosion in the building's electrical supply room left the entire building without water and electricity for ten days.

From the late 1990s, the building became a commercial magnet for migrants from all over the world, who set up small import/ export business. It has also become a refuge for illegal immigrants, providing them with cheap accommodation, a place to work, and basic services—all without them ever having to leave the building. Today, Chungking Mansions continues to flourish as an entry point for immigrants from developing countries into Hong Kong.

Amidst the glittering shopping malls of wealthy Hong Kong, Chungking Mansions is not the city's most glamorous building, but certainly its most globalized.

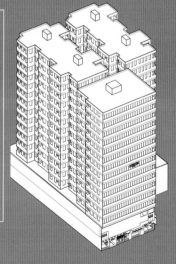

Address
36–44 Nathan Road, TST
Kowloon
Developer
Hang Lung Properties
Architect
Lamb Hazeland & Co.
Construction
Completion: 1962
Site Area
4,699 m²
Gross Floor Area / GFA
60,923 m²
Floor Area Ratio / FAR
12.9
Building Height
+9.5 m / 57 m (Podium/Tower)
Blank Wall at Ground Level
8 percent (Front Facade)

D
Chungking is known for its authentic Indian, Pakistani, Malaysian, African, and Middle Eastern cuisine. It is also a great place to talk with the cosmopolitan restaurant owners.

Seller—Nelson (age 65)

I was born in Hong Kong in 1945 and I have been working in Chungking (Mansions) for 35 years now. Even though I don't have a fixed schedule, I work very hard, as most people in Chungking do. Thirty-five years ago, 90 percent of Chungking's residents were Chinese workers, and only 10 percent from other places. Today, it's the opposite. Now 90 percent are Indian, Pakistani, African, and other nationalities, and maybe 10 percent Chinese. Back then there was not that much competition, because there were many things to sell. But nowadays most people sell the same goods and it becomes very difficult to make enough money to pay rent for my shop, house and cover my living expenses.

Despite all this, I enjoy my life in Chungking. I like the daily exercise of lifting things and moving them around. I go to Chungking every day (no holiday for me) from 10:30 a.m. to 7:30 p.m. I take one day off every two months to visit my good friend in Macao. Working in Chungking is a very demanding job for a 65-year-old man. Moreover, the shop has no air-conditioning, which makes it an inferno during the hot and humid summer.

I receive my customers from all nationalities with a wide smile. Although being here every day may seem boring, it is not so. Interacting with so many people from different cultures makes me a global-minded person, while I get to practice my English, Mandarin, Cantonese, and Spanish. Chungking has taught me histories of India, Pakistan, and a wide variety of other countries.

M
The Mall

A
Everything from phone repair services to restaurants, and from Middle Eastern souvenirs to pirated DVDs can be found in Chungking Mansions's little stores.

B
Due to the illegal conversion of residential apartments into guesthouses and restaurants, haphazard electrical wires and plumbing cover Chungking's ceilings.

C
Foreign exchange offices at the building's main entrance offer some of Hong Kong's most competitive rates.

Hong Kong's First Computer Market

GOLDEN SHOPPING CENTRE

Golden Shopping Centre, located in Sham Shui Po, consists of two markets that sell computer related products: Golden Computer Centre (1/F) and Golden Computer Arcade (G/F and L/G). It forms the base of five 12-story residential towers.

Completed in 1980, the center first sold clothes. But as Hong Kong developed its electronics industry, the center began to sell electronics, video games, and IBM PCs. It became Hong Kong's first computer market, and infamous for illegal computer clones and pirated software.

As the government began to carry out computer education, Golden Centre's reputation began to spread in Hong Kong.

Although other similar markets exist today, for Hongkongers "Golden" has become synonymous with computers.

With stricter government supervision today, the center has cleaned up its act, but retains its reputation for cheap computers, components, peripherals, and cell phones.

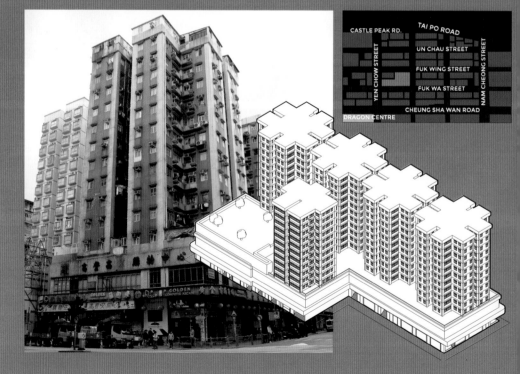

CASTLE PEAK RD. TAI PO ROAD
UN CHAU STREET
YEN CHOW STREET FUK WING STREET NAM CHEONG STREET
FUK WA STREET
CHEUNG SHA WAN ROAD
DRAGON CENTRE

Address
146-152 Fuk Wa Street,
Sham Shui Po, Kowloon
Developer
Proposed Commercial / Cinema
and Domestic Complex
Architect
Kwan Wing Hong
Construction
Initiation: 1978
Completion: 1980
Site Area
3,115 m²
Gross Floor Area / GFA
18,948 m²
Floor Area Ratio / FAR
6.1
Building Height
11.5 m / 45.5 m (Podium/Tower)
Blank Wall at Ground Level
35%

R
Residential

Residential 70%
Retail 30%

**Golden Mansion
Block 1**

Block 2

Block 3

Block 4

**Golden Mansion
Block 5**

Apartment A, 7th Floor
Flat size: 42.5 m²
Flat cost: 2.5 million HKD
Cost per m²: 60,000 HKD
Windows per floor area: 14%
Operable windows: 41

Compared to other residential
buildings in Hong Kong, Golden
Mansion is relatively old with
fewer stories. But it has a
convenient location close to
the subway station.

1/F

G/F

KWEILIN STREET

FUK WA STREET

FUK WING STREET

YEN CHOW STREET

LG

Worker—Mr. Fung (age 30)

*I have worked here for
five years. Although the
transportation in Sham Shui Po
is convenient, the surrounding
facilities are very old. Take this
complex as an example: this
building was built in the 1980s.
Every three years it needs
repair. For the neighbor next to
my shop, the problem is more
severe. His ceiling sometimes
has water leakage, so he needs
to replace it every one or
two years. Since the leakage
does not originate from his
own place, he has no way to
solve it. His upstairs neighbor
refuses to fix the leak. This is a
very common problem in this
complex. It needs to be rebuilt.*

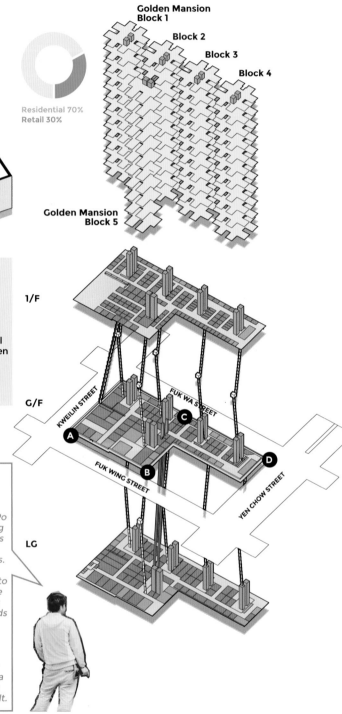

A
Golden Shopping Centre lies in Sham Shui Po, a district known for its street market with electronics, a place to go "geek shopping."

M
The Mall

B
Although the two malls are within the building, they have separate entrances.

C
The five entrances to the residential buildings are independent from the shopping malls.

D
On weekends, the center's narrow corridors fill up with predominantly men looking for cheap computer products.

D

Tuen Mun Town Plaza, established in 1988 and built over many phases, is the largest mall in this area of the New Territories, with more than 1 million square feet of retail. Of all Hong Kong's large malls it lies closest to Mainland China, and has a large transport interchange for light rail and buses. The five-story mall, which is partially built over a road, is known for its wide variety of brands, including Zara, H&M, Aeon, and Sa Sa Cosmetics.

Over the past decade, the developer Sino Group, one of Hong Kong's largest property companies, has spent millions renovating the mall. Through its location, tenant mix, and promotional activities it manages to draw more than 300,000 customers per day from far and wide.

Address
1 Tuen Shun Street, Tuen Mun
Developer
Sino Group
Architect
Benoy (Renovation)
Construction
Initiation: 1987
Completion: 1988
Site Area
21,375 m²
Gross Floor Area / GFA
207,391 m²
Floor Area Ratio / FAR
9.7
Building Height
+24.5 m / 99.5 m (Podium/Tower)
Blank Wall at Ground Level
40%

Mall on the Road
TUEN MUN
TOWN PLAZA

TUEN MUN
GOVERNMENT
OFFICE

LIGHT RAIL
TOWN CENTRE
STATION

TUEN MUN
CENTRAL LIBRARY

TUEN MUN TOWN
HALL

PRIVATELY OWNED PUBLIC SPACE

TUEN MUN
ROAD

CASTLE PEAK
ROAD

TUEN YAN
STREET

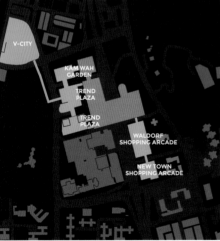

V-CITY

KAM WAH
GARDEN

TREND
PLAZA

TREND
PLAZA

WALDORF
SHOPPING ARCADE

NEW TOWN
SHOPPING ARCADE

Visitor—Mr. Wei (age 30+)

I am from Mainland China and now live in Shenzhen near Guomao station. I usually come to Hong Kong twice a week. Not unlike other mainland visitors, shopping in Hong Kong has become a part of my daily life. I come here to buy items I cannot find in Shenzhen or are more expensive there, such as small appliances, clothes, health products, and toys for my three-year-old son. Most of the staff speak Mandarin very well, which makes it much easier for me to go shopping. Sometimes I come here immediately after work at 5:30 p.m. and go back two hours later, thanks to direct buses between Tuen Mun and the border.

A change in visa policy had made shopping in Hong Kong more convenient for Shenzhen residents. More and more people living in Shenzhen now come to Hong Kong, and especially to Tuen Mun, for their daily essentials. Tuen Mun Town Plaza is becoming ever more popular among mainland customers.

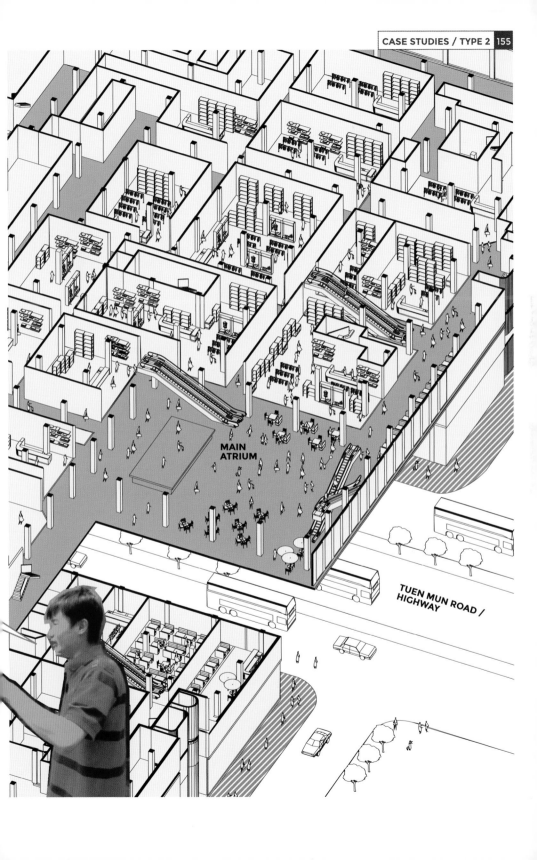

MAIN
ATRIUM

TUEN MUN ROAD /
HIGHWAY

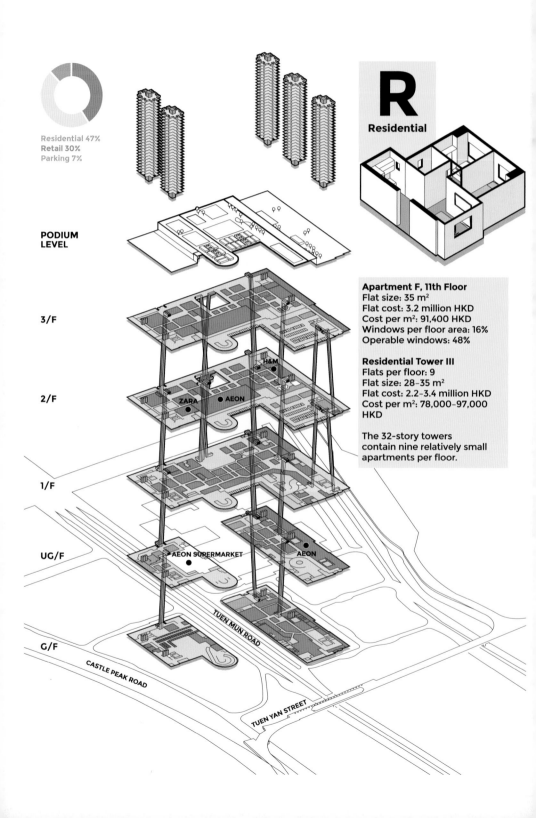

Residential 47%
Retail 30%
Parking 7%

PODIUM
LEVEL

3/F

2/F

1/F

UG/F

G/F

H&M

ZARA   AEON

AEON SUPERMARKET   AEON

TUEN MUN ROAD

CASTLE PEAK ROAD

TUEN YAN STREET

R
Residential

Apartment F, 11th Floor
Flat size: 35 m²
Flat cost: 3.2 million HKD
Cost per m²: 91,400 HKD
Windows per floor area: 16%
Operable windows: 48%

Residential Tower III
Flats per floor: 9
Flat size: 28–35 m²
Flat cost: 2.2–3.4 million HKD
Cost per m²: 78,000–97,000 HKD

The 32-story towers contain nine relatively small apartments per floor.

A
Extensive renovations make the relatively old mall appear modern.

M
The Mall

B
Private cars and buses can easily access Tuen Mun Town Plaza via the ground level roads.

C
The podium crosses the main road and connects the two parts of the estate as a "bridge."

D
The central plaza is used as an exhibition space and for special activities. In the 1990s it was European themed with neo-classical storefronts, a fountain, and a faux blue sky ceiling.

A Mall for Public Housing Residents

LOK FU PLAZA

Lok Fu Plaza, called Lok Fu Centre when it first opened in 1985, was constructed and managed by the Hong Kong Housing Authority. Before the development of Lok Fu Centre, no commercial facilities had been planned for the resettlement estates of Lok Fu. Shops and workshops were only provided later in ground floor bays because of concern over the lack of employment opportunities for tenants. Until then, on-street hawking was common in many Kowloon central estates.

In 1975, a Town Planning Office study recommended the establishment of a district

shopping center in Wang Tau Hom / Lok Fu together with the construction of a MTR station. The Housing Authority chose to build Lok Fu Centre on top of the MTR Lok Fu Station.

After only two years, the Housing Authority decided to expand Lok Fu Centre's mall with a wider variety of shops, no longer perceiving Lok Fu's public housing residents as poor working-class households, but rather as shoppers with purchasing power.

The Housing Authority eventually sold Lok Fu Centre to the private Link Real Estate Investment Trust, Hong Kong's

first real estate investment trust, and today Asia's largest. As a consequence, the estate changed from public to private ownership. In 2007, Link started a renovation program that would cover every corner of Lok Fu Plaza with shops.

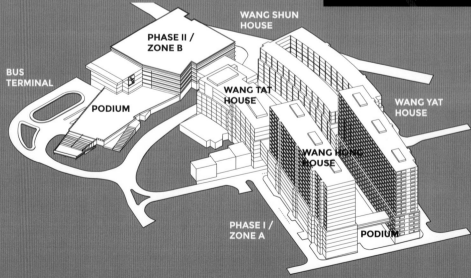

R

Residential

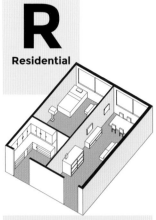

Residential 48%
Retail 37%
Eateries 15%

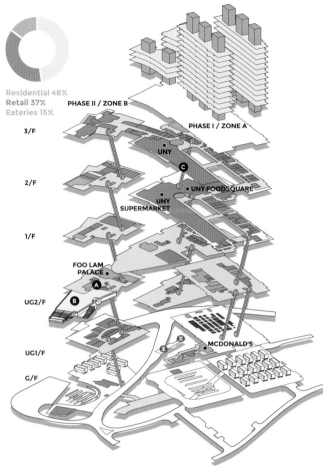

PHASE II / ZONE B

PHASE I / ZONE A

3/F

2/F

UNY

C

UNY FOODSQUARE

UNY
SUPERMARKET

1/F

FOO LAM
PALACE
A

UG2/F   B

UG1/F

MCDONALD'S

G/F

Wang Yat House Apartment
Flats per floor: 20–26
Flat size: 35–80 m²
Flat cost: 1.75–8.0 million HKD
Cost per m²: 50,000–100,000 HKD

Address
198 Junction Road, Wang Tau
Hom, Kowloon
Developer
The Hong Kong Housing
Authority (Before)
The Link Property Limited
(Now)
Architect
Rocco Design
Construction
Initiation: 1989
Renovation Completion: 2011
Site Area
300,000 m²
Gross Floor Area / GFA
1,160,800 m²
Floor Area Ratio / FAR
3.9
Building Height
+20.5 m / 25 m (Podium/
Tower)
Blank Wall at Ground Level
30%

A
To facilitate promotional
activities, the atrium of Lok Fu
Plaza's second phase mall is
more spacious.

B
The public podium is available
to residents, but also attracts
other people into the complex.

C
The wide circulation paths
around the oval atrium
facilitate pedestrian flows and
allow for the placement of
different commercial kiosks.

A

B

C

A Green Mall

CITYWALK

Citywalk, located in Tsuen Wan on the former site of the Four Seasons Estates owned by the Hong Kong Housing Society, is a joint development between the Urban Renewal Authority and Sino Land, a member of the Sino Group.

A three-story mall forms the base of Vision City, five residential towers rising up to 52 stories, containing 1,466 residential units. The green courtyard, a 40,000 square feet "Citywalk Plaza," and abundance of green space, sets the mall apart from other developments. The mall's exterior façade even includes an 8,000 square feet Vertical Garden.

In 2008, the Hong Kong Building Environmental Assessment Method (BEAM) Society rated the project platinum, its highest rating, for the distinctive green features including the vertical garden, the open plaza, and the large amount of permeable surface areas.

Address
1 Yeung Uk Road, Tsuen Wan
Developer
Sino Land
Urban Renewal Authority
Construction
Completion: December 2007
Site Area
28,600 m²
Gross Floor Area / GFA
229,440 m²
Floor Area Ratio / FAR
8.0
Building Height
+22.5 m / 195 m (Podium/
Tower)
Blank Wall at Ground Level
85%

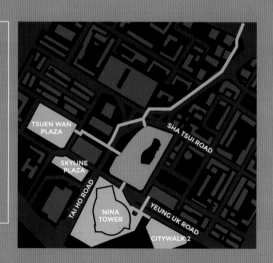

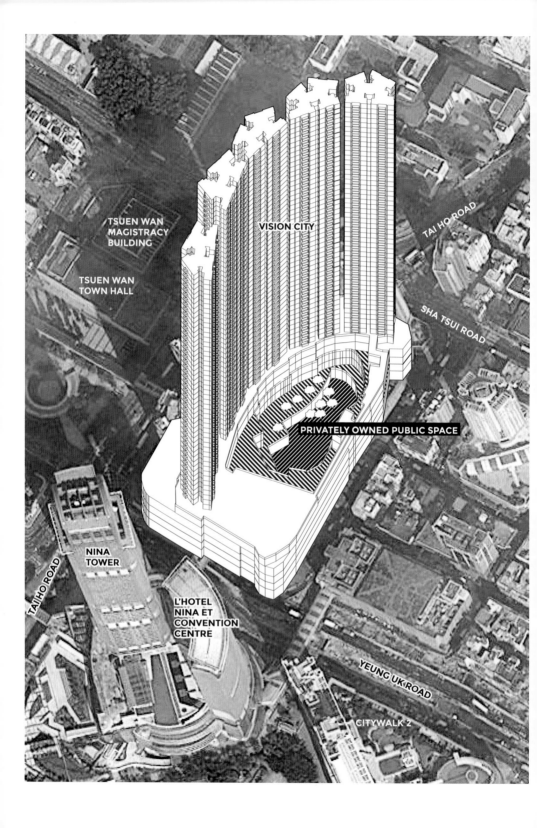

TSUEN WAN
MAGISTRACY
BUILDING

TSUEN WAN
TOWN HALL

VISION CITY

TAI HO ROAD

SHA TSUI ROAD

PRIVATELY OWNED PUBLIC SPACE

NINA
TOWER

TAI HO ROAD

L'HOTEL
NINA ET
CONVENTION
CENTRE

YEUNG UK ROAD

CITYWALK 2

R

Residential

M

The Mall

VISION CITY

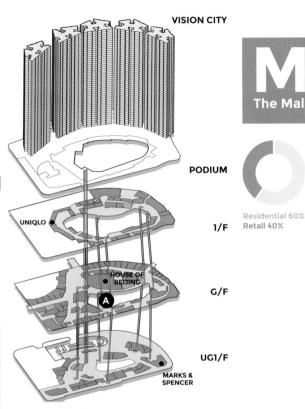

PODIUM

UNIQLO •

HOUSE OF
BEIJING •

Ⓐ

MARKS &
SPENCER

1/F

G/F

UG1/F

Residential 60%
Retail 40%

Apartment C, 12th Floor
Flat size: 102 m²
Flat cost: 8 million HKD
Cost per m²: 78,170 HKD
Windows per floor area: 32%
Operable windows: 36%

Vision City Tower I
Flats per floor: 7
Flat size: 62–155 m²
Flat cost: 2.4–10.4 million HKD
Cost per m²: 38,700–67,000 HKD

HERE
Vision City consists of five
residential high-rise towers
containing 1,446 units and
about 300 parking spots. The
units range from two to five
bedrooms, ideal for a family
of four or more. Completed
in 2007, the 52-story towers
rise far out of the shopping
podium, forming a skyscraper-
wall.

A
The exterior courtyard attracts
many visitors and provides
an attractive view to the
surrounding mall. Each floor
has its own seating area
facing the green courtyard.
Citywalk is not just a mall but
also a place that encourages
interaction between people.

1982

1983

1986

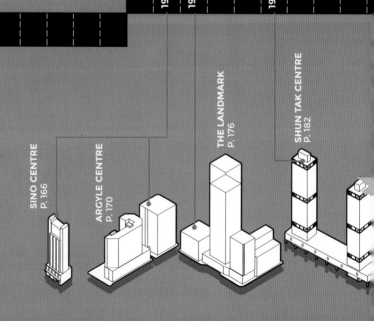

SINO CENTRE
P. 166

ARGYLE CENTRE
P. 170

THE LANDMARK
P. 176

SHUN TAK CENTRE
P. 182

1994

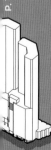

P. 188

2007

MEGABOX
P. 194

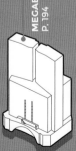

The Trendy Hub

SINO CENTRE

Sino Centre is located on Nathan Road in Mong Kok, one of Hong Kong's most crowded shopping districts. While its shops initially sold pictures of pop stars, by the late 1990s it had become infamous for its pirated CDs and pornography.

Today, after the crackdown on piracy, Sino Centre is known for its trendy Asian youth products, including *manga* comic books, *gashapon* capsule toys, video games, DVDs, and watches. There are also shops that rent out holiday flats.

Sino Centre enjoys such a great popularity that some shops have moved from the mall into the lower office floors, including travel agencies and toy stores.

Address
582-592, Nathan Road
Mong Kok, Kowloon
Developer
Sino Group
Architect
Wong & Ouyang Associates
Construction
Initiation: 1979
Completion: 1982
Site Area
797 m²
Gross Floor Area / GFA
11,939 m²
Floor Area Ratio / FAR
14.9
Building Height
+20 m / 81.5 m (Podium/
Tower)
Blank Wall at Ground Level
53%

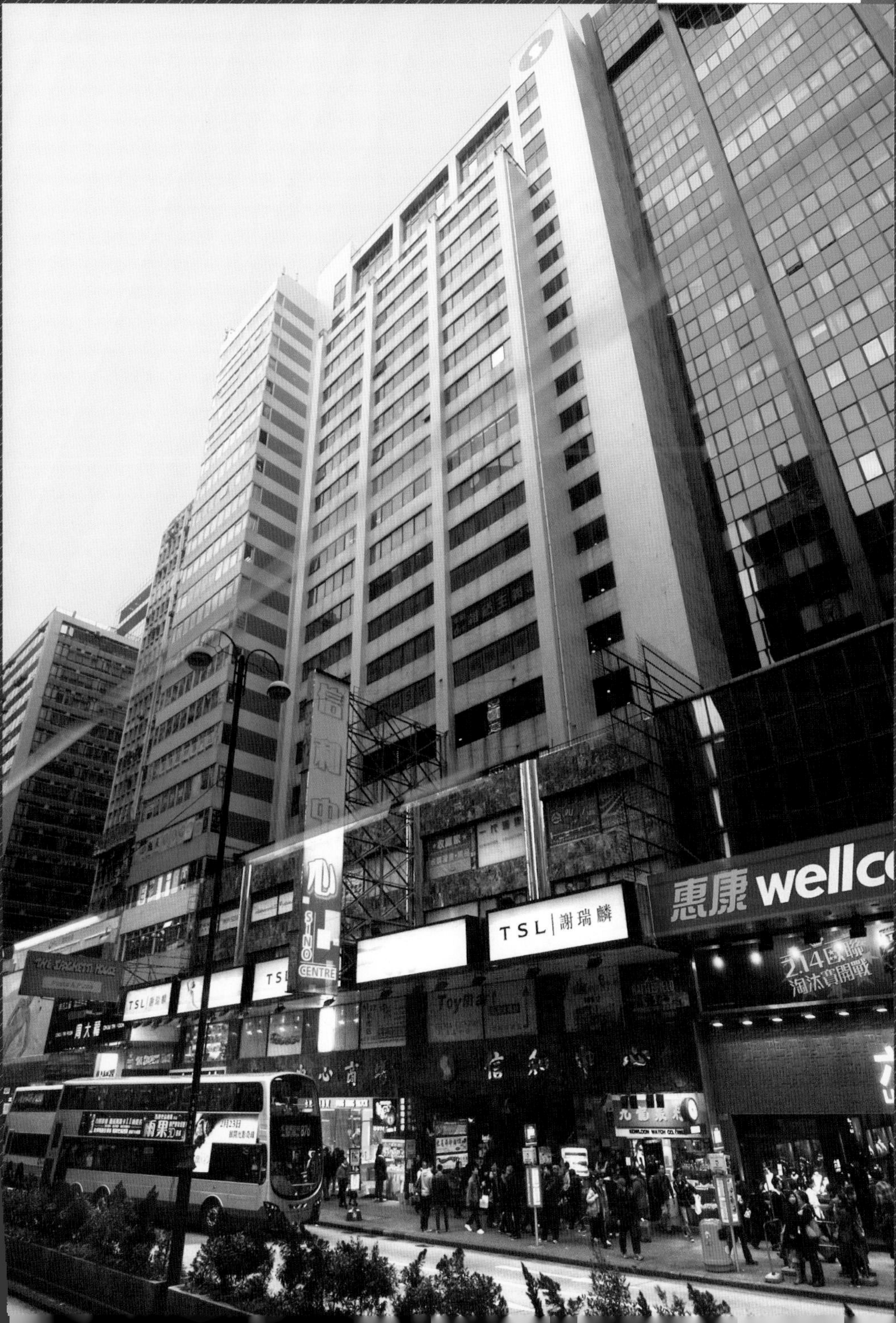
TSL 謝瑞麟
惠康 wellc
SINO CENTRE

B

C

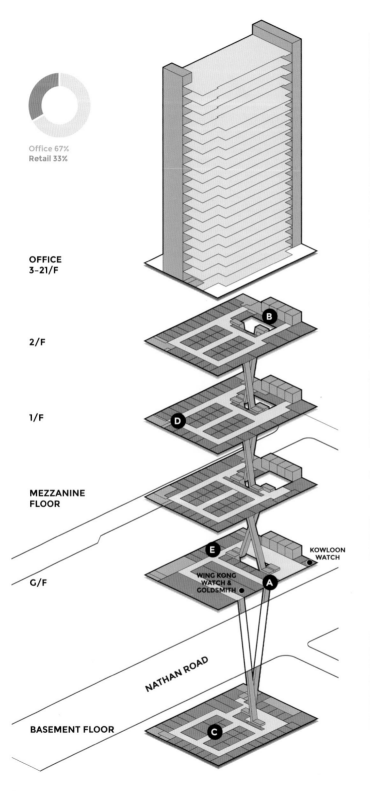

Office 67%
Retail 33%

OFFICE
3–21/F

2/F

1/F

MEZZANINE
FLOOR

G/F

KOWLOON
WATCH

WING KONG
WATCH &
GOLDSMITH

NATHAN ROAD

BASEMENT FLOOR

M
The Mall

Sino Centre is a haven for Asian pop culture, dazzling with Japanese cartoons, skin flicks, video games, watches, and *gashapon* toy figures.

D
The "cube shop," a unique store type, contributes to the wide array of products within Sino Centre. Individual boxes can be rented by anyone wanting to sell goods.

E
The cube shop-owner is tasked to sell products of each of these mini-stores, and will maintain the diversity of the offerings on display.

D

E

Trendy and Affordable Women's Fashion

ARGYLE CENTRE

Argyle Centre Phase I and Phase II (now called Trade and Industry Department Tower) are connected by a bridge. Argyle Centre Phase I, completed in 1982, includes a 14-story office building that accommodates predominantly medical clinics and beauty stores. The 6-story mall used to be a department store, but was gradually split into a series of mini-shops selling clothes, shoes and bags, accessories, and snacks.

Today, called Mong Kok New Town Mall, it has more than 200 stores selling mostly women's fashion, except for the gaming arcade in the basement, and the karaoke boxes on the upper floors. Especially during evenings and weekends, young women flock to the mall where they can find the latest fashion trends from Taiwan, Korean, and Japan, while DJs provide shoppers with loud music.

Address
688 Nathan Road
Mong Kok, Kowloon
Developer
Hang Lung Properties
Architect
CRE Property Ltd.
Construction
Completion: 1982
Site Area
2,265 m²
Gross Floor Area / GFA
33,980 m²
Floor Area Ratio / FAR
15
Building Height
+18.5 m / 67.5 m (Podium/Tower)
Blank Wall at Ground Level
45%

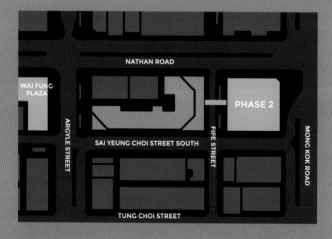

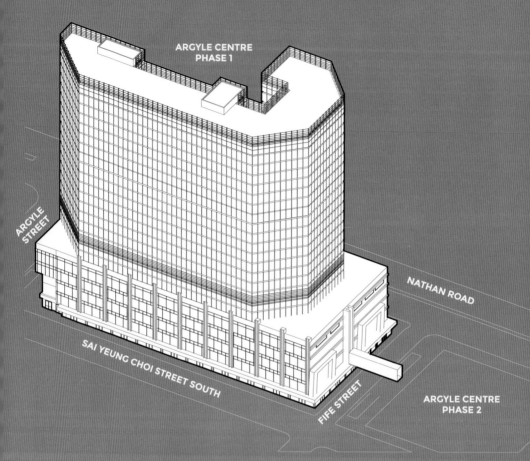

ARGYLE CENTRE
PHASE 1

ARGYLE STREET

NATHAN ROAD

SAI YEUNG CHOI STREET SOUTH

FIFE STREET

ARGYLE CENTRE
PHASE 2

E
The former department store has been split into many mini-shops, most of them dedicated to women's fashion.

1/F
2/F

Visitors - Ms. Gong (age 20+)

I am an exchange student from Shanghai. I like to come here for shopping since my dormitory is near. Argyle Centre has three floors of shops selling low-priced clothes and shoes.

It is usually crowded because it is located right next to the Mong Kok MTR station. Every time I pass through the MTR station, I'll go upstairs and come here, even if it is just for window-shopping.

The other reason why Argyle Centre is so popular, particularly among young people, is that the clothes here are very fashionable while still being affordable.

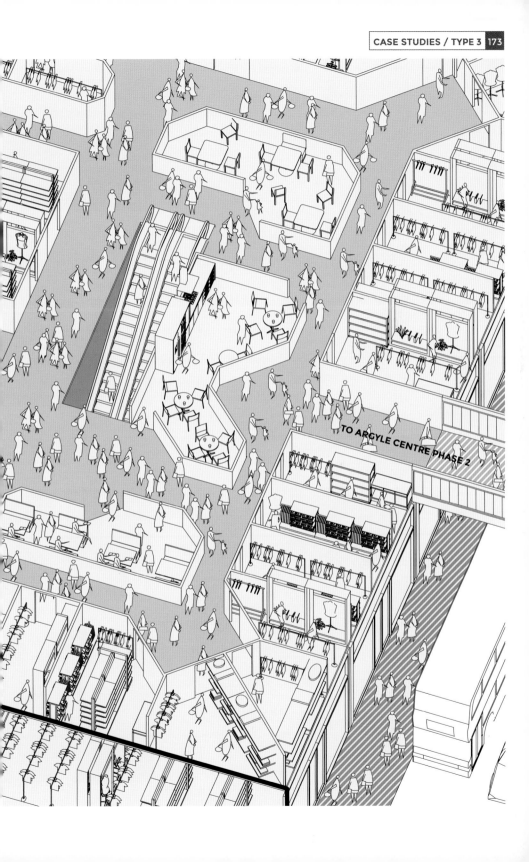

TO ARGYLE CENTRE PHASE 2

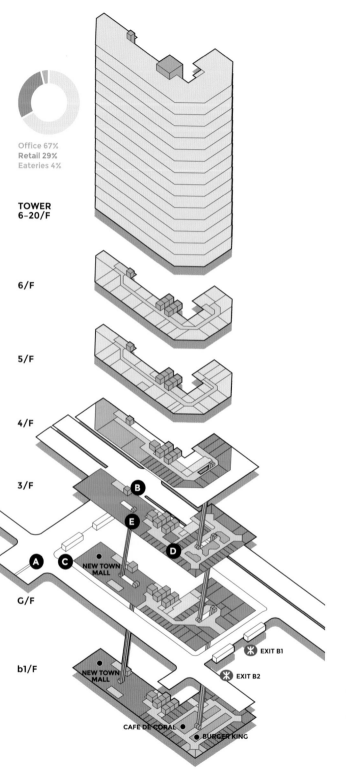

Office 67%
Retail 29%
Eateries 4%

**TOWER
6–20/F**

6/F

5/F

4/F

3/F

B

E

A C
NEW TOWN
MALL

D

G/F

b1/F

NEW TOWN
MALL

✳ EXIT B1

✳ EXIT B2

CAFE DE CORAL ● ● BURGER KING

The Mall

A
While the ground floor of Argyle Centre's mall is open with shops, all upper floors are covered in advertising.

B
Argyle Centre lies on the intersection of the busy Nathan Road and Argyle Street.

C
Five MTR exits (Mong Kok Station) adjacent to Argyle Centre ensure the mall with incessant pedestrian flows.

D
Argyle Centre's mall is known for its trendy and affordable women's fashion.

Hong Kong's First Atrium
THE LANDMARK

Address
11 Pedder Street, Central
Developer
Hongkong Land
Architect
KPF
P+T International (Phase I)
Aedas (Phase II)
Construction
Phase I: Late 1970s
Completion: 1983
Renovation: 2002–2006
Site Area
1.9 ha
Gross Floor Area / GFA
187,972 m²
Floor Area Ratio / FAR
9.9
Building Height
+29 m / 192 m (Podium/Tower)
Blank Wall at Ground Level
32%

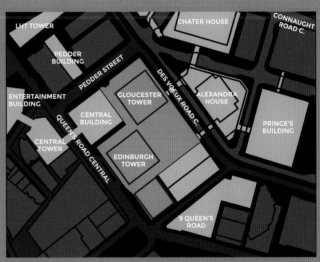

The Landmark is a mall, office, and hotel complex. The mall is known for its high-end international fashion and jewelry brands, and upscale restaurants. Hongkong Land initiated the project to capitalize on the new MTR station in Central, giving the mall direct access to the subway system at the basement level. Completed in 1983, the Landmark introduced the atrium to Hong Kong's malls by building a focal point between the twin office towers (the Edinburgh and Gloucester Towers), enclosed by a series of multilevel shops.

In 2002, a $210 million renovation enlarged the mall and the atrium with two stories, and introduced the five-star hotel The Landmark Oriental Hotel into one of the office towers. A pedestrian bridge network on the second floor connects the complex to other major malls owned by Hongkong land, including Chater House, Alexandra House, and Prince's Building.

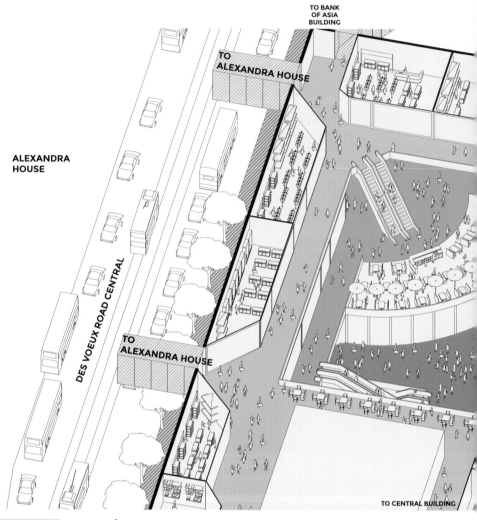

TO BANK
OF ASIA
BUILDING

TO
ALEXANDRA HOUSE

ALEXANDRA
HOUSE

DES VOEUX ROAD CENTRAL

TO
ALEXANDRA HOUSE

TO CENTRAL BUILDING

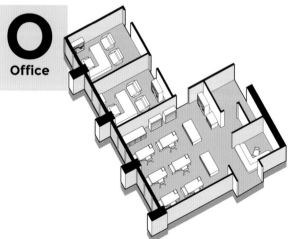

O
Office

Gloucester Tower / avg. per floor
Offices per floor: 3
Office size: 120 m²
Office cost: 15.3 million HKD
Cost per m²: 127,500 HKD
Windows per floor area: 20%
Operable windows: 58%

The development consists of
three office towers: the 48-story
Gloucester Tower, the 47-story
Edinburgh Tower, and the
14-story York House.

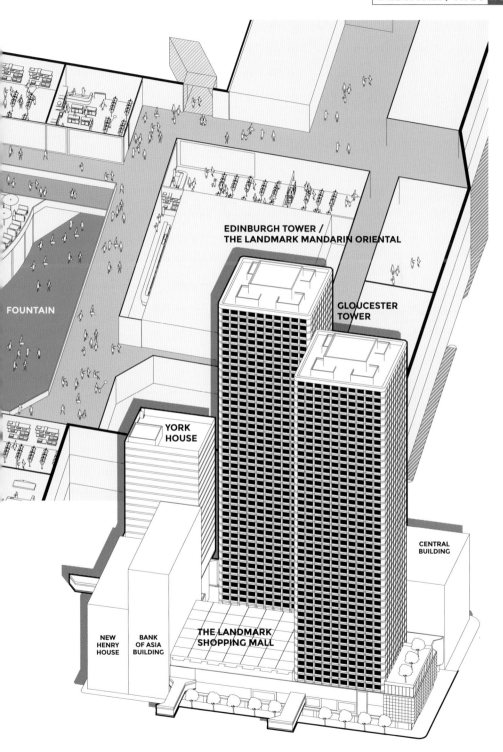

FOUNTAIN

EDINBURGH TOWER /
THE LANDMARK MANDARIN ORIENTAL

GLOUCESTER
TOWER

YORK
HOUSE

CENTRAL
BUILDING

NEW
HENRY
HOUSE

BANK
OF ASIA
BUILDING

THE LANDMARK
SHOPPING MALL

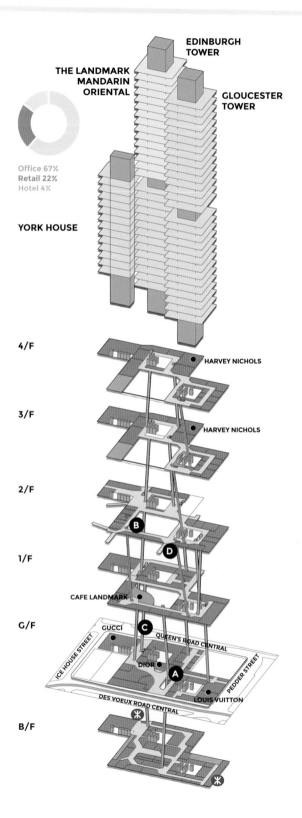

EDINBURGH TOWER

THE LANDMARK MANDARIN ORIENTAL

GLOUCESTER TOWER

Office 67%
Retail 22%
Hotel 4%

YORK HOUSE

4/F

HARVEY NICHOLS

3/F

HARVEY NICHOLS

2/F

B

D

1/F

CAFE LANDMARK

G/F

GUCCI

C

QUEEN'S ROAD CENTRAL

ICE HOUSE STREET

DIOR

A

PEDDER STREET

DES VOEUX ROAD CENTRAL

LOUIS VUITTON

B/F

Shopping Guide—Mr. Yao (age 40+)

I am one of Landmark's shopping guides. We work on weekdays and weekends. Our duty is to provide shopping suggestions to our clients, including information about deliveries, shop locations, and discounts. Our clients are mainly from Mainland China and Hong Kong.

Landmark's atrium is part of a larger central shopping network— including Chater House, Alexandra House, and Prince's Building—all linked by pedestrian bridges on the second floor. As everyone knows, Landmark sells famous international fashion labels and leading jewelry and watch brands. In addition, some shops sell art, lifestyle and personal care products, and household gifts.

Sometimes you can see performances, exhibitions, and fashion shows staged in the atrium. The basement floor specializes on men's products, and is very easy to reach.

A
Landmark also has a smaller atrium where escalators connect the office towers to the MTR, through the mall.

M
The Mall

B
The atrium, a gathering space for upscale shoppers, accommodates high-end restaurants and cafés.

C
After the 2006 upgrade, the Landmark's exterior façade was remodeled to feature Harvey Nichols, a new luxury flagship store within the mall.

D
The Landmark is part of the central shopping network, linked with footbridges to Chater House, Alexandra House, and Prince's Building.

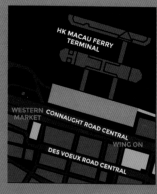

Transportation Giant

SHUN TAK CENTRE

Address
168-200 Connaught Road
Central
Developer
Shun Tak Holdings Limited
Architect
Spence Robinson Ltd.
Construction
Initiation: 1983
Completion: 1986
Site Area
8,603 m²
Gross Floor Area / GFA
70,500 m²
Floor Area Ratio / FAR
8.2
Building Height
+22.5 m / 184 m (Podium/
Tower)
Blank Wall at Ground Level
65%

Shun Tak Centre is a transport and office complex located on the northern shore of Hong Kong Island. It includes a 4-story mall, two 38-story office towers, a parking garage, and the Hong Kong–Macau Ferry Terminal. A major transportation hub, Shun Tak Centre has a direct exit to the MTR Sheung Wan Station, lies next to a bus terminal, and is connected to the Central Elevated Walkway. The centre connects to destinations throughout the Pearl River Delta, but above all to Macao, to which passengers can take a jetfoil, hydrofoil, hovercraft, and even a helicopter.

The Shun Tak Group is headquartered in the building. This Hong Kong conglomerate in transportation, property, hospitality, and investments is owned by the Macao casino mogul Stanley Ho. The company also owns TurboJET, whose ferries bring gamblers to Macao casinos, many of them owned by Ho.

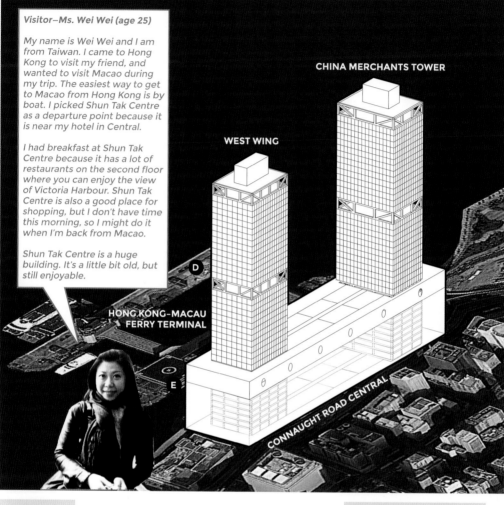

Visitor—Ms. Wei Wei (age 25)

My name is Wei Wei and I am from Taiwan. I came to Hong Kong to visit my friend, and wanted to visit Macao during my trip. The easiest way to get to Macao from Hong Kong is by boat. I picked Shun Tak Centre as a departure point because it is near my hotel in Central.

I had breakfast at Shun Tak Centre because it has a lot of restaurants on the second floor where you can enjoy the view of Victoria Harbour. Shun Tak Centre is also a good place for shopping, but I don't have time this morning, so I might do it when I'm back from Macao.

Shun Tak Centre is a huge building. It's a little bit old, but still enjoyable.

CHINA MERCHANTS TOWER

WEST WING

HONG KONG-MACAU FERRY TERMINAL

CONNAUGHT ROAD CENTRAL

D

E

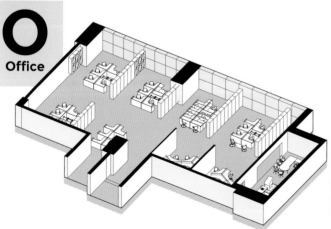

⭕ Office

Apartment E, 50th Floor
Office size: 571 m²
Office cost: 42 million HKD
Cost per m²: 73,600 HKD
Windows per floor area: 16%
Operable windows: 46%

Sorrento Tower II
Offices per floor: 10
Office size: 302–671 m²
Office cost: 22.6–42.1 million HKD
Cost per m²: 59,000–84,000 HKD

The two office towers are covered in mirrored glass to take full advantage of the sea views.

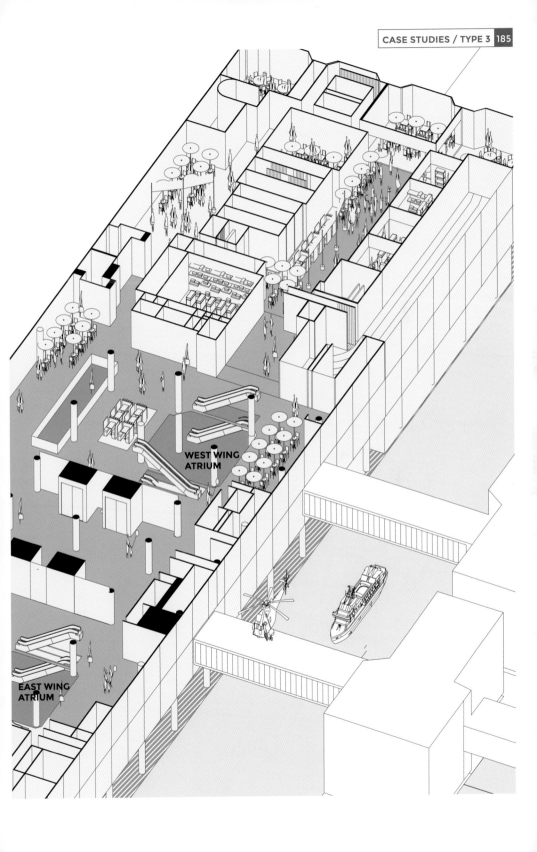

WEST WING
ATRIUM

EAST WING
ATRIUM

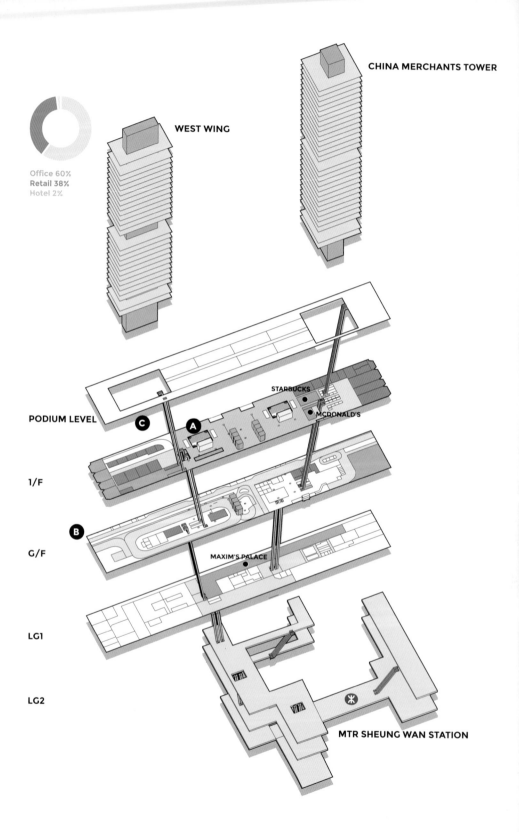

CHINA MERCHANTS TOWER

WEST WING

Office 60%
Retail 38%
Hotel 2%

STARBUCKS

McDONALD'S

PODIUM LEVEL

C

A

1/F

B

G/F

MAXIM'S PALACE

LG1

LG2

MTR SHEUNG WAN STATION

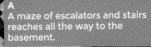

A
A maze of escalators and stairs reaches all the way to the basement.

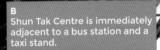

M
The Mall

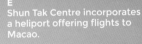

B
Shun Tak Centre is immediately adjacent to a bus station and a taxi stand.

C
On the ground floor, Shun Tak Centre can be reached via private cars, taxis, minibuses, shuttles, and trams. The Central Elevated Walkway brings pedestrians into the complex on the second floor.

D
After buying a ticket on the second floor, passengers move through a long hall, pass the immigration point, and reach the ferry.

E
Shun Tak Centre incorporates a heliport offering flights to Macao.

Times Square is located on the former site of the tram depot in Causeway Bay. The Wharf Group acquired and developed the site, which was approved for a commercial, non-residential development by the Town Planning Board in 1987, at a time when the area was predominantly residential.

Times Square opened in 1994 as the first vertical mall in Hong Kong. It has a 14-story podium and six basement levels for retail, cinemas, and parking. The complex includes two office towers: the 33-story Tower One and the 26-story Tower Two. An escalator connects the basement to a tunnel leading to Causeway Bay MTR Station.

Only 60 percent of the total ground floor area is built area, which frees up the remainder for open space to be used for promotional activities and public events. This privately owned public space (POP) was a place of controversy in 2008 after the complaints that private security guards prevented people from lingering in the area. That year the government sued Wharf over charging exorbitant rents for the use of public space.

Today, Times Square is a major shopping destination in what has become one of Hong Kong's most popular shopping areas for locals and tourists. Times Square ignited the conversion of Causeway Bay into a district with the most expensive retail rental in the world.

The First Vertical Mall

TIMES SQUARE

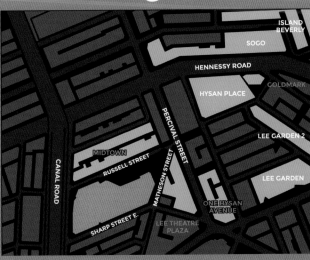

Address
1 Matheson Street, Causeway Bay
Developer
Wharf Properties Ltd.
Architect
Wong & Ouyang Associates
Construction
Initiation: 1988
Completion: 1994
Site Area
10,445 m²
Gross Floor Area / GFA
183,506 m²
Floor Area Ratio / FAR
17.5
Building Height
+70.5 m / 134.5 m (Podium/Tower)
Blank Wall at Ground Level
88%

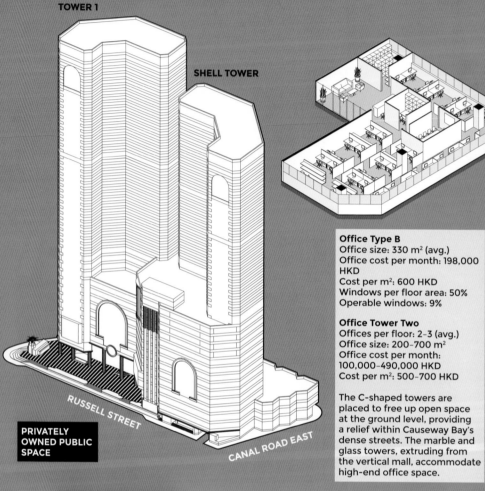

TOWER 1

SHELL TOWER

RUSSELL STREET

CANAL ROAD EAST

PRIVATELY OWNED PUBLIC SPACE

Office Type B
Office size: 330 m² (avg.)
Office cost per month: 198,000 HKD
Cost per m²: 600 HKD
Windows per floor area: 50%
Operable windows: 9%

Office Tower Two
Offices per floor: 2–3 (avg.)
Office size: 200–700 m²
Office cost per month: 100,000–490,000 HKD
Cost per m²: 500–700 HKD

The C-shaped towers are placed to free up open space at the ground level, providing a relief within Causeway Bay's dense streets. The marble and glass towers, extruding from the vertical mall, accommodate high-end office space.

Visitor—Mr. Marco (age 25)

I was born and grew up in Hong Kong. Nine years ago I migrated to Canada with my parents, but now I have come back for business. When I was a boy I used to gather with my friends at Times Square after school.

Times Square was a convenient place to meet since it had everything we needed. I usually took MTR to get here, and met with buddies in front of the clock tower or under the advertisement sign, which is now a huge video screen. We chatted about everything, even smoked and drank, went to the cinema, played video games,
or just tried some food on the upper floors.

I remember how we once drank on the rooftop of a building opposite Times Square. Looking down to the square at night was so different from the busy square by day. We were so excited to see this great empty space amid Hong Kong's crowded streets.

Today everything seems to be the same. Every time I go shopping here, this square, this space, these plant boxes, and even these steps remind me of my childhood.

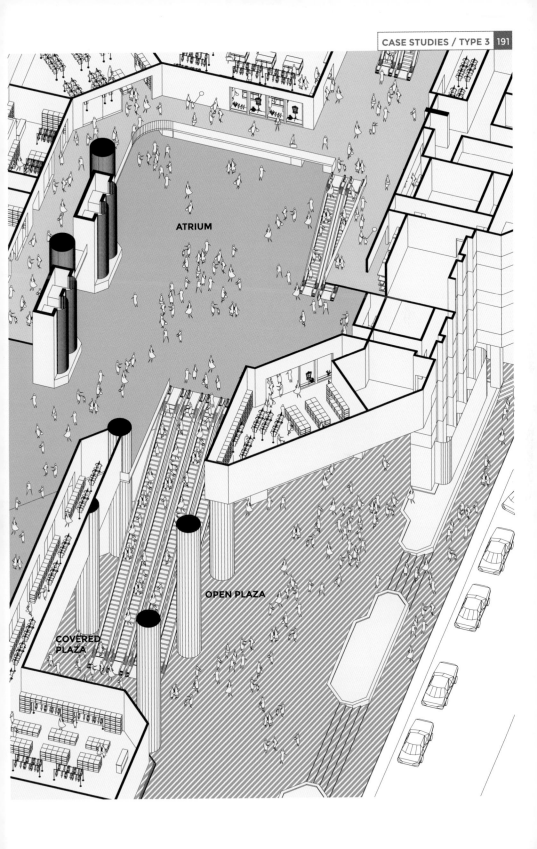

ATRIUM

OPEN PLAZA

COVERED
PLAZA

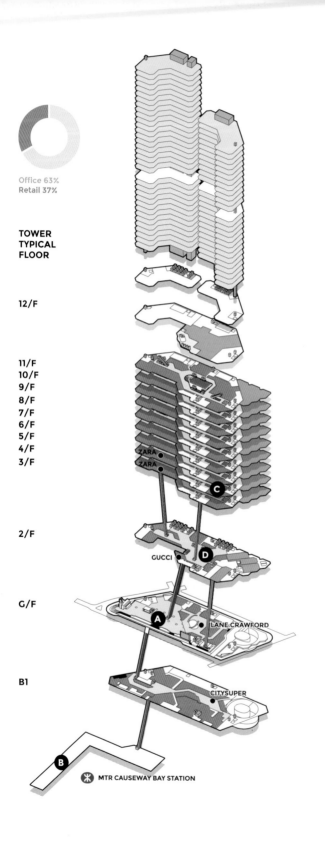

Office 63%
Retail 37%

**TOWER
TYPICAL
FLOOR**

12/F

11/F
10/F
9/F
8/F
7/F
6/F
5/F
4/F
3/F

ZARA
ZARA

C

2/F

GUCCI   D

G/F

A   LANE CRAWFORD

B1

CITYSUPER

B   🚇 MTR CAUSEWAY BAY STATION

A
Even though a large part of the mall's facade has blank walls, the open space on the ground floor creates convenient access and contributes to an active ground.

C
Vertical circulation within the tall mall is arranged through bullet elevators, single-story escalators, and a recent addition—the multistory "expresscalator."

M
The Mall

B
A tunnel directly connects the basement level shopping area to the Causeway Bay MTR station.

D
The second floor atrium space, an indoor "square" connected to the outdoor square by long escalators, is frequently used for promotional events.

Hong Kong's Big Box with a Ball and Beehive Atrium

MEGABOX

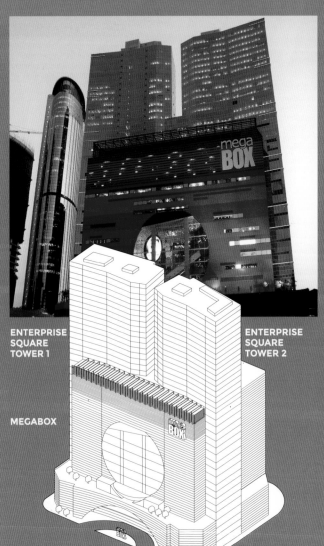

ENTERPRISE
SQUARE
TOWER 1

ENTERPRISE
SQUARE
TOWER 2

MEGABOX

MegaBox is located at the center of the rapidly growing East Kowloon district, which the government plans to develop into a new Central Business District. MegaBox is the only project within the area that contains major retail, entertainment, as well as two office towers called Enterprise Square 5.

Designed by the Jerde Partnership, the MegaBox redefines Big Box retail in a high-density city. Big Box retail such as IKEA and Toys'R'Us, along with restaurants and entertainment, has been stacked in a 19-story mall. MegaBox is divided into four thematic areas for different demographics: fashion zone, home improvement zone, electrical products, and an entertainment and restaurant zone called EATertainment, which includes an IMAX theater, and an indoor ice rink that looks out to the city through a 30-meter-tall curtain wall.

A system called Totally Connected Modules (TCM) attempts to ease vertical people flows within the tall structure. Pedestrians are moved quickly between zones through express escalators that cut across multiple stories. Private cars can go all the way to the top zone with only three loops.

Unlike other large commercial developments in Hong Kong, MegaBox is not connected to Hong Kong's metro station, but offers a free shuttle bus service to the nearest MTR station.

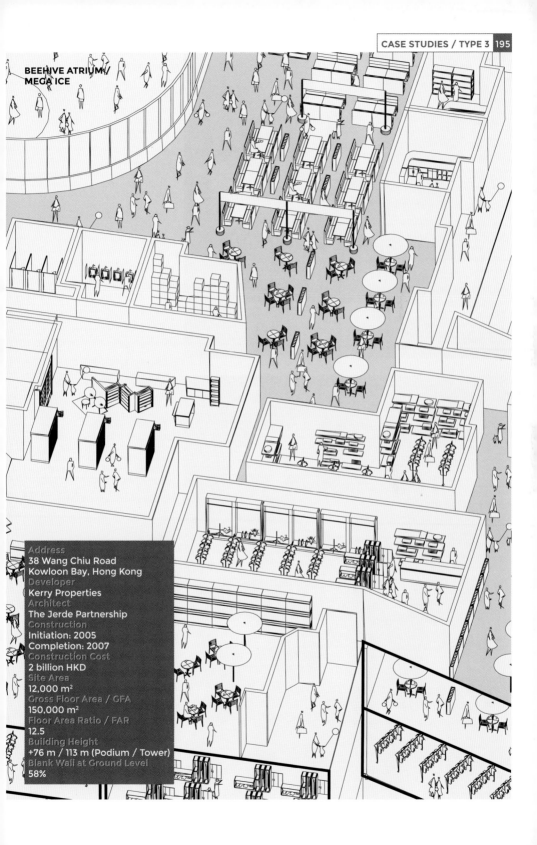

BEEHIVE ATRIUM /
MEGA ICE

Address
**38 Wang Chiu Road
Kowloon Bay, Hong Kong**
Developer
Kerry Properties
Architect
The Jerde Partnership
Construction
**Initiation: 2005
Completion: 2007**
Construction Cost
2 billion HKD
Site Area
12,000 m²
Gross Floor Area / GFA
150,000 m²
Floor Area Ratio / FAR
12.5
Building Height
+76 m / 113 m (Podium / Tower)
Blank Wall at Ground Level
58%

A
MegaBox's "Ball Atrium" breaks the big box with a six-story-tall glass facade that lets in sunlight and gives visitors a view of Kowloon.

B
Deep red colors, bright lights, reflective surfaces, and electronic messages augment the mesmerizing maze of escalators. Separately themed areas add to the vertical retail experience.

Visitors—Johnny Lee (age 38) and Alan Lee (age 6)

I came to MegaBox to spend quality time with my son on a Sunday afternoon. There are few places in Hong Kong where both my son and I can be entertained at the same time without much worrying. We both are frequent visitors of MegaBox. My son finds the interior full of colors, so much colors that it sometimes makes him "dizzy," and there are many fun activities and adventures. I asked him why he likes MegaBox and he replied, "Many cool lights and cool cartoon characters! Many things to play and the furniture is my size!" (the children levels feature life-size cartoon figures and children's furniture).

I am happy that my son is excited and the surrounding environment arouses his imagination. It is rare in Hong Kong to find a place with so many activities, including ice-skating, an Imax theater, and a video game arcade, without being too crowded. I also appreciate that MegaBox has an IKEA and Suning electrical store where I can check up on the latest products while my son is happily occupied.

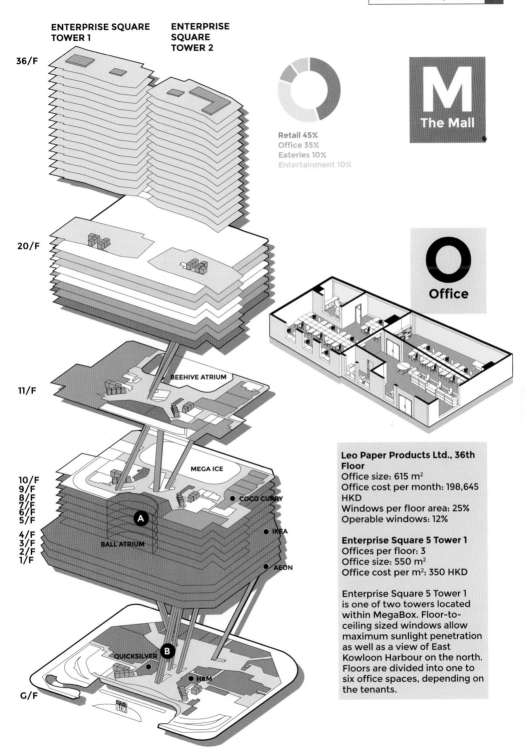

ENTERPRISE SQUARE
TOWER 1

ENTERPRISE
SQUARE
TOWER 2

36/F

20/F

11/F

10/F
9/F
8/F
7/F
6/F
5/F
4/F
3/F
2/F
1/F

G/F

BEEHIVE ATRIUM

MEGA ICE

COCO CURRY

IKEA

A

BALL ATRIUM

AEON

QUICKSILVER

B

H&M

Retail 45%
Office 35%
Eateries 10%
Entertainment 10%

M
The Mall

O
Office

Leo Paper Products Ltd., 36th Floor
Office size: 615 m²
Office cost per month: 198,645 HKD
Windows per floor area: 25%
Operable windows: 12%

Enterprise Square 5 Tower 1
Offices per floor: 3
Office size: 550 m²
Office cost per m²: 350 HKD

Enterprise Square 5 Tower 1 is one of two towers located within MegaBox. Floor-to-ceiling sized windows allow maximum sunlight penetration as well as a view of East Kowloon Harbour on the north. Floors are divided into one to six office spaces, depending on the tenants.

1966

1969

1977

1982

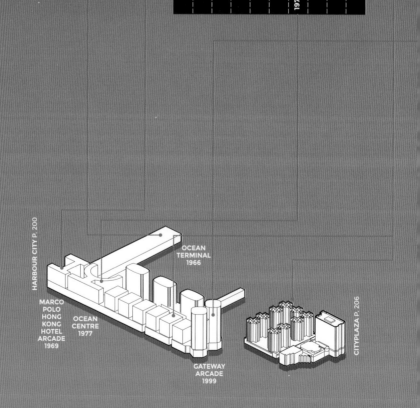

HARBOUR CITY P. 200

OCEAN
TERMINAL
1966

MARCO
POLO
HONG
KONG
HOTEL
ARCADE
1969

OCEAN
CENTRE
1977

GATEWAY
ARCADE
1999

CITYPLAZA P. 206

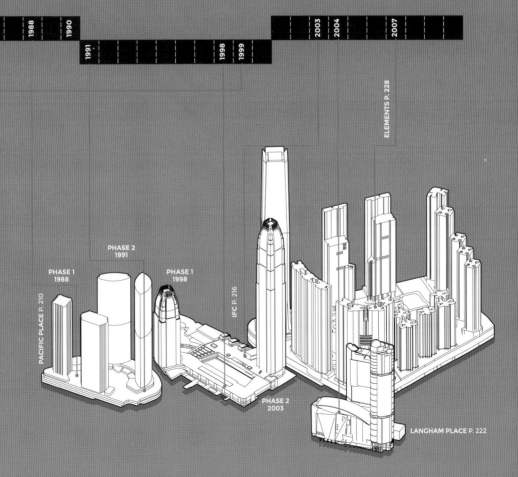

1988
1990
1991
1998
1999
2003
2004
2007

ELEMENTS P. 228

PACIFIC PLACE P. 210

PHASE 1
1988

PHASE 2
1991

PHASE 1
1998

IFC P. 216

PHASE 2
2003

LANGHAM PLACE P. 222

Harbour City, a complex that includes retail, office, hotel, and residential, is built on the site of the original wharf and warehouses of the Wharf Group. In 1966, in what would become a forerunner of worldwide waterfront developments, the company converted the harbor docks into retail space by building Ocean Terminal. The largest mall in Hong Kong at the time, it particularly served travelers coming from the Cruise Terminal built that same year on the wharf pier.

Wharf gradually added buildings: the Marco Polo Hotel in 1969, the Ocean Centre mall in 1977, the Harbour City Shopping District in 1987, the Gateway mall and office development in 1999.

Harbour City is known for its wide variety of international brands within a single complex, providing customers with a one-stop shopping experience. There are over 450 shops, including 50 restaurants, two cinemas, and 2,000 parking spaces.

Although not directly connected to the MTR, its proximity to the Star Ferry piers and the Hong Kong China Ferry Terminal makes the mall directly accessible from the Mainland.

TYPE

4

Hybrid

All Brands under One Roof

HARBOUR CITY

Address
3–27 Canton Road
Tsim Sha Tsui
Developer
The Wharf (Holdings) Limited
Architect
Eric Cumine Associates
Construction
Completion:
Ocean Terminal: 1966
Marco Polo Hong Kong Hotel:
1969
Ocean Centre: 1977
The Gateway: 1999
Site Area
185,800 m²
Floor Area Ratio / FAR
20.8
Building Height
+20.0 m / 132 m (Podium/
Tower)
Blank Wall at Ground Level
37%

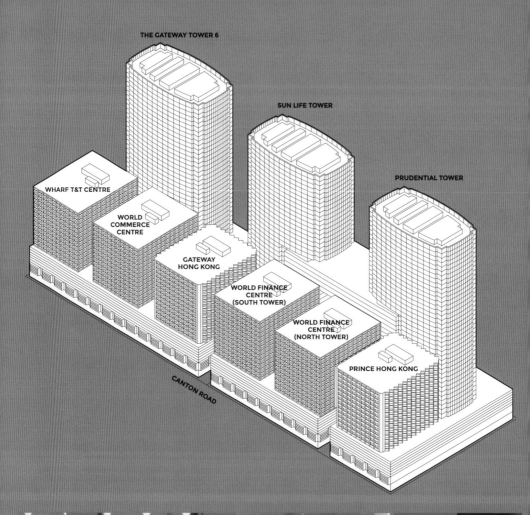

THE GATEWAY TOWER 6

SUN LIFE TOWER

PRUDENTIAL TOWER

WHARF T&T CENTRE

WORLD COMMERCE CENTRE

GATEWAY HONG KONG

WORLD FINANCE CENTRE (SOUTH TOWER)

WORLD FINANCE CENTRE (NORTH TOWER)

PRINCE HONG KONG

CANTON ROAD

Visitor—Mr. Wang

I am from Hangzhou. Shopping is one of my favorite activities in Hong Kong. The currency exchange rate is declining, so compared to the Mainland the prices of many products here are lower. Their quality is also better. Moreover, clothing here is more fashionable than in Mainland China. Hong Kong is a paradise for fans of luxury goods. Almost all of the luxury brand stores are here. Now I just take a few minutes to line up to get into Louis Vuitton.

Harbour City is too large to visit all the shops in a couple of days. When I go shopping, I like to bring an oversized trolley case rather than a dozen of bags, so that I can buy anything that I want.

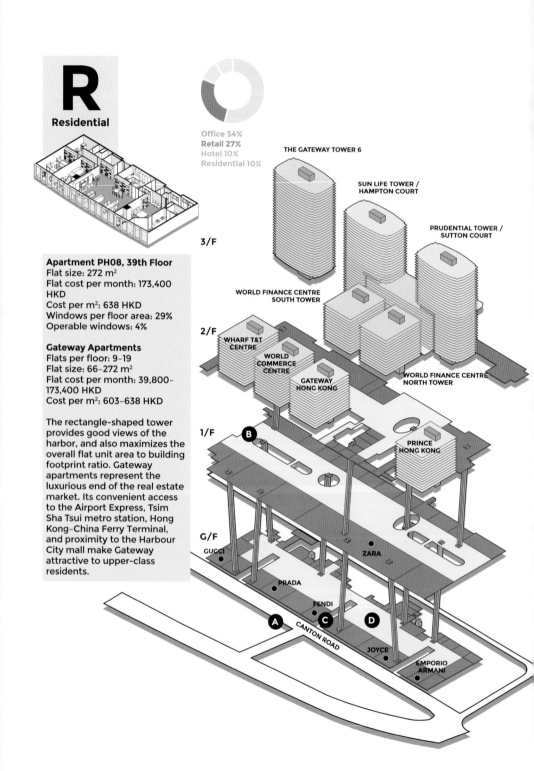

R
Residential

Office 54%
Retail 27%
Hotel 10%
Residential 10%

3/F

THE GATEWAY TOWER 6

SUN LIFE TOWER /
HAMPTON COURT

PRUDENTIAL TOWER /
SUTTON COURT

Apartment PH08, 39th Floor
Flat size: 272 m²
Flat cost per month: 173,400 HKD
Cost per m²: 638 HKD
Windows per floor area: 29%
Operable windows: 4%

WORLD FINANCE CENTRE
SOUTH TOWER

2/F

WHARF T&T CENTRE

WORLD COMMERCE CENTRE

GATEWAY HONG KONG

WORLD FINANCE CENTRE
NORTH TOWER

Gateway Apartments
Flats per floor: 9–19
Flat size: 66–272 m²
Flat cost per month: 39,800–173,400 HKD
Cost per m²: 603–638 HKD

The rectangle-shaped tower provides good views of the harbor, and also maximizes the overall flat unit area to building footprint ratio. Gateway apartments represent the luxurious end of the real estate market. Its convenient access to the Airport Express, Tsim Sha Tsui metro station, Hong Kong–China Ferry Terminal, and proximity to the Harbour City mall make Gateway attractive to upper-class residents.

1/F

B

PRINCE HONG KONG

G/F

GUCCI

ZARA

PRADA

FENDI

A **C** **D**

CANTON ROAD

JOYCE

EMPORIO ARMANI

M
The Mall

B
"The Gateway" of Harbour City, the lower-level shopping arcade, bustles with activity as a crossroads for residents, hotel guests, office workers, and shoppers.

C
Open-air walkways extend into the mall and allow for exterior entrances into shops, and for a place where office workers like to come during their break.

D
Habour City's interiors are themed with decoration and sculptures.

A
Along Canton road are Harbour City's most expensive shops. The sidewalks are crowded with people lining up to get into the luxury stores, such as Louis Vuitton.

The Center of Taikoo Shing
CITYPLAZA

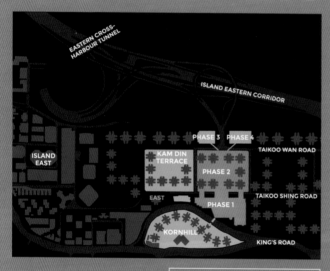

EASTERN CROSS-HARBOUR TUNNEL

ISLAND EASTERN CORRIDOR

PHASE 3   PHASE 4

ISLAND EAST

KAM DIN TERRACE

TAIKOO WAN ROAD

PHASE 2

EAST

PHASE 1

TAIKOO SHING ROAD

KORNHILL

KING'S ROAD

Address
18 Taikoo Shing Road
Taikoo Shing, Hong Kong
Developer
Swire Properties
Architect
Wong Tung and Partners Ltd.
Construction
Completion: 1982 (Phase 1)
Site Area
65,000 m²
Gross Floor Area / GFA
274,000 m²
Floor Area Ratio / FAR
4.2
Building Height
+20 m / 100 m (Podium/Tower)
Blank Wall at Ground Level
11%

Cityplaza is the town center and lifeblood of Taikoo Shing. Taikoo Shing is one of the early examples of Hong Kong's podium-style residential development, with residential towers built on top of retail.

Swire Properties started construction of Taikoo Shing in 1975, planning to replace the old Taikoo dockyards with a residential development of 61 towers. In 1983, it completed the first phase of Cityplaza, the shopping mall component of Taikoo Shing. The original building incorporated six levels and included retail, restaurants, an ice-skating and a roller-skating ring. At this stage, the mall was only accessible by bus as the subway to Taikoo Shing was not constructed until 1985. In 1987, the second phase of the mall was completed including nine residential towers on the podium of the newest phase of the mall. Two office buildings were subsequently built in 1992 to the north of the mall, with skybridges linking them to the mall. Large-scale renovations of the mall occurred in 1997, 2000, and 2014. Today, Cityplaza is Hong Kong Island's largest and most family-friendly mall.

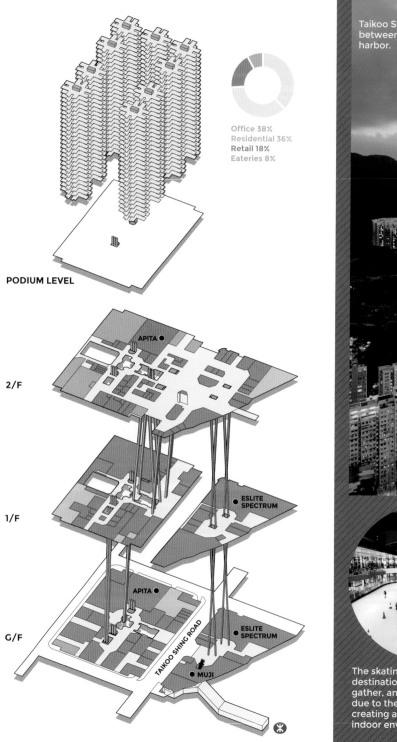

Office 38%
Residential 36%
Retail 18%
Eateries 8%

PODIUM LEVEL

2/F

APITA ●

1/F

ESLITE
SPECTRUM ●

G/F

APITA ●

TAIKOO SHING ROAD

ESLITE
SPECTRUM ●

● MUJI

✳

Taikoo Shing and Island East,
between the hills and the
harbor.

The skating rink is a popular
destination for people to meet,
gather, and people watch
due to the high ceiling atrium
creating a bright and open
indoor environment.

M
The Mall

Resident—Ms. Lau

I've lived here for about 20 years now. Cityplaza is like the town center of Taikoo Shing. I have to walk through here almost every day, either to get to the MTR station, buy groceries, eat at one of the restaurants, or shop at one of the stores. I even used to work at a company based in one of Cityplaza's office buildings. I never used to even have to leave the confines of Taikoo Shing!

As a child it was great living here. There are many parks and gardens on ground level and on the podiums. My friends and I used to go swimming in one of the podium swimming pools and go rollerblading along the harborside promenade. The mall itself also has a number of activities for children. There is an amusement center here that used to have a mini-rollercoaster. There is also an ice-skating ring here, and many years ago a roller-skating ring also existed on the top floor of the mall. I have so many good memories of living here when I was a child and teenager. I have access to just about every service I need to survive in Taikoo Shing. In general, I'm very happy living here.

Connector in the City

PACIFIC PLACE

Address
88 Queensway, Admiralty
Developer
Swire Properties Ltd.
Architect
Wong & Ouyang (HK) Ltd
Construction
Initiation: 1985
Completion:
One Pacific Place: 1988
JW Marriott Hong Kong: 1988
Pacific Place Mall: 1990
Conrad Hong Kong: 1991
Pacific Place Apartments: 1991
Island Shangri-La Hong Kong: 1991
Two Pacific Place: 1991
Three Pacific Place: 2004
Site Area
92,000 m²
Gross Floor Area / GFA
505,000 m²
Floor Area Ratio / FAR
5.5
Building Height
+21 m / 228 m (Podium/Tower)
Blank Wall at Ground Level
11%

Pacific Place, a premier mixed-use development owned and managed by Swire Properties, is located in the central business district of Hong Kong. It includes an upscale shopping mall, three Grade-A office towers, luxury serviced apartments, and four five-star hotels: Conrad Hong Kong, Island Shangri-La Hong Kong, JW Marriott Hong Kong, and The Upper House.

Built on the site of Victoria Barracks, one of the first military compounds in Hong Kong, Swire developed the project for a total cost of US$1 billion. The integrated complex is highly accessible by car and well-connected to the public transport network, including buses, minibuses, and trams. Pacific Place is directly connected to the Admiralty MTR interchange station via air-conditioned pedestrian

walkways, a major connection across the harbor and to the rest of the city.

Pacific Place serves as pleasantly a node in the city as a connection between Admiralty, Wan Chai, and the higher elevated Hong Kong Park. Due to the selection of upscale shops, however, the mall excludes itself from the mainstream public of Hong Kong as an agglomeration of high-purchasing power.

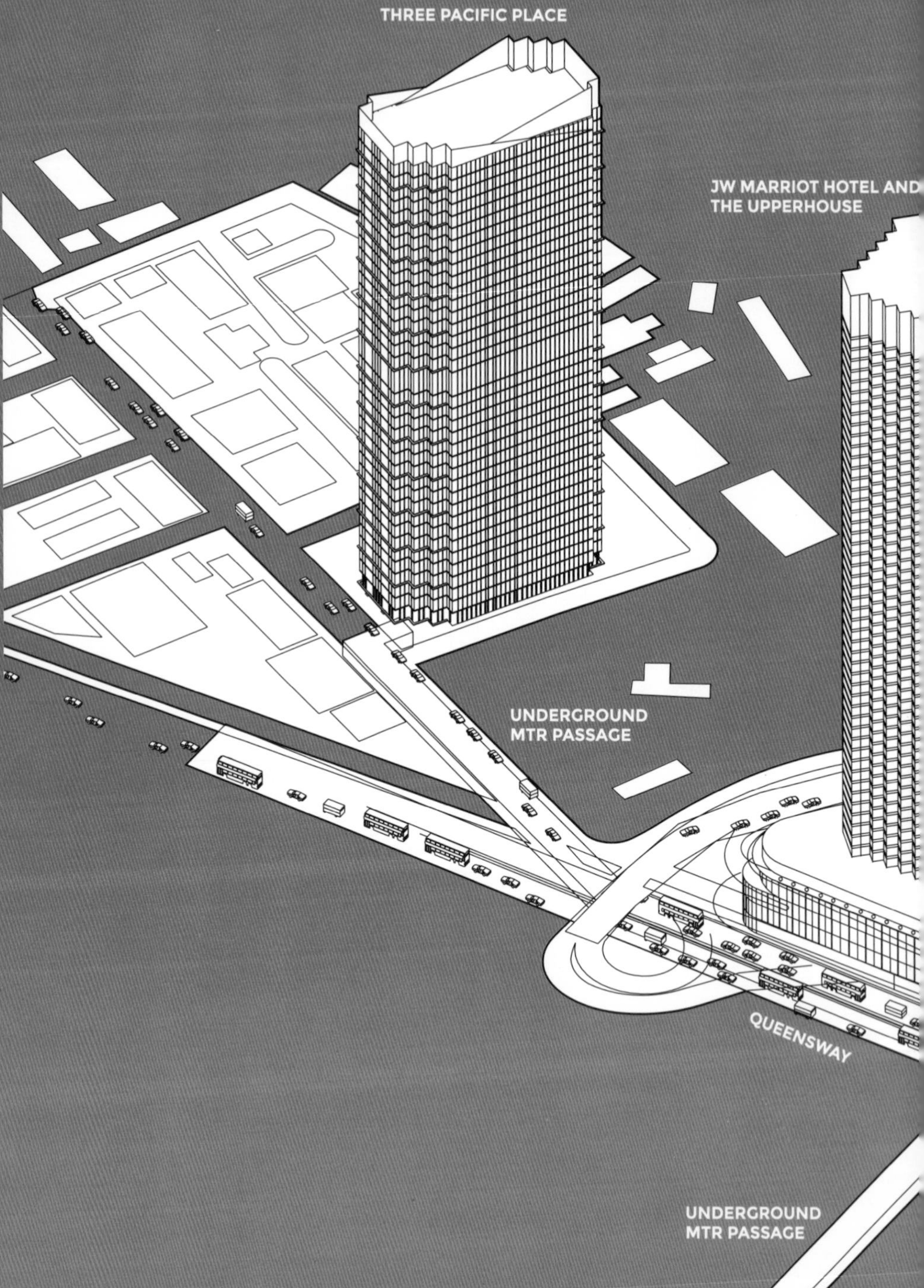

THREE PACIFIC PLACE

JW MARRIOT HOTEL AND
THE UPPERHOUSE

UNDERGROUND
MTR PASSAGE

QUEENSWAY

UNDERGROUND
MTR PASSAGE

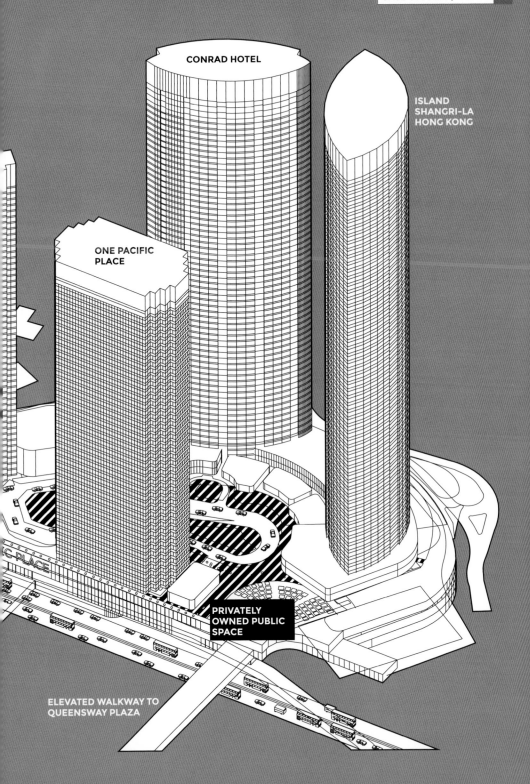

CONRAD HOTEL

ISLAND SHANGRI-LA HONG KONG

ONE PACIFIC PLACE

PRIVATELY OWNED PUBLIC SPACE

ELEVATED WALKWAY TO QUEENSWAY PLAZA

...IC PLACE

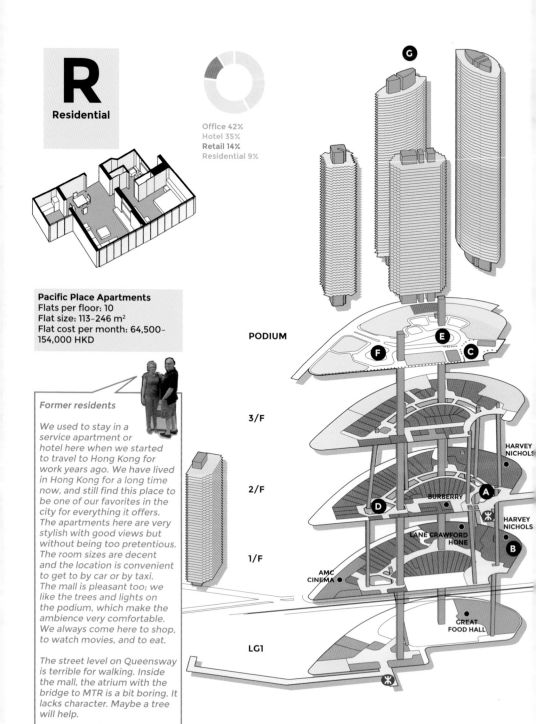

R

Residential

Office 42%
Hotel 35%
Retail 14%
Residential 9%

Pacific Place Apartments
Flats per floor: 10
Flat size: 113–246 m²
Flat cost per month: 64,500–154,000 HKD

Former residents

We used to stay in a service apartment or hotel here when we started to travel to Hong Kong for work years ago. We have lived in Hong Kong for a long time now, and still find this place to be one of our favorites in the city for everything it offers. The apartments here are very stylish with good views but without being too pretentious. The room sizes are decent and the location is convenient to get to by car or by taxi. The mall is pleasant too; we like the trees and lights on the podium, which make the ambience very comfortable. We always come here to shop, to watch movies, and to eat.

The street level on Queensway is terrible for walking. Inside the mall, the atrium with the bridge to MTR is a bit boring. It lacks character. Maybe a tree will help.

G

PODIUM

E

F

C

3/F

HARVEY NICHOLS

2/F

BURBERRY

A

D

HARVEY NICHOLS

LANE CRAWFORD HONE

B

1/F

AMC CINEMA

LG1

GREAT FOOD HALL

A
The west atrium often holds public exhibitions in the center. The periphery is used as a public resting place.

B
Zigzagging escalators weave together the multi-tiered shopping mall, nourishing all shops with pedestrian flows.

M
The Mall

C
A cinema and shops flank the east atrium, which occasionally holds exclusive events.

D
The banyan tree on the podium level is preserved from the original site, and featured as a highlight of the new development.

E
High-end hotel and office towers rise up from the podium.

F
Greenery camouflages the parking entrance at the podium.

G
Elevators connect the mall's interior to the public open space on the podium level.

Bastion of Footbridges
IFC

The Hong Kong Station Development, known as International Finance Centre (IFC), is a comprehensive commercial complex in Hong Kong's central business district occupying a 5.7-hectare site, and located adjacent to the scenic Victoria Harbour. The development comprises two sites: the northern site and the southern site, connected by two air-conditioned retail walkways at podium level. The construction of the southern site was completed in 1998 with the opening of the office tower One IFC, and the shopping area of IFC Mall. The construction of the shopping mall at the northern site and the office tower, Two IFC, was completed in 2003. In 2005 the last phase was completed: a luxury hotel and serviced apartment suites.

Although the IFC development provides limited pedestrian connectivity at grade, it is seamlessly integrated into its surroundings at the upper level, connected to Exchange Square, the Central Elevated Walkway, footbridges that lead to the piers, and to the Central Market. In addition, it is linked to the MTR and contains the Airport Express station, where passengers can conveniently check in their luggage and continue to shop before they travel to the air terminal.

Address
8 Finance Street, Central
Developer
Sun Hung Kai Properties Ltd.,
Henderson Land Development
Co. Ltd.,
The Hong Kong and China Gas
Co. Ltd.
Architect
Cesar Pelli & Associates
Rocco Yim
Construction
Initiation: 1997
Completion: 1998 (Phase 1) /
2003 (Phase 2)
Site Area
57,100 m²
Gross Floor Area / GFA
402,145 m²
Floor Area Ratio / FAR
7.1
Building Height
+29 m / 420 m (Podium/Tower)
Blank Wall at Ground Level
91%

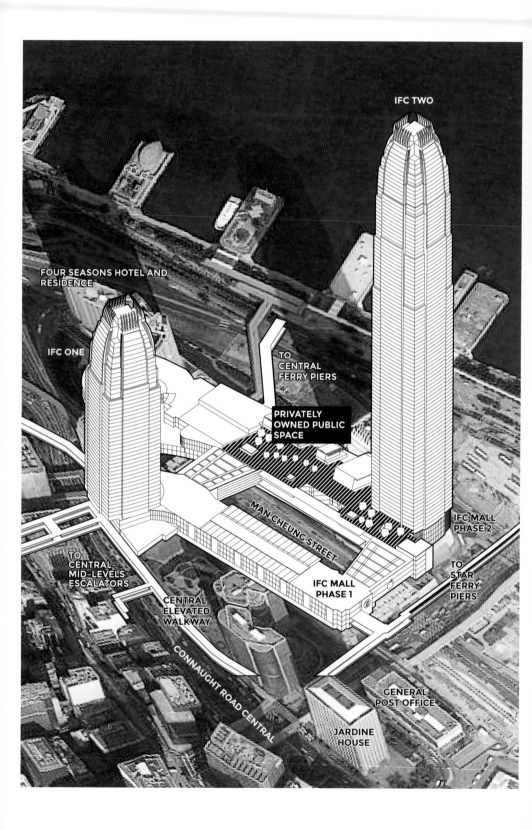

IFC TWO

FOUR SEASONS HOTEL AND RESIDENCE

IFC ONE

TO CENTRAL FERRY PIERS

PRIVATELY OWNED PUBLIC SPACE

MAN CHEUNG STREET

IFC MALL PHASE 2

TO CENTRAL–MID-LEVELS ESCALATORS

IFC MALL PHASE 1

TO STAR FERRY PIERS

CENTRAL ELEVATED WALKWAY

CONNAUGHT ROAD CENTRAL

GENERAL POST OFFICE

JARDINE HOUSE

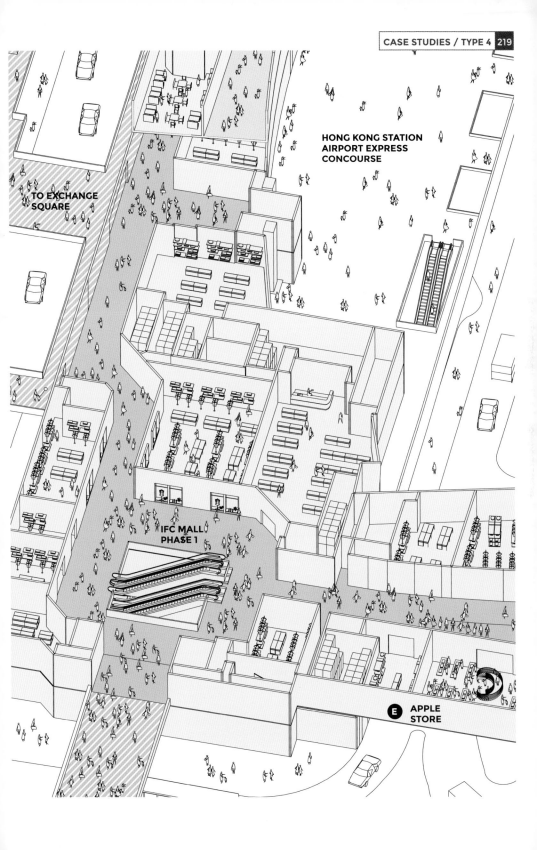

HONG KONG STATION
AIRPORT EXPRESS
CONCOURSE

TO EXCHANGE
SQUARE

IFC MALL
PHASE 1

E APPLE
STORE

M
The Mall

A
Apple Store

B
The podium roof of IFC is a public open space, privately managed and publicly accessible. The plaza is well designed, decorated with trees, vegetation, lighting installations, and plenty of seating.

C
Access to the roof garden is only possible by going through the mall, for instance, by taking the escalator in the oval atrium.

D
The first floor of IFC One connects to three of Hong Kong's elevated pedestrian walkways.

E
The west side of IFC is directly linked to the ferry terminal.

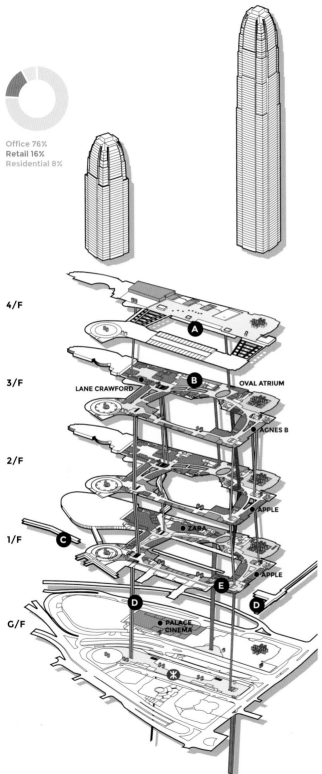

Office 76%
Retail 16%
Residential 8%

4/F

3/F

LANE CRAWFORD Ⓑ OVAL ATRIUM

AGNES B

2/F

APPLE

ZARA

1/F Ⓒ

APPLE

Ⓔ

Ⓓ Ⓓ

G/F PALACE CINEMA

Ⓐ

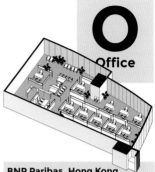

Office

BNP Paribas, Hong Kong Branch, 63rd Floor
Office size: 6,000 m²
Office cost per month: 7.2 million HKD
Cost per m²: 1,200 HKD

IFC Two
Offices per floor: 0.7 (avg.)
Office size: 3,140 m² (avg.)

The plan of the tower is convex-shaped and steps back in the middle, giving the tower a beveled and rounded look, known by the nickname "the razor." Thanks to its prime central location and easy access to the Hong Kong International Airport, the tower is a highly prestigious business location, home to many international financial institutions.

Financier—Mrs. Fong

I am a Hongkonger and this is the second year I work for BNP Paribas in IFC Two. I feel sophisticated to work in this top office building in Hong Kong. If you are a tourist, it is not a good idea to have lunch here during workdays, because people who work here usually have lunch then. You can also bring your own lunch from home, or grab take-away, and take it up to the roof garden, where there is plenty of seating. You can enjoy an awesome view of the harbor or a unique perspective of Central's buildings from within the city, while having lunch or chatting with your friends.

Mong Kok's Vertical Mall

LANGHAM PLACE

L angham Place is a business and commercial complex in Hong Kong that took 16 years to develop and finally opened in 2004. It was a major urban renewal project covering several blocks led by the Urban Renewal Authority, and co-developed by the Great Eagle Group. In what was a lengthy process, it displaced the historic bird market and the homes of about 6,000 people. When the buildings were cleared away, six blocks were combined into two, and Nelson Street was closed off between its Canton Road and Portland Street junctions. With little regard to context, the 42-story hotel and 59-story office tower dwarf the lower surroundings. Jerde designed the 15-story vertical mall, innovating with long "Xpresscalators" that cover multiple stories and bring people up quickly. He also designed a four-story corkscrew-shaped "Spiral" mall. Langham Place has become a model of vertical mall design in Hong Kong.

Address
8 Argyle Street, Mong Kok
Developer
Urban Renewal Authority
(URA)
Great Eagle Group
Architect
Brian Honda (Mall)
Wong & Ouyang (HK) Ltd.
(Office Tower, Hotel)
Construction
Initiation: 1999
Completion: 2004
Site Area
14,400 m²
Gross Floor Area / GFA
167,000 m²
Floor Area Ratio / FAR
11.6
Building Height
+21 m / 255 m (Podium/Tower)
Blank Wall at Ground Level
15%

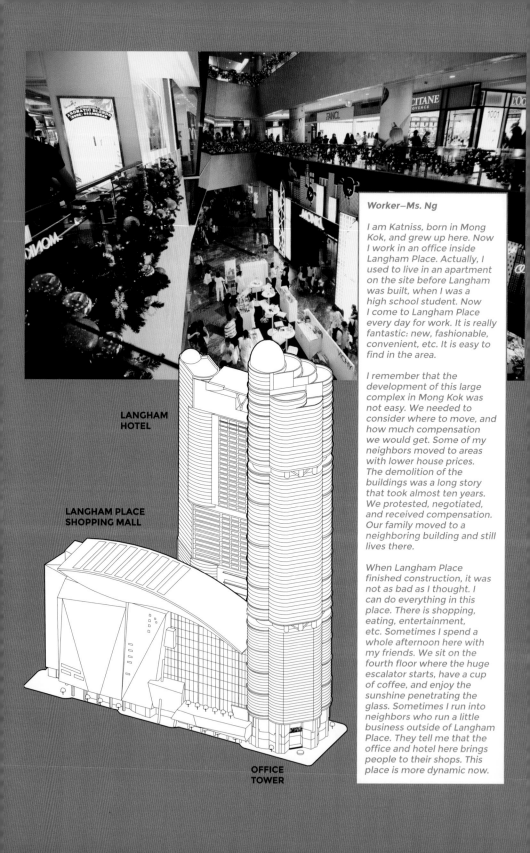

LANGHAM HOTEL

LANGHAM PLACE SHOPPING MALL

OFFICE TOWER

Worker—Ms. Ng

I am Katniss, born in Mong Kok, and grew up here. Now I work in an office inside Langham Place. Actually, I used to live in an apartment on the site before Langham was built, when I was a high school student. Now I come to Langham Place every day for work. It is really fantastic: new, fashionable, convenient, etc. It is easy to find in the area.

I remember that the development of this large complex in Mong Kok was not easy. We needed to consider where to move, and how much compensation we would get. Some of my neighbors moved to areas with lower house prices. The demolition of the buildings was a long story that took almost ten years. We protested, negotiated, and received compensation. Our family moved to a neighboring building and still lives there.

When Langham Place finished construction, it was not as bad as I thought. I can do everything in this place. There is shopping, eating, entertainment, etc. Sometimes I spend a whole afternoon here with my friends. We sit on the fourth floor where the huge escalator starts, have a cup of coffee, and enjoy the sunshine penetrating the glass. Sometimes I run into neighbors who run a little business outside of Langham Place. They tell me that the office and hotel here brings people to their shops. This place is more dynamic now.

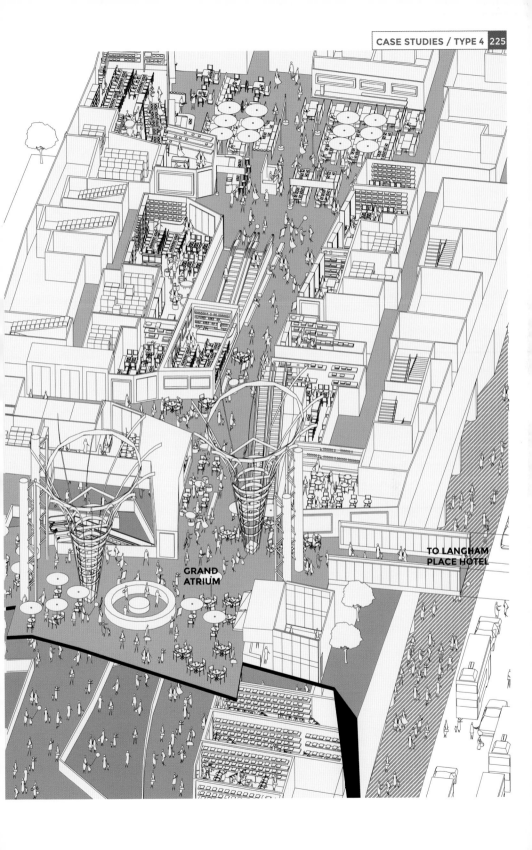

GRAND
ATRIUM

TO LANGHAM
PLACE HOTEL

Office

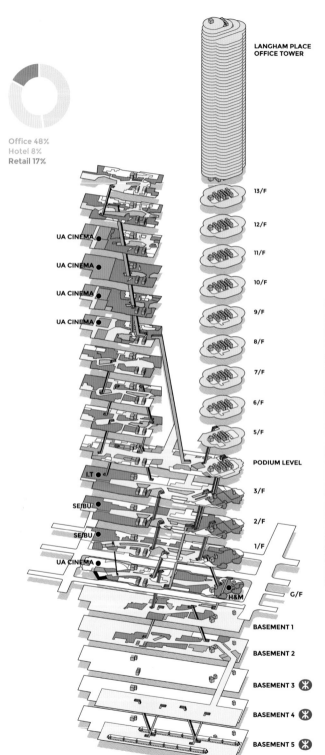

LANGHAM PLACE
OFFICE TOWER

13/F
12/F
11/F
10/F
9/F
8/F
7/F
6/F
5/F

PODIUM LEVEL

3/F
2/F
1/F
G/F

BASEMENT 1
BASEMENT 2
BASEMENT 3 ✳
BASEMENT 4 ✳
BASEMENT 5 ✳

UA CINEMA ●
UA CINEMA ●
UA CINEMA ●
UA CINEMA ●

I.T ●
SEIBU ●
SEIBU ●
UA CINEMA ●
H&M ●

Office 48%
Hotel 8%
Retail 17%

Office Tower, 23rd Floor
Flat size: 304 m²
Flat cost per month: 121,600 HKD
Cost per m²: 400 HKD
Windows per floor area: 82%
Operable windows: 35%

Office Tower
Flats per floor: 1–8
Flat size: 152–1,700 m²
Flat cost per month: 629,000–731,000 HKD
Cost per m²: 370–430 HKD

At 59 floors tall, the Grade-A office tower stands as the defining landmark in the heart of Mong Kok. Floor plans can be customized to meet the individual tenant's needs. From within the mirrored glass facade, the tower offers panoramic views of Victoria Harbour and the whole Kowloon Peninsula.

A
The 9-story glass atrium underneath the office tower maintains a light and airy appearance. It provides for all sorts of activities and restaurants, while linking the retail, office tower, and the hotel. It is also the starting point of the "Xpresscalators," a mega escalator that moves shoppers up over four levels in one shot.

B
A second set of "Xpresscalators" leads from the 8th floor up to the 12th floor, where The Spiral is located, a continuous downward spiraling series of youth-oriented shops.

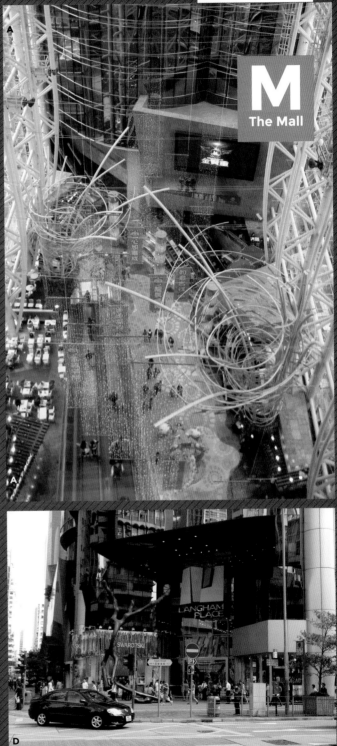

M
The Mall

C
A stage on the sky terrace level hosts live performances and singers, attracting young adult crowds.

D
Happy Man, a 2,700 kg sculpture by the artist Larry Bell, enlivens Langham Place's entrance.

Mega-Development

ELEMENTS

Union Square is an ambitious mega-development with seven project phases. Kowloon Station is situated within the heart of the complex.

In executing this project, the Hong Kong government had put together a project team of four developers, Sun Hung Kai Properties, Hang Lung Group, Wharf Holdings, and Wing Tai Asia in collaboration with Mass Transit Railway Corporation Limited (MTRC). Terry Farrell & Partners lead the overall design. Past precedents, such as Sha Tin New Town Plaza, Taikoo Shing, Pacific Place, and Kowloon Tong provided benchmarks for the Union Square development.

Elements Mall and the International Commerce Centre (ICC), a 484-meter-tall tower, represent Phase 5 and Phase 7 in the overall development of Union Square. Elements Mall provides retail services and connects the office and residential towers to Kowloon Station and the Airport Express. The mall functions as a transport hub for buses, taxis, and other modes of ground vehicular transport. The podium level of the complex accommodates circulation of vehicles and pedestrians, and contains a public space with restaurants, called Civic Square.

This complex is an example of a self-contained, mega-block island-city. It disengages itself from the surrounding context with bare podium walls and few ground level linkages.

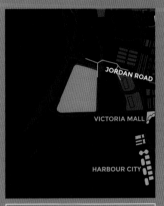

Address
1 Austin Road West, West Kowloon
Developer
MTR Corporation Limited
Sun Hung Kai Properties Ltd.
Hang Lung Group
Wharf Holdings
Wing Tai Asia
Architect
Benoy (Mall)
KPF (ICC)
Construction
Initiation: 1994 (Station)
Completion: 2010 (ICC)
Site Area
135,400 m²
Gross Floor Area / GFA
1,090,026 m²
Floor Area Ratio / FAR
8.1
Building Height
+36.5 m / 484 m (Podium/Tower)
Blank Wall at Ground Level
89%

ICC
INTERNATIONAL COMMERCE
CENTRE / RITZ-CARLTON HONG
KONG

THE CULLINAN 2 /
W HOTEL / THE
HARBOURVIEW
PLACE

THE
CULLINAN 1

SORRENTO

THE
HARBOURSIDE

PRIVATELY
OWNED PUBLIC
SPACE

THE
ARCH

THE
WATERFRONT

AUSTIN ROAD WEST

HIGH SPEED RAIL STATION /
UNDER CONSTRUCTION

WEST KOWLOON CULTURAL DISTRICT /
UNDER CONSTRUCTION

AUSTIN ROAD WEST

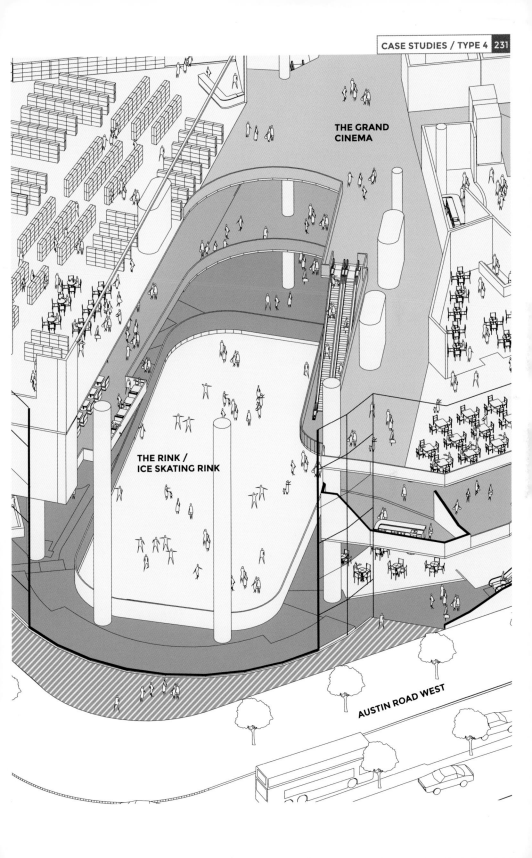

THE GRAND
CINEMA

THE RINK /
ICE SKATING RINK

AUSTIN ROAD WEST

M

The Mall

A
The ice-skating rink is a popular destination for people to meet and watch the activities on the ice. A high ceiling atrium creates a bright and open indoor environment.

B
Blank walls characterize the exterior environment of Elements, making the urban context bleak and dull.

C
Inside Elements, seating is provided for shoppers and passers-by. The seating arrangement is oriented more for solitary use than for creating interaction between users.

D
The privately owned public space on the south side of the podium roof has little community use other than pedestrian circulation.

E
Escalators lead to the International Commerce Centre (ICC).

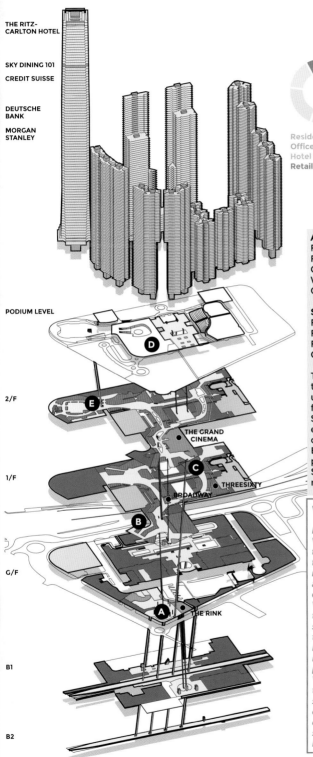

THE RITZ-
CARLTON HOTEL

SKY DINING 101

CREDIT SUISSE

DEUTSCHE
BANK

MORGAN
STANLEY

PODIUM LEVEL

2/F

THE GRAND
CINEMA

1/F

THREESIXTY

BROADWAY

G/F

THE RINK

B1

B2

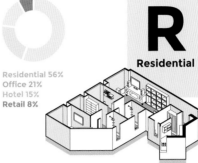

Residential 56%
Office 21%
Hotel 15%
Retail 8%

R
Residential

Apartment E, 50th Floor
Flat size: 107 m²
Flat cost: 18.9 million HKD
Cost per m²: 176,600 HKD
Windows per floor area: 18%
Operable windows: 43%

Sorrento Tower II
Flats per floor: 8
Flat size: 107-120 m²
Flat cost: 15.3-19.8 million HKD
Cost per m²: 142,000-165,000 HKD

The cruciform-shaped tower optimizes
the maximum window frontage to
unit ratio. It also maximizes the overall
flat units within the building footprint.
Sorrento represents the luxurious
end of the real estate market. The
convenient access to the Airport
Express, Kowloon metro station, and
proximity to Elements Mall make
Sorrento attractive to many upper-
middle-class residents.

Visitors—Mr. & Mrs. Cheung

*My wife and I are long retired seniors.
We live in Kwun Tong, but we come
to Elements Mall every so often due
to its spacious interior environment,
relatively less crowded atmosphere,
and good amount of seating areas. It is
easy for us to spend a few hours here.
We usually come here on Sundays and
take the bus on the "two-dollar trip"
senior fare discount. It is comfortable
to sit inside the mall as it is clean and
has sunlight. With the air conditioning
in the summer time, this mall is a great
place for us to get away from the heat.
We do not use the podium gardens
though as the sun is too strong. The
shops and restaurants at the mall are
expensive, so we sometimes bring our
own food. We then look for a good
sitting place, and spend two to three
hours inside the mall.*

CREDITS

Cover Design
Anthony Lam

Layout Design
Anthony Lam

Graphic Editing
Anthony Lam

Infographics
Footprints; Cross-sections; 312 Malls in Hong Kong; F.A.R. (Floor Area Ratio);
Blank Wall Ratio: Anthony Lam
17 Mall City Case Studies: Chi Fung Chan, Marty Chun Kit Chan

Case Studies
Chungking Mansions: Bibiana Gomez Dangond
Golden Shopping Centre: Dong Lu
Tuen Mun Town Plaza: Li Yapeng
Lok Fu Plaza: He Yuan
Citywalk: Camille Anne Ang Tang
Sino Centre: Chi Fung Chan
Argyle Centre: Sun Cong
The Landmark: Wang Lin
Shun Tak Centre: Li Li
Times Square: Loc Hoi Tran
MegaBox: Marco Ng
Harbour City: Wang Xiachen
Cityplaza: Tara McGready
Pacific Place: Audrey Ma
IFC: Ye Xinxin
Langham Place: Wu Yue
Elements: Marty Chun Kit Chan